The Motivated Worker

The Motivated Worker

*A Manager's Guide
to Improving Job Satisfaction*

BRAD WARD

McFarland & Company, Inc., Publishers
Jefferson, North Carolina

This book has undergone peer review.

LIBRARY OF CONGRESS CATALOGUING-IN-PUBLICATION DATA

Names: Ward, Brad, 1980– author.
Title: The motivated worker : a manager's guide to improving job satisfaction / Brad Ward.
Description: Jefferson, North Carolina : McFarland & Company, Inc., Publishers, 2021 | Includes bibliographical references and index.
Identifiers: LCCN 2020047311 | ISBN 9781476680217 (paperback : acid free paper) ∞
ISBN 9781476641614 (ebook)
Subjects: LCSH: Employee motivation. | Job satisfaction. | Organizational behavior.
Classification: LCC HF5549.5.M63 W375 2021 | DDC 658.3/14—dc23
LC record available at https://lccn.loc.gov/2020047311

BRITISH LIBRARY CATALOGUING DATA ARE AVAILABLE

ISBN (print) 978-1-4766-8021-7
ISBN (ebook) 978-1-4766-4161-4

Front cover image © 2020 Shutterstock

Printed in the United States of America

McFarland & Company, Inc., Publishers
Box 611, Jefferson, North Carolina 28640
www.mcfarlandpub.com

Acknowledgments

I would first like to thank my wife Angela and my children: Leah, Ethan, Aaron, and Evan. They supported me throughout this journey and it is for them that I write. My family was an encouragement to me—my parents, sisters and immediate and extended families.

Legendary pinball artist John Youssi recrafted my illustrations, and his artistry undoubtedly improved the quality of this book. Brad and Sara Hammond were the undergraduate students who heard me lecture on Two Factor theory and gave me the inspiration to finish the proposal and submit it to McFarland.

Dr. Paul Gratton and Dr. Craig Johnson both let me bounce ideas off of them before I started writing this book. Their optimism impacted me greatly. Allison Davis performed the initial proofread of this book and dialogued with me regarding the policy chapter.

Dr. Steve Song, Dr. Gene McKay and Dr. Paul Shelton were professors who gave me a passion and knowledge for data analysis and survey creating. My current office colleagues were also supportive of me as I wrote this book.

Regarding the Universal Dual-Factor Survey, upon which this book is constructed, I have more people to thank. Dr. Joy Drinnon provided early critiques of the UDS that proved to make it a more robust instrument. Dr. Bill Greer helped me set up the UDS banking study location, which led to testing the reliability of the instrument. And colleague Cindy Wymer assisted by setting up the Qualtrics survey for the UDS banking study.

Table of Contents

Table of Contents

Section IV.
Measuring Employee Job Satisfaction

Preface

Why I Wrote This Book and How It Can Help You

The reason I am intrigued by workplace motivation is that I want to know why so many of the employees I interact with are bitter and miserable. For instance, in my previous career in automotive manufacturing, I continually came across coworkers who were unhappy, and I wanted to know why. I heard phrases like "If I was only paid a dollar more an hour, I'd be happy" or "Why does our shift always work harder than first shift and why aren't we noticed for it?" or "Why do our benefits keep getting taken away? Does management care about us?" When I looked internally, I realized that I was not happy with my job as well. Currently, I am a professor and could not imagine a better occupation. But why do I like this job compared to previous jobs? In the past I had decent, good-paying jobs, yet I struggled to find meaning in my work. I wanted to discover for employees, as well as for myself, the factors that make work meaningful. I believed there could be a model "out there" that explains the various reasons employees lack motivation and job satisfaction.

I am sure that you have encountered workers (perhaps yourself) who feel like they are "doing time" instead of thriving in their work. Perhaps you (or your coworkers) feel that you do not have a noteworthy career and are just getting by in a dead-end job. Regardless of position, job title, or industry, I have noticed that workers are often miserable with their employment. A recent *Forbes* article supports this notion as more than half of all U.S. workers are not happy at work.[1] This statistic, and my experiences, led me to ask questions like the following: Why are so many employees unhappy with their jobs? Is management solely responsible for worker dissatisfaction? Is there a way in which both the employer and employee can flourish together? Instead of quid pro quo, "the employer provides a job and the employee provides labor," is there

1

a way to improve the manager/employee relationship? Can productivity and efficiency increase as a result of a motivated workforce?

Regarding my previous careers, after I completed my undergraduate degree, I went directly into the workforce via a temporary agency. I did not have my dream job lined up; rather, I worked as a manual laborer in a factory. As an aside, I would not necessarily recommend this career path, but this experience enlightened me. I got to experience what it felt like to be a "cog in the machine" firsthand. I had previously worked menial jobs as a high schooler, but all were part time. After a few months of laboring 10-hour shifts in the factory I was hired by a contractor. This contractor made me a team leader and my career took off from there. As a 23-year-old who was now a boss and directing the work of baby boomers, generation Xers, and the upcoming millennials (age-wise I am on the generation X/millennial border), I continued observing that, while some workers were content with their jobs, many were unhappy. It occurred to me that some of the differences may be generational, yet, at the core, there seemed to be something else going on. Were there underlying factors, or predispositions, that led to employee dissatisfaction?

I climbed my way into middle management while working for the contractor and for a future employer. I had a couple of different job titles. The first was field administrator, which required me to oversee the work of a 70-person workforce. The other job was titled "new product introduction quality engineer." My primary responsibility was to focus on systems and coordinate engineers, production supervisors and assembly line workers, production control, and sales staff. Regardless of my position in the company or department in which I worked, I frequently noticed there was a contingent of miserable workers present. The unhappiness did not just occur at the lowest levels of the organizations; it was present in supervisory levels and beyond. As I reflected on my own job satisfaction, I realized that I had a high quality, sustainable job, yet I was dissatisfied. My employers treated me well and I liked my coworkers, but something was missing. As I finally transitioned into higher education and became a professor, I once again noticed that some of my colleagues were happier than others. Regardless of where I worked, this problem persisted, and I was intrigued to solve the mystery. To add to my fascination with this quandary, my wife would mention how nursing turnover (she is a nurse) was abundant at her employer.

Enter Two Factor theory. Created in 1959, the Two Factor theory is a model that comprehensively defines what factors satisfy an employee at work. "Employees" refers to those working at any level in the firm, not just the lowest levels. The Two Factor theory, like Maslow's Hierarchy of Needs, has stayed relevant over the previous decades and is still studied and applied in organizations today. Essentially, Two Factor theory asserts that (a) employees are motivated by internal factors such as achievement or personal growth at work and (b) external factors, such as a clean working environment or job security, are demanded of employers, but they do not actually motivate employees.

I have taught Two Factor theory to my students for nearly a decade, mostly in Principles of Management, Organizational Behavior, and Operations Management classes. When I teach this model in the classroom, students are quick to engage in conversation as to how it relates to their schoolwork and careers. The students like the theory and can make immediate applications to their lives. Two of my students, who would eventually marry, liked the theory so much that we discussed it in more detail after class, and they proofread the book proposal. Their interest in and passion for the topic provided me the encouragement I needed to finish this book.

Can a theory from the mid−20th century be relevant in today's ever-changing business landscape? A 2005 study, in which 3,200 employees in government, utilities, services, retail, manufacturing, financial services, and police sectors were surveyed, confirmed that Two Factor theory is here to stay and is relevant in the fast paced 21st century world.[2] Additionally, a 2017 study states that "in today's context the relevance of Herzberg's theory stands true; the importance of motivators (internal factor) and hygiene factors (external factors) to job satisfaction has not changed."[3] Thus, Two Factor theory is relevant to those working in virtually any industry today.

This text is set up so that practitioners can quickly assess employees' attitudes about their jobs and make swift changes to improve worker satisfaction. Professors will be able to use it as a supplement for Human Resource Management, Organizational Behavior, Principles of Management, or Introduction to Research classes (there is a survey methods section at the end of this book). Finally, employees will be equipped to improve their own motivation at work.

In addition to walking you through the Two Factor theory and how it can better improve worker motivation, the text presents and applies current examples to modern generations (primarily the millennial generation). Finally, I provide a survey that can be used to quickly assess and improve employee motivation. This book is a bit more rigorous than

Preface

typical popular press management textbooks yet is written with the practitioner in mind. It bridges the gap, in a concise manner, between the theoretical and the practical. Two Factor theory changed the way in which I approach motivation, both personally and professionally. My life has improved because of it and I hope yours will too.

Introduction

Managers today are completely overwhelmed. Smartphone notifications and emails are piling up and countless meetings disrupt the workday. Compliance with accrediting agency standards and adhering to ever-changing laws force employers to hire more staff-level employees while works loads, in general, increase. Customers are expecting businesses to be more socially responsible while efficiently innovating and creating customizable products. The job itself is becoming more complex due to globalization, improvements in information technology, big data, and supply chain communications. Typical managers are simply trying to keep their heads above water: trying to achieve various productivity, efficiency, and quality goals. In this volatile, uncertain, complex, and ambiguous (VUCA) work environment resulting from globalization and the digital age, employee morale is often ignored. In VUCA environments especially, improving employee job satisfaction and motivation should be a primary focus of management.[1] When employees are dissatisfied with their jobs, managers add more tasks to their schedules as they deal with human resources functions such as hiring, firing, training, and disciplining employees.[2] It is important to note that managers of all organizational levels, team leaders through CEOs, are affected by employee motivation.

Is there a way to improve the working lives of managers? Absolutely! A properly motivated workforce makes managers' lives easier. For example, empowered workers can make decisions and implement changes on the fly without interrupting management. Well trained employees can assist with data analysis, use contemporary technology, deal directly with customer inquiries, troubleshoot and fix problems, and make improvements to work processes. Investing in employees will result in a more satisfied workforce. Workers who are satisfied with their jobs are more productive and less likely to quit.[3] Unfortunately, many managers believe that employees are either unwilling to take on more responsibility or are simply not competent enough to participate in "higher level" management work.[4] Or, managers are just too busy with their day-to-day challenges as they are pressured to meet short-term financial goals. Managers, then, may overlook investing in the long-term growth and development of their employees because they are simply trying to survive in the VUCA work environment. They may also assume that workers do not want to put in the effort to advance in their careers.

Evolving worker expectations and attitudes are also a challenge for managers. The millennial generation is comprised of 76 million persons born after 1980 and they are the "fastest-growing segment of workers today!"[5] Millennial workers expect large salaries, robust benefits packages, flexible work hours, and frequent promotions and raises.[6] Younger workers freely question leadership decisions and they expect managers to act like coaches, not bosses.[7] If dissatisfied with their jobs millennials are likely to job hop, seeking better employment opportunities.[8] In a nutshell, millennial workers want to be employed at a company that helps them succeed in their careers, support their growth as human beings, and pay them well for their knowledge and contributions. Although new generational titles beyond "millennial" are emerging, such as generation Z or post-millennial (those born in 1995 or later)[9] this book will focus primarily on studies and company policies that are evolving to meet the needs of the millennial workforce. In addition, post-millennials are quite like millennials regarding work expectations.[10]

Employees are quitting their jobs at record rates, in part, due to job dissatisfaction: Nearly 3.5 million workers quit in the United States each month![11] The purpose of this book is to provide a framework that managers can use to motivate modern workers in hopes of reducing this negative trend. Employees will also benefit from this book as they discover which factors are related to their own job satisfaction.

This book is built upon the classic Two Factor theory and includes a *Modern Worker Focus* at the end of each chapter. The Two Factor theory is a simple yet effective framework that managers can reference and apply to the workplace. Although this theory has existed for decades and is still being studied by researchers, very few managers are aware of its merits or applicability.[12] Using the Two Factor model as a guide, contemporary examples from small, medium, and large organizations will be provided. Each chapter will end with application questions that will help managers assess their current work environment. Questions are designed from both a quantitative and qualitative perspective to help managers more holistically analyze their employees' job satisfaction.

This text concludes with the ready-to-go *Universal Dual-Factor Survey (UDS)*. The UDS is a short-form survey based on the Two Factor theory and can be used in most organizations. Managers can quickly assess their employees' attitudes and take immediate actions to improve morale and productivity. The UDS is also accompanied by a Microsoft Excel data analysis section. Descriptive statistics are foundational to organizational decision making. Managers will learn how to quickly evaluate job satisfaction (no previous statistical training is required) and translate outcomes into easily readable charts and graphs. Although this book is written for business managers and practitioners, its contents are applicable to employees as well as managers of nonprofit organizations. Additionally, this text is meant to be a supplement for higher education business management related classes (Organizational Behavior, Human Resources, or Principles of Management) or an introductory research methods class.

SECTION I

Two Factor Theory for Managers

1

From Taylor to Herzberg

Why Motivation Matters

To understand how employees are motivated, a review of classical theory is necessary. Management education, and the workplace in general, are still impacted by research that was conducted during the 20th century. For example, time study and continuous improvement techniques derive from the work of Frederick Taylor, employee empowerment and team-building were promoted by Mary Parker Follett, Elton Mayo investigated the impact that working conditions had on employee performance, and Abraham Maslow and Frederick Herzberg created motivational theories, which are popular in high school and college texts today. Herzberg's Two Factor theory is the foundation of this book. Following is a brief history of worker motivation.

Motivational Theory History

At the turn of the 20th century, employers were primarily concerned with worker productivity. The process, or the job itself, was the primary focus of researchers. Scientific management, a philosophy credited to Frederick Taylor, pervaded factories after the industrial revolution. The primary focus of scientific management was to find the "one best way" to do a job. For any job, then, there was only one method that resulted in maximum productivity. Managers, via the time study method, would study how workers moved when completing tasks. When extra steps, or movements, were eliminated, production speeds drastically increased. For example, Frank Gilbreth, a scientific management disciple, studied bricklayers and noticed that each worker had his own way of doing the job. Some workers had better methods and others were slow. As a result of time studies, Frank was able to reduce the motions to lay a brick from 18 to 4.5. One of his improvements was the development of a scaffold that standardized how employees bent and lifted bricks.[1]

Although scientific management practitioners had good intentions, at least in part, the psychology of the worker was ignored. The brick laying example is illustrative, in a general sense. At first glance, the brick laying improvements would have been beneficial to employees. The job became easier, ergonomically speaking, leading to fewer injuries. The job could be completed faster, meaning that if employees were paid for performance (i.e., managers paying for the number of bricks laid instead of paying for hours worked), they could complete more jobs and earn more pay. Piece rate was a popular pay method of scientific management practitioners: employees were paid for each unit produced. Finally, employees could work fewer hours and get more time off to recuperate. But workers realized that completing jobs faster would lead to layoffs.[2] Workers tended to slow down production as a matter of self-preservation. Workers were deemed too incompetent to uncover the "one best way" to perform their jobs which led to a natural boundary between workers and managers: the workers worked and the managers managed.[3] Additionally, a major drawback for workers was that jobs were simplified and broken down into extremely repetitive remedial components.[4] Workers, at this point in history, were considered to be cogs in the machine and managers primarily motivated workers by giving them the right tools to do the job and pay for exceptional performance. Workers were not able to use many of their natural talents at work, which led to boredom and fatigue.

Taylor's methods were considered to be so extreme, by unions especially, that he was taken before Congress to discuss the principles of scientific management. At the core of the investigation, workers felt dehumanized by time studies. They also felt humiliated and believed they worked in a hostile work environment. One of the main contentions was Taylor's philosophy: "there was only one best man for each job." Critics were mostly concerned with the second-best person (or third, etc.). What was to become of those who were not most exceptional? Taylor was only concerned about the best employees as he figured the less-skilled workers could find employment elsewhere.[5] Simply stated, Taylor's focus was on creating the one best way, via time studies, and finding the one best person to work each job. This approach reflected the Darwinian survival of the fittest mindset of the day. Organizations that created the best processes and hired the best talent would survive.

In contrast to Taylor, Mary Parker Follett was mostly concerned with the psychology of the worker and did not believe in top-down management domination. This is also known as the "power-with" instead of "power-over" power-sharing ideology.[6] Follet believed that workers could find meaning in the work itself (a concept later promoted by Herzberg) and that they should be empowered to assist managers in the decision-making process.[7] Employees, then, were considered to be valuable assets that could make contributions beyond producing a product. Follet was also a supporter of group, or team, reward structures versus the individualized incentives promoted by Taylor.

While Follett's work was concluding, Mayo, in the 1920s and 30s, studied workers at Western Electric to determine if working conditions impacted employee productivity.[8] Mayo's infamous "Hawthorne Studies" lasted six years. The studies focused on women working in a relay assembly room. Experiments included adjusting temperature and lighting conditions in the assembly room, moving lunch break start times and altering their duration, and shifting the time at which the workers could end their day. Mayo discovered that productivity increased, regardless of negative modifications to the work environment. The reason productivity increased was that the workers received recognition and were able to participate (responsibility) with management.[9] Responsibility and recognition, which Herzberg would later suggest, are motivating agents. Researchers such as Herzberg and Maslow, who followed in the 1940s and 50s, created motivational theories based on worker psychology studies like those of Mayo.

Maslow's Theory in the Workplace

Maslow's famous Hierarchy of Needs pyramid is often used as an employee motivation template. Created in the 1940s, this theory attempted to explain the biological and psychological needs that human beings possess and has since been adapted to demonstrate the motivational needs of workers. Figure 1 depicts the Hierarchy of Needs pyramid and its general levels. At the foundational level, human beings have physiological needs, like eating and sleeping. Once these needs are met, by eating, for example, a new set of needs emerge. Now, the human being can move up to the second level of the pyramid, concentrating on building a sustainable life, for example. Human needs also revert down the pyramid when a previously fulfilled need (i.e., hunger) arises. There are three more sets of needs that emerge in sequence as each lower level is met, including social, esteem, and self-actualizing needs. The person will have a desire to fit in and be loved by friends and family (social needs), followed by a desire to be respected (esteem needs), and ultimately will try to find and fulfill their calling and purpose in life (self-actualization needs).[10] Of course, this is a simplified explanation of the theory since many micro needs exist within each level, but the progression is what is important for managers and employees to recognize.

What is interesting about this theory is that individuals will not be concerned with the needs at the top of the pyramid if the base of the pyramid is cracked. In other words, if her day-to-day sustenance needs are not met, she will not be able to focus on self-esteem needs, etc. From a business perspective, the pyramid looks like Figure 2.

The worker, like the human being who is trying to survive, will need the base of the pyramid to be solid before climbing to higher level needs. For example, Chip Conley, CEO of Joie de Vivre hotels, did not lay off employees following the 9/11 attacks, even though hotel sales, in the industry, were tanking. To keep the bottom of the pyramid from crumbling, Chip did not take a salary for three years and senior executives

Figure 1.

Figure 2.

took a 10 percent reduction in pay.[11] Chip realized that if pay, benefits, and safe working conditions were inadequate, his workers would not be interested in long-term employment. Thus, the higher-level needs, such as building meaningful relationships with coworkers (affiliation), seeking promotions and job title changes (respect), and attempting to fulfill career ambitions, would not matter to employees who were underpaid and working in understaffed departments.

Regardless of the generation to which workers belong, they want to be satisfied with their jobs and make meaningful contributions to society. Managers often shortsightedly assume that workers simply want decent pay and benefits. In a competitive economy, employees will seek employers who address more levels of the Employee's Hierarchy (as in Figure 2). For example, if two employers offer a similar wage but one has a well-defined career path and is well respected in the community, employees would rather work for this organization.

Modern Worker Focus—Generational Differences

Before moving on, it is important to note that this book makes broad generalizations about each generation and primarily focuses on the millennial generation. Not every individual within a generation will share the exact same values and beliefs. However, on average, the members will have similar beliefs or values. Thus, this book generalizes but does not stereotype. Managers should be careful not to apply one size-fits-all policies considering generational differences.

Social scientists have noted that there are four distinct generational groups. First, the traditionalists were born before 1945 and they were the generation working at the time of Herzberg's and Maslow's research. The second and third generations are the baby boomers (born between 1946 and 1964) and generation Xers (born between 1961 and 1980). Finally, the millennials were born after 1980.[12] Additionally, new generation titles are emerging such as the iGeneration, Homeland Generation, and Generation Z (those born between 1995 and 2015), yet individuals associated with these titles share similar characteristics with millennials.[13] Each generation has been subjected to a few major life-changing events that impact how they view the nature of work. For example, the traditionalists were impacted by the Great Depression and World War II and were not exposed to exponential increases in technology.[14] Notable inventions in the 1940s included a 35-ton computer that could add numbers, Elmer's Glue, and a turbo-prop engine.[15] Due to harsh economic, global, and business environments, traditionalists were extremely loyal to their companies and valued hard work. Career changes were infrequent and frowned upon by society.

In contrast, the millennials have experienced quite different life events, especially regarding advances in technology. Millennials have grown up with an abundance of innovations such as smartphones and immersive televisions, multiple forms of computing devices and high-speed Internet (unconnected), and traveling the world has never been easier due to advances in transportation and logistics. Concerning war, millennials have experienced more regarding terrorism and less regarding major world wars. Due to technological innovations, jobs are routinely created, destroyed, or outsourced, so millennials have no problem changing careers as the odds that any employer will survive the long term are minimal. For example, the average age of a company listed on the S&P 500 Index was 60 years in 1950. Today, it is 20 years old, meaning company life spans are closer to this mark.[16] Millennials are likely to be loyal to employers who make meaningful contributions to society and to worker development.[17] Since outsourcing and temporary employment are so common, workers feel exploited and do not typically feel a need to be loyal to an organization.

Although there are contextual differences between traditional-ists and millennials, the theories of Maslow and Herzberg, who cre-ated their theories during the traditionalist period, still apply today. However, each generational cohort may interpret their constructs, i.e., the pyramid, differently, through their own cultural lens. For example, imagine how workers from the 1950s would interpret the Employee's Hier-archy compared to millennial workers today. The traditionalists were so loyal to their companies that they believed their hard work would pay off and lead to promotional opportunities within the company. Their career needs may involve working long hours and putting in their dues to secure long-term employment, hopefully leading to a promotion a few years down the road. Millennials, in contrast, may expect to be pro-moted relativity quickly if they are higher skilled than their coworkers. Putting in their dues is unnecessary since their current job is a step-ping stone to a more advanced position in another company. The millen-nial employee, then, is responsible for doing good work at their current employer in the short term, but does not really owe the employer long-term loyalty. Even if an employer invests in the employee through addi-tional training, it's simply the cost of doing business. Thus, "career needs" are important to both traditionalists and millennials but they interpret what this term actually means with their own generational lens.

Chapter Summary

This chapter briefly overviewed Maslow's Hierarchy of Needs the-ory from the 1940s and noted its relevance to the workplace today. Maslow's theory, when viewed in a workplace context, is still relevant today. However, each generation will interpret the needs at each level in light of their own experiences. Regarding the four main generational cohorts, and emerging generations, vintage (classic) theory from the mid–20th century is still relevant today. In the next chapter, this text will unveil Herzberg's Two Factor theory. This theory emerged about a decade after Maslow's hierarchy. Two Factor theory is more applicable to the modern workplace, yet is easier to understand and apply consid-ering Maslow's work.

Application Questions, Chapter 1

1. Analyze the bottom two levels of your organization's pyramid. In the first column, list the factors such as pay, benefits, working conditions, job security, etc. You may want to review "hygiene factors" in the following chapter to help you make a list of factors. Then, weight each factor in the second column. **All weights should total 1**. The weights represent how important each factor is for workers. For example, of all potential factors, pay is quite important and given a weight of .35. In the third column, rate how well your company is addressing the factor when compared to competitors, on a scale from 1 to 4, 1 being "poorly" and 4 being "excellent." When the first three columns are filled in, multiply across each row. For example, the top row has a score of 1.05. Then, add all scores from column four to reach a total weighted score. An average total weighted score is 2.5; 4.0 is the maximum and 1.0 is the lowest possible total weighted score.[18] Based on your results, how can your organization improve your total weighted score? Is there certain improvement that can make immediate impact? *Note, if you need a more efficient method, simply list the factors and rank them in order of importance and discuss which you want to address.

Factors (i.e., pay)	Weights (i.e., .35)	Rating (i.e., 3)	Score (i.e., 1.05)

1. From Taylor to Herzberg

Factors (i.e., pay)	Weights (i.e., .35)	Rating (i.e., 3)	Score (i.e., 1.05)
	Total of Weights = 1.00		Total Weighted Score=

2. Does your organization have a career planning center? What programs could you create that would allow employees to pursue their higher-level needs within your organization? Make a list below.

3. Most companies use scientific management principles in one way or another. Have you ever been guilty of treating workers as if they were cogs in a machine? What can you do to promote employee well-being?

4. If an employee asked you why his job mattered, how would you respond?

5. Have you noticed any generational differences in the workplace? In what ways can you promote positive working relationships between workers from different generations?

2

The Two Factor Theory
Why Vintage Theory Is Relevant

Chapter 1 provided a brief workplace motivation history. Taylor was primarily concerned with process efficiency, Mayo studied the impact that the work environment had on employee motivation, and Maslow was concerned with the psychological needs of the individual. In the late 1950s, Frederick Herzberg emerged, and he wanted to know which factors, if any, led to employee job satisfaction. Herzberg studied accountants and engineers in the Pittsburgh area and asked them to describe times when they felt exceptionally good or bad about their jobs.[1] What Herzberg discovered was that the needs on the bottom of Maslow's pyramid (see previous chapter for reference), if fulfilled in a work context, would not lead employees to job satisfaction. In other words, improving factors on this level would not motivate employees. For example, employees will not be motivated if employers provide a safe and clean working environment. It is a basic assumption that the work area will be hazard free, well maintained, and ergonomically designed. Managers do not get a pat on the back for taking care of the physical safety needs of their employees. If managers do not provide a safe work environment, however, workers will be upset, and rightfully so. Workers, then, are not motivated by safety but its absence is demotivating. No laborer gets excited to go into work because their workspace is clean and safe. The work environment is not a motivating agent. Take away a well-maintained workplace, though, and employees will not be happy. The work environment, as Herzberg discovered, is a hygiene factor.

The Hygiene Factors

Herzberg believed that Mayo and Taylor's studies focused on what he identified as hygiene factors or needs like those at the bottom of Maslow's pyramid.[2] This section of the pyramid is primarily concerned with survival needs. The hygiene factors are like the foundation of a house. When purchasing a new home, buyers expect the foundation to be firm. If the foundation is cracked, leaking, or crumbling, the buyers will walk away from the sale. But the foundation itself is not what prompts the buyers to take out a mortgage and buy the home. When searching real estate websites for the perfect dream home, most families look for attributes such as a big yard, hardwood floors, vaulted ceilings, or a certain style of kitchen and bath. They buy because they can see themselves enjoying the house, and those features, now and in the future. The foundation of a home is a "must have" but it is not a motivating agent. Similarly, pay, safe working conditions, and good interpersonal relationships at work are "must haves" for employees but they do not motivate the employee to excel at their jobs. These are considered hygiene factors. See Figure 3 for a visual representation of the hygiene factors.

There are six workplace hygiene factors[3]:

- working conditions—adequate or inadequate workspace, technology, ergonomics
- company policy and administration—adequate or inadequate personnel policies (performance reviews, pay schedules, etc.), poor or rich communication channels
- supervision—management's willingness or unwillingness to teach employees, maintain technical competence, or delegate workloads
- interpersonal relationships—positive or negative interactions between peers, superiors, and subordinates

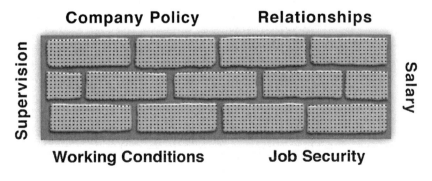

Figure 3.

- salary—fair or unfair wages, increase or decrease in compensation
- job security—company stability or instability, tenured positions

It is important to note that the hygiene factors can be identified in a positive or negative light. If a hygiene factor is "present," this refers to the negative description of the term. For example, if the hygiene factor "job security" is present, workers may believe that the company is financially unstable or that their jobs are easily expendable. Employers should be aware that employees expect hygiene factors not to be present at work. According to Herzberg, managers cannot increase employee job satisfaction by eliminating hygiene factors, but the presence of hygiene factors will result in job dissatisfaction.[4] An employee will not be satisfied at work simply because she has a great boss. However, the presence of an incompetent or demeaning boss will lead to employee dissatisfaction. Figure 4 is a visual depiction of how hygiene factors (in this case, supervision) relate to job satisfaction.

Understanding how hygiene factors function is an extremely important concept in this text. To further illustrate, imagine a famous pop band. The fans can recite the lyrics and they get emotional when they hear the song. They may even think of a time they heard this song, in the past, and instantly feel the nostalgia associated with this remembrance. The lyrics, melody, or "vibe" of the song hold a special importance to the fan. What is interesting is that the common listener cannot pick out each instrument as it plays; they only feel the general rhythm of the song. Now, take away a steady drum beat or have the bassist play inconsistent notes and the song loses its feel. The listener expects the song to be played in time, in tune, and to be well produced. These factors

Good Supervisor　　　　　**Bad Supervisor**
No Job Dissatisfaction　　**Job Dissatisfaction**

Figure 4.

do not motivate the listener to like the song, though. Take away the foundation, i.e., consistent bass player, and the listener will no longer like the song. This is the essence of hygiene factors.

As previously mentioned, the presence of a hygiene factor is like a crack in the foundation of a house. If there are too many smaller cracks, or too large individual cracks, employees will be dissatisfied. Akin to the foundation example, the absence of a major factor, salary, for instance (large crack), will lead to dissatisfaction. Or perhaps the salary is "OK" but most of the factors are not great (small cracks). Again, dissatisfaction will result. The most important point regarding hygiene factors is that workers will not try to excel at their jobs, or try to advance in the company, if hygiene factors are not addressed by management.

The Motivating Factors

Once employee survival needs are met, they will begin to seek job satisfaction. Resembling the top of Maslow's pyramid, employees are motivated by higher level needs such as personal growth and meaningful work. Two Factor theory contrasts with the Hierarchy of Needs theory because workers will not become motivated until negative hygiene factors are removed. In Maslow's pyramid, once a need on the lower level is fulfilled, a new need emerges and becomes a motivator. Thus, motivation happens on every level. Herzberg called the higher-level factors "motivators." The motivators are like the features of a property that entice the purchaser to make a buying decision. Using the previous real estate example, a buyer may dream about getting a four-bedroom home with a mountain view and screened in porch. These checklist items would be analogous with motivators. A firm foundation would be analogous with hygiene factors. A buyer would not be motivated to buy if the foundation was cracked, warped, or had leaking issues. The foundation itself is not the motivating agent like the mountain view. Both the mountain view and firm foundation are needed for a successful purchase, they just serve different functions. See Figure 5 below.

There are five workplace motivators[5]:

- recognition—acts of praise from employees at any level of the organization

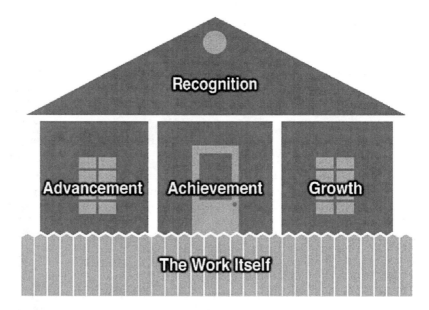

Figure 5.

- achievement—success in one's job, the ability to make meaningful contributions at work
- growth potential—the ability to receive a change in status or learn new skills
- advancement—an actual change in an employee's status or position
- the work itself—the ability to complete an entire task, positive or negative feelings about daily job duties

Herzberg (1966) believed that employees' job satisfaction would increase with the presence of motivators. A recent study shows that motivation and engagement (happiness and energy) are related to each other and both are related to job satisfaction,[6] as Herzberg would presume. The absence of motivators, or engagement, however, would only lead to no job satisfaction. Figure 6 shows the presence of recognition.

On the continuum, an employee lacking recognition will not necessarily be dissatisfied, he simply will not be satisfied. In other words, he would feel emotionally monotone about his job but would not necessarily be upset. On the other hand, if he was regularly praised for a job well done, he would be satisfied with his job.

24

Frequent Recognition   **Lacking Recognition**
Job Satisfaction   **No Job Satisfaction**

Figure 6.

Having no motivators but a solid foundation at work (no hygiene factors present) is like living in a high functioning efficiency apartment. It may not be a dream home, but it is functional. The renter will not be dissatisfied because her survival needs are met, but the efficiency apartment lacks the dream home aspect, so she will not be totally satisfied either. If the motivators are present, and the negative hygiene factors are removed, it is like living in a dream house with no foundational issues. The buyer loves the house and wants to work hard to maintain the property. See Figures 7 and 8 for a visual representation of the Two-Factor Theory.

Figure 7.

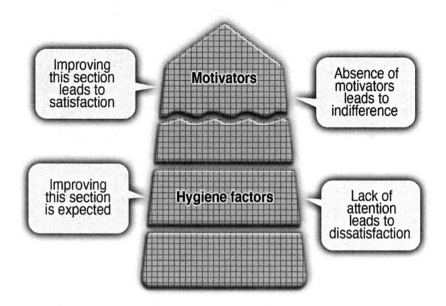

Figure 8.

Modern Worker Focus—Employees Expect the Standard of Living to Increase

One major difference between the 1950s and 60s, when Herzberg gained prominence, and today, is that the standard of living has drastically increased. Families require more goods and services than ever before. The more goods or services a family requires, the higher the wage must be to support the family. In 1960, consumers spent approximately 32 percent of their income on non-necessities. In 2003, consumers spent approximately 50 percent of their income on non-necessities, which is a dramatic shift.[7] For example, a typical U.S. consumer today spends almost $6,000 per year on entertainment and eating at restaurants.[8]

U.S. citizens have incurred overhead expenses they did not have at the time of Herzberg. In the 1960s families had basic expenses such as electricity, transportation (usually one car per household), food, and entertainment (primarily radio/TV in the home), but did not have a laundry list of additional expenses like Internet, cable TV and/or streaming channels, additional vehicles and transportation costs, smartphone payments, and so on. As a result, dual income families

26

have also risen from 25 percent in 1960 to approximately 60 percent today.[9] Although this list of expenses is not exhaustive, it is clear that millennials have more expected expenses than previous generations.

In addition to the quantity of expenses increasing from Herzberg's era, the standard of living, measured by real GDP per capita (average income per person), has consistently risen as well. In the 1960s, the average income per person was $17,253 and in 2016 it was $51,549.[10] Since "real" GDP per capita is being reported here, inflation is taken into account. Thus, the average income per worker has risen almost three-fold since 1960.

So, what does a higher standard of living have to do with managers? First, employers must realize that employees will continually expect wages to increase (or be at least livable in today's standards). Reverting wages will lead to dissatisfaction. Second, employees will expect employers to fund not only wages, but also fringe benefits and personal expenses. Many companies are now offering additional benefits such as subsidizing smartphone bills, home and auto insurance, hotels and vacation expenses, cable services, financial services, automotive services, computers and electronics, and the list goes on.[11]

Chapter Summary

The most important concept from this chapter is that managers cannot motivate workers by minimizing hygiene factor presence. Workers simply expect decent pay, good working conditions, competent supervisors, and so on. Two Factor theory differs from Maslow's Hierarchy of Needs in this regard.

Application Questions, Chapter 2

1. Make a list of expectations that your employees have regarding pay and benefits. Compare how your organization subsidizes these demands verses your closest competitors. What improvements can your firm make?

Section I—Two Factor Theory for Managers

Employee Expectations i.e., $15/hr	Your Organization i.e., $13/hr	Competitor A i.e., $16/hr	Competitor B i.e., $14/hr	Competitor C i.e., $15/hr

2. Which type of fringe benefits would be most affordable and relevant to your workers? (Make a table below.)

Benefit, i.e., Term Life Insurance and Potential Carriers	Monthly Cost to Employer	Monthly Cost to Employee

3. Briefly describe how your organization addresses each motivator and hygiene factor below:

2. The Two Factor Theory

Motivators	Actions or Policies That Address Each Factor	Overall, Is Your Organization Strong, Average, or Weak, Addressing Each Factor?
Achievement		
Recognition		
Work Itself		
Responsibility		
Growth		
Advancement		
Hygiene Factors		
Salary and Benefits		
Job Security		
Supervision		
Relationships		
Working Conditions		
Policy		

SECTION II

The Foundation: Hygiene Factors

3

Salary and Benefits

Why Union Workers Aren't Happy

When reviewing factors related to Two Factor theory it is important to begin by addressing salary. As a survival need, most employees are initially concerned with pay over all other factors. For example, students primarily select college degrees and career paths based on the potential salary they can earn.[1] But will employees who earn an expected wage from their employer truly be happy and less likely to quit their job? The following story will illustrate why incentives, such as generous bonuses, salaries, and benefits packages, do not truly motivate employees in the long term.

One day an elderly gentleman was enjoying his quiet time when two of the neighborhood kids began playing on his lawn. The gentleman was not overly fond of these kids and he really liked the look of his nicely manicured lawn. He tried yelling at the children and even threatened to call their parents, but they would not stop playing in his yard. After a few days of torment, he decided to start paying the children each time they trampled through his yard. The first payment was $5 each. The kids roared with excitement and they made big plans to spend this hard-earned money. The next day the kids came back, romped through the yard, and the gentleman paid them $4 each. Although this payment was not as much as the previous day, the children were still excited to spend their earnings. This process continued, with the old man eventually paying the children $1. At this point the kids got upset. They could not understand why the pay continued to be reduced. Finally, the gentleman offered them 50 cents on their next visit and the kids were so mad they stopped playing in his yard.[2]

So how did the elderly gentleman win the battle against the neighborhood children? He realized that children have a natural inclination to run through neighbors' yards. It is exciting and energizing. When the gentleman realized that the kids had an internal drive to play on his

33

grass, he was able to switch their focus to an external motivator: money in this instance. Now, the children came to play on the grass not because they enjoyed it, but to get paid. As the payments declined, so did their motivation. In a similar vein, educators often have trouble motivating children to learn as they get older. When young kids first arrive at school, they have a natural curiosity and want to learn. Children are quite eager and cannot wait to go study new concepts and spend time with their friends. However, when their natural motivation (internal) is removed and making the grade becomes the motivator (external), children seek the easiest/quickest method to earn grades. They no longer care about learning.[3] Likewise, pay (external) does not motivate workers long term. Employees naturally want to work jobs that fit their skillsets and personality. Internal motivation is far superior to external motivation; albeit, both are necessary to operate a functioning workforce.

Salary Is Not a Motivator: Union Case Studies

If decent pay and benefits are good motivators, union employees should be happy since they are paid more and receive better benefits than nonunion employees, on average.[4] However, studies show that union workers are not as happy as nonunion employees. For example, nonunion employees at a large research university were less satisfied than nonunion employees in virtually every aspect of the job including recognition, the work itself, advancement and growth opportunity, level of responsibility, good feelings about the organization, clarity of mission, management and supervision, relationships with coworkers, organizational values, and salary and pay![5] How could this be? The reason is that mandatory bargaining subjects, at least in the U.S., are wages, work hours, and working conditions,[6] also known as hygiene factors.

A classic Ford Motor Company (FMC) example is illustrative of salary not being a long-term motivator. In the early 1900s, workers from all over the world flocked to FMC. Interestingly, this is partly why the greater Detroit area is so diverse today, with sections such as Greektown, Polish influenced Hamtramck, and the largest Middle Eastern population in the U.S. located in nearby Dearborn.[7] In 1914, Ford was paying workers up to $5 per day, which was unheard of at that time.[8] Comparatively, farm workers in the U.S. were paid approximately $1.50 per day.[9] Thus, workers were flooding into Detroit to work for Ford. The reason

Ford paid $5 per day, though, was that the annual turnover rate (employees quitting) was 370 percent, primarily due to worker boredom. Initially, skilled craftsmen were needed at FMC, but as the assembly line began to take hold, jobs became extremely mundane and routine. Jobs were so simple, in fact, that any employee, regardless of skill level, could be an expert with less than 10 minutes of training. Ford, then, offered $5 per day to combat employees quitting. Although the annual turnover was temporarily decreased to 16 percent in 1916 after the implementation of the $5 workday, which was quite an impressive reduction, workers were still not happy with their jobs. Eventually, workers went on strike and the United Auto Workers (UAW) union won their certification election in 1941.[10] Regardless of well-above average pay and benefits, workers still wanted union representation.

Fast forwarding to more recent events, unionized Kellogg's workers in Memphis, Tennessee, in 2013 were locked out when negotiations reached an impasse. Similar to FMC, workers in the Memphis plant were paid much more than most workers in the area. Kellogg's management was attempting to pay temporary workers $6 less per hour than associate employees. Although paying temporary workers less than associates is a common practice in virtually every industry, workers were upset that such a profitable organization would attempt to improve profit margins via reducing wages. The average wage for a Memphis Kellogg's employee in 2014 was $28/hour with generous benefits including a fully funded employer health care plan. The typical Kellogg employee would earn $58,240 per year without working any overtime, plus benefits. The average pay in Memphis, in 2014, was $40,477 per year, with fewer benefits.[11] If the $6 per hour pay reduction was implemented, temporary employees would make $22/hour, equating to an annual wage of $45,760, plus benefits, albeit a bit more modest than their current benefits.[12] The associate and temporary employees, then, would still make more than the typical worker in Memphis.

When one considers the previous story of the kids trampling the elderly gentleman's grass, it makes sense that a reduction in wages or benefits would lead to employee dissatisfaction. Workers are not truly motivated by salary. Initially, salary is a great recruiting tool, but employees get used to the salary and simply expect it to increase. From a hygiene factor perspective, salary and benefits did not motivate the Kellogg's workers, but the lack (or reduction) thereof, demotivated workers. As a *Harvard Business Review* article puts it, "You can't buy higher job satisfaction."[13]

Expected Salary Is Subjective

Intriguingly, workers do not evaluate the fairness of their salary using a global lens. It would not be hard for workers to look abroad and see the unlivable working conditions and wages experienced by millions of employees. Rather, they compare their wage to employees within their organization first. Then, they compare their wages to workers outside of their firm: within the community, then the region, and finally the nation. The previous Kellogg's example illustrates this point. Workers not only felt that it was unfair that temporary workers in the same facility were paid less but they were also unhappy with executive pay. Seldom do the employees of industrialized countries compare their wages to those who work outside of their country. From a global perspective, annual net income of temporary Kellogg's workers is in the top 1 percent of wage earners in the world.[14] Although being a top 1 percent (world) wage earner does not necessarily mean that there are not wage inequities in the U.S., or at Kellogg's, it is apparent that workers continually expect salaries to rise, regardless of prevailing economic conditions in their locale.

Employers have a systemic problem that looks like this: employees expect wages to rise, resulting in higher production costs, resulting in higher priced products and services, resulting in decreased sales. Of course, this is a simplified explanation of wages as they relate to sales, but this issue is exacerbated by increased societal pressures not to outsource to lower wage countries. Balancing consumer price expectations with wage expectations is not an easy feat.

Employees and employers need to be aware of both local and global economic developments when discussing wages. The U.S. is still a world power in regard to output (GDP), but their role in the global economy has declined 50 percent since the 1960s.[15] GDP, from a global perspective, has greatly increased. More countries, then, are successful at contributing to global GDP than in the past. But it is not reasonable for U.S. citizens to continue to expect both benefits and pay to increase in perpetuity while U.S. GDP declines (relative to other countries) and developing economies grow their GDP. Additionally, as globalization and free trade become the norm, businesses in industrialized nations cannot compete with foreign competitors who do not compensate employees as well. For example, the average wage in India, using real GDP/capita as a proxy, is approximately $6,500 per year compared to the U.S. at $58,000 per year. Another example is that wages in Mexico are approximately

$18,000 per year.[16] Workers, though, may not consider external country salary norms when seeking their expected wage.

Internal Motivators Are Superior

Intuitively, it seems that salary would be the number one workplace motivator for most employees. However, intrinsic motivators typically are more important. The Boston Consulting Group surveyed over 200,000 people from around the world and discovered that the following factors related to employee happiness[17] (a satisfaction proxy):

1. Recognition
2. Interpersonal relationships
3. Work-life balance
4. Supervision
5. Job security (company financial stability)
6. Growth
7. Job security (fair worker treatment)
8. Salary
9. The work itself
10. Company values

Although the hygiene factors and motivators are not "in order," as researchers Evans and Olumide-Aluko[18] suggest due to differences in job satisfaction factor priorities between industrialized (which is the focus of this book) and developing countries, it is clear that salary takes a back seat to other factors. To further illustrate the point that salary is not a prime motivator, two studies will be discussed. First, internal motivators like work engagement (the work itself), respect, autonomy (responsibility), were more important to master of library science students, than external motivators, including pay.[19] Likewise, in a study of Japanese civil servants, internal motivators related to the work itself (matching skills to job tasks), were more important than working conditions or pay.[20] Although salary is an important factor, managers who increase salaries in hopes of motivating employees will fail, in the long run, if other factors are not addressed.

Benefits

Benefits, like salary, are not true motivators. Although the cost of benefits is a major concern to both employers and employees, modern day employees simply expect benefits to increase in both quantity and quality. Herzberg noted this in *Work and the Nature of Man*[21] when he stated that the government and/or corporations are expected to subsidize benefits based not on employee performance but out of obligation to society. In other words, businesses are expected to provide for employee needs, beyond salary, out of duty. He is not making a prescription in his text but was stating a reality. In Herzberg's day, citizens of the U.S. expected the government to at least partially supplement retirement and unemployment wages, especially following the Social Security Act of 1935. Additionally, workers expected businesses to provide pensions and fringe benefits since U.S. industry dominated global production, accounting for an astonishing 40 percent of world GDP by 1960.[22]

Benefits Are Costly to Employers

Although there is an expectation from modern day employees that businesses provide sufficient wages and benefits, the cost of employee benefits has skyrocketed from 3 percent to over 30 percent of payroll, 1929–2017.[23,24] The following bar chart (Figure 9), based upon data from the Bureau of Labor Statistics,[25] shows percentages of typical pay and

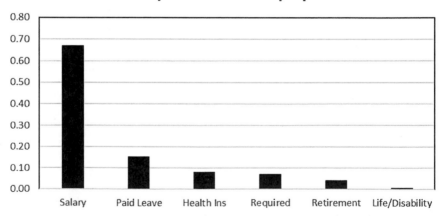

Figure 9.

benefits that employers pay out of total compensation. Salary accounts for approximately 67 percent and combined benefits account for 33 percent of total compensation. Breaking down benefits, legally required benefits, such as social security, Medicare, and worker's compensation account for 7 percent, health insurance accounts for 8 percent, life and disability insurance account for 1 percent, retirement accounts for 4 percent, and paid leave accounts for 15 percent of total employer compensation.

From the chart above, the two most notable benefit expenses are health care and paid leave. From a national perspective, the U.S. has the highest cost of health care, by far, compared to other industrialized countries. The average costs per person in the U.S. is greater than 2.5 times that of most industrialized nations.[26] Paid leave typically consists of paid time off, sick and personal days, and vacation. FMLA is unpaid up to 12 weeks in the U.S. and the employer indirectly pays, via temporarily replacing and training workers, this expense. The U.S. is one of few countries that does not offer paid maternal leave.[27] There is mounting pressure on government officials to pass government subsidized paid time off for working parents and this will continue to be an expectation of the modern worker.

Supplementing Retirement with Defined Contribution Plans

Pensions are nearly extinct today. Most businesses can no longer afford to fully fund retirement plans as they could in their heydays of the 1960s. Retirement costs for modern employers, as a percentage of total compensation, is relatively low. To further illustrate the decline of pensions, aka defined benefit plans, only 4 percent of private sector companies currently offer pensions compared to 60 percent in the early 1980s; with the bulk of current pension holders being baby boomers.[28] 401ks and other defined contribution plans are a relatively inexpensive way for employers to provide retirement benefits. The employer essentially outsources the retirement plan to a third party, like TIAA Cref or Prudential, and has employees work directly with advisors about specific retirement strategies. For example, an employee may select a mix of debt and equity investments that align with their risk profile and expected capital gains. The company, via human resources, then sets up a matching (contribution) percentage that the employer will pay into the employee's retirement plan. An employee may divert up to 6 percent of her pre-tax paycheck, for instance, and put it into the 401k plan. Then, the employer will match their 6 percent contribution. Assume the worker, pre-tax, earns $4,000 per month. Six percent, or $240, will be placed into the 401k, which the employer will match. Now, if the same employer offered a defined benefit plan (i.e., pension), the estimated employer monthly cost would be at least $720[29] per month, which is three times more expensive than the defined contribution plan. The interesting trend is that employees, for some reason, seem to be willing to accept defined contribution plans as the norm. Perhaps the rationale is that the government, through social security, has picked up some of the retirement tab. Employees do expect employers to help with retirement but not fully fund it as in the past.

Pay and Benefits Are Hygiene Factors

The most important point from this chapter is that, once a pay or benefits package is implemented, workers will expect the plan to never revert backwards. A national example of this is enlightening. The French retirement age was raised from 60 to 62 years of age in 2010. Lawmakers raised the age to offset the costs of many baby boomers retiring. The 60-year-old retirement age was established in 1982. Employees of the 21st century grew up with the expectation that retirement should commence at 60; it was the norm.[30] Workers considered it unfair that the age was raised, thus leading to many protests and riots.

Following is an example relevant to smaller firms. Imagine that an employer wants to give a "one-time" $200 holiday bonus. Suppose it has been an exceptionally strong net profit year and managers want to share the wealth with their hard-working employees. Management should be careful to award this bonus as workers will expect it, or more, the following year. This will be the case with any added benefit. If the company provides a benefit, but for economic reasons can no longer sustain the benefit, employees will develop a "they keep taking our benefits away" attitude. This is not to say managers should forgo bonuses altogether, but they should ensure that the level of said bonuses can be sustained in future years.

Modern Worker Focus—The Evolving Minimum Wage

One of the major themes of the 2016 presidential election was the case for $15/hour minimum wage. The federal minimum wage at this time was $7.25/hour.[31] One industry that received highlighted attention during the build-up to the election was the fast-food industry. Workers from 270 cities walked out and protested for the $15 minimum wage.[32] The notion was that an employee making the national minimum wage of $7.25 per hour could not support a family. In addition, many companies, due in part to the Affordable Care Act, had reduced workers hours to 27 or less per week to dodge the insurance mandate. Thus, many minimum wage workers were not making a livable wage as well as not being able to afford benefits such as health care and 401ks. Since $15 an hour was more than double the national minimum wage, many commentators made a case that employers would either ramp up automation or outsourcing to offset salary costs. It is important to note that walkouts/strikes have been a common expression of worker dissatisfaction throughout U.S. history and that this is not a new phenomenon. For example, 185,000 workers at the United Parcel Service, consisting of traditionalists, baby boomers and generation Xers, went on strike to protest for higher wages. At the time, the average driver earned $19.95/ hour, which was negotiated to approximately $23.05 per hour during the strike.[33]

In response to wage-hike pressures, companies like Amazon felt pressure to raise wages. In October of 2018, Amazon made an announcement that they would raise worker wages to $15/hour. As previously mentioned, wages are not a motivator in the long term and the reaction at a Tennessee fulfillment center supports this notion. According to the Washington Post, workers did not applaud the $15 an hour announcement as they had many more concerns than praises. Since newer workers would also make similar wages, veterans of the Murfreesboro fulfillment center felt slighted by the announcement.[34] This is a contrasting position, when compared to Kellogg's workers, who were upset about wage inequities between temporary and full-time workers.

One example of a small- to medium-sized business that is being proactive regarding employee wages is Zingerman's, a bakery in Ann Arbor, Michigan. Zingerman's is an archetypal example of how a business can create satisfied employees through training programs and empowerment (motivators similar to responsibility and growth). Co-founder Paul Saginaw was honored by the White House for his attempt to increase wages,[35] but the organization still does not pay lower skilled workers $15/hour.[36] Interestingly, Zingerman's has annual revenues of approximately $58 million per year[37] yet cannot afford to set their wages at $15 per hour. As an aside, the fact that Zingerman's motivates with empowerment and training, and not salary, reinforces the notion that salary is not necessarily a prime motivator.

Chapter Summary

Regardless of economic implications, workers, in general, will continue to demand higher wages. Just as consumers demand the businesses they patronize to provide updated technology, products, and services (consumer expectations typically do not regress), employees will continue to expect businesses to provide higher wages and added benefits. When trying to determine an appropriate wage, a manager should do the following. First, understand the cost of living in the general area. For example, the $15 an hour minimum wage idea is primarily focused on larger cities, such as New York City and Seattle, where the cost of living is quite high compared to rural areas. One resource a manager can use to determine the cost of living differences between cities is Bankrate.com's Cost of Living Calculator. A manager can simply enter two cities for comparison as well as a base wage. For example, an employee earning $50,000 per year in Buffalo (metro), New York, would need to make $119,307 per year in New York City to have an equivalent wage! Houses in New York City are approximately four times as expensive and home energy costs are nearly 1.5 times greater than that of Buffalo, among other expenses. Therefore, simply following the $15 per hour suggestion in both Buffalo and New York City is unrealistic. The cost of living calculator also provides comparative costs of various food/beverages as well as lifestyle costs including clothing, hygiene products, entertainment, etc.

Second, competitor wages should be examined in the region to determine how salary and benefits compare. Employees performing similar work will notice salary differences and, if the differences are notable, will consider it unfair to be offered the lower wage.[38] Undoubtedly, an organization's profitability is the main factor to consider, but modern employees will still demand competitive wages. Finally, the cost of goods and services, as they rise or decline, in general, should be monitored. The Consumer Price Index, which is produced by the Bureau of Labor Statistics, essentially tracks the cost of goods and services, over time, and determines if there is inflation. For example, imagine placing items into a basket, perhaps from this point in time last year, taking the average price of the goods in the basket, then, comparing it to the average price today. Typical items include food, energy, housing, apparel, transportation, health care, recreation, and education.[39] If the price for the basket of goods increases, inflation is present.

Application Questions, Chapter 3

1. Perform a cost of living search for your area and a neighboring larger, or smaller, city. First, make a hypothetical wage allocation for housing in column one. For example, if take home pay is $2,500 per month, perhaps 30 percent, or $750, could be placed into the first column. Thirty percent of the salary would be spent on housing. The second column would list typical costs in your region. The third column would list the total cost in the comparison region.

Wage Allocation Housing	Costs in Your Region i.e., Food, Gas, Utilities	Cost of Living in Comparison Region

2. Do the wages provided, for your region, adequately cover employees' living expenses?

3. Are there benefits that you could add that have minimal direct costs? For example, do employees demand more work/life balance? Are there ways to tweak policies to provide flex scheduling?

4. Take a look at the Consumer Price Index (CPI). What is the average rate of inflation, each year, over the past three years? How much should wages increase next year (if the inflation pattern holds)?

4

Supervision
Why the Cavaliers Booted Blatt

"Leadership is lifting a person's vision to high sights, the raising of a person's performance to a higher standard, the building of a personality beyond its normal limitations."[1] The preceding quote comes from management guru Peter Drucker. If this quote is unpacked into two components, it first describes a leader as a visionary. The leader sets a path that employees didn't already know existed. The leader, then, removes the blinders that employees wear, since they are not typically aware of the big picture. The leader helps employees realize that they are part of a larger story that has meaning, with yet-to-be achieved goals. Second, a leader can influence workers to improve their performance beyond what they thought was possible. A good leader can inspire workers. The first aspect requires professional aptitude: being able to have the conceptual skills necessary to set a direction for a company, department, or team, while possessing the relevant technical skills to complete and assign relevant tasks. The second aspect requires the leader to be able to inspire workers via personality (likability) or by effectively allocating rewards for acceptable employee performance and behavior.[2]

Leaders Versus Supervisors

The term "leader" can apply to any influential person.[3] Volunteers, employees, supervisors, and contract workers can make a positive or negative impact on an organization. Although leaders can exist at any level, they do not have legitimate power, as do managers, to give orders or make policy decisions. As employees are promoted within the organization, though, subordinates expect these newly minted supervisors to possess leadership skills. Supervisors, then, should be people that employees can look up to and respect. Often, employees are promoted based on technical ability related to a specific job, not because they possess team building or leadership abilities. It cannot be overstated that employees, or new hires, should not be placed into positions of authority if they have negative attitudes or are not others' focused. Technical skill alone is not a robust enough reason to promote a worker to a position of leadership or supervision. To further illustrate this point, poor supervision is deemed one of the leading causes of employees quitting their jobs.[4] It is estimated that 35 percent of workers quit their job due to dissatisfaction with managers.[5]

Herzberg identified supervision as a hygiene factor, but not specifically leadership, per se. There has been much written about leadership since the 1960s and there are countless degrees focusing on the subject. Undoubtedly supervisors should possess leadership skills. This book will use the terms "supervisors," "managers," and "leader" interchangeably, although there are nuanced differences between each of these terms.

David Blatt and the Cleveland Cavaliers

In the previous chapter, a case was made for salary not being a long-term motivator. Workers simply expect decent wages, but they will not be internally fulfilled just because their pay level is acceptable. Similarly, managers are expected to be inspiring (motivating) as well as competent in their decision-making abilities. Workers will be dissatisfied if managers are uninspiring or incompetent, but the presence of a good manager should be a given. For example, players from the 2015 Cleveland Cavaliers, one of the elite teams in the National Basketball Association (NBA), earned near-record breaking multi-million-dollar annual contracts. This team won a conference title and made it to the 2015 NBA finals under head coach David Blatt. Although the team was on a championship run in 2016, players were not celebrating wins and were disconnected in the locker room. At the core, players did not respect Blatt as coach and leader, even though he possessed competence: he had previously won over 700 games overseas and an Olympic medal.[6] In this case, players were motivated by achievement (internal factor) more so than salary (external factor) or leadership. Achievement, in this case, was winning the NBA championship. The championship, the internal motivator, trumped the hygiene factors of salary and supervision. The manager, leader, or coach, in this instance, served as a conduit for players to reach their internal goals. A coach or leader's inspiration or competence cannot fully motivate employees in the long term. Employees must be able to fulfill internalized ambitions, and the coach simply helps them get there by aligning an organization's and employee's goals.

Using a more relatable example, imagine a student who has been motivated by a teacher. In the short term, the teacher inspired the student by providing a mentorship that enabled him to develop skills beyond his own aspirations. To make this happen, the teacher possessed competence and leadership ability. Parents and students, though, expect teachers to be good leaders in the classroom; it is their job. Of course, parents can be grateful to the teacher, but the expectation is proficiency. Even if a student has the best teacher, at some point, the student will need to have an internal drive to remain motivated. If the student does not have an internal desire to excel at the given subject (i.e., math), the teacher can only inspire to a given point. Or, if the student loves math, the teacher acts as the conduit for advancing this skill. In the long term, the student will ultimately be responsible for excelling in their studies. For example, a high school music teacher can help the student learn music theory and the technical aspects of playing the instrument, as well as provide encouragement and inspiration, but at some point, the student will need her own personal goals, perhaps a career in music, to maintain motivation.

Now, imagine that the teacher is incompetent. A hygiene factor is present: the student will be demotivated. Simply stated, students do not get excited to come to class because teachers are good at their jobs. But, if teachers are bad at their jobs, students will not want to come to class. Students may think they do not like certain subjects, i.e., math, as well, but it may be the result of a present hygiene factor: a dreadful teacher.

Vintage Theory in Modern Practice— X and Y Managers

Once again, vintage theory is relevant and helpful to managers. While Herzberg was studying job satisfaction in the 1960s the typical boss possessed a Theory X mentality. The four assumptions of Theory X managers are employees inherently dislike work and hope to avoid it, employees must be forced to work and threated with punishments, employees will avoid responsibility and seek direction whenever possible, and employees are most concerned about job security.[7] When considering the previous music student example, a Theory X teacher would assume that students are lazy and unmotivated. To combat poor student attitudes, the teacher would offer rewards for learning the assigned skills or reprimands when skills are not learned in time. Theory X leadership was the natural style resulting from scientific management practices. As previously mentioned in the opening chapter, workers were cogs in the machine and supervisors dictated orders to subordinates during and following the industrial revolution. A prime example of this is Henry Ford. Skilled craftsman at Ford Motor Company were no longer needed as the assembly line was constructed. Jobs were broken down into mundane, simplistic tasks, that workers simply did not like perform.[8] Ford used a dictatorial, hard-nosed style to manage the low-skilled workforce.[9] Teachers of Ford's day also possessed this Theory X mentality.

Workers today prefer Theory Y supervisors. The four assumptions of Theory Y leaders are employees view work as a natural part of life, workers want to exercise self-direction and control, the average person seeks responsibility, and innovative decisions can occur from anywhere, not just the top of an organization.[10] Millennials prefer supervisors who communicate well, coach instead of dictate, empower workers, and involve employees in decision making.[11] Referring back to the music student example, a music teacher would assume students want to learn, that they want to excel at playing their instruments, and that they want to be challenged. The teacher, then, would act as an encourager, more so than a boss, to get students to perform at a higher rate. This does not mean that all students will be self-directed or that there are not occasions where Theory X will apply, but in general, the teacher would act more like a coach than dictator.

Theory Y in Action—Zingerman's Deli and Pal's Sudden Service

A prime example of Theory Y leadership is Zingerman's Deli, mentioned in the previous chapter. Zingerman's leaders believe that power should not be hoarded by executives and that it is management's role to put workers first so they can perform at high levels.[12] Note Zingerman's guiding principles and abbreviated descriptions.

1. Great Food!
   -A food driven business

2. Great Service!
   -Great service is an honorable profession
3. A Great Place to Shop and Eat!
   -Provide a dazzling environment for customers and staff
4. Solid Profits!
   -Be fiscally responsible
5. A Great Place to Work!
   -Empowerment, treat and compensate staff well, provide opportunity for growth and advancement, involve employees in running the business, continuous improvement, learn from errors and correct them, create a safe workplace, have fun, embrace diversity
6. Strong Relationships!
   -Build long term relationships with customers and staff, celebrate employee (group/individual) achievement and success
7. A Place to Learn!
   -Educate customers, staff, and managers
8. An Active Part of Our Community!
   -Zingerman's is here to stay and participates in community service[13]

Zingerman's addresses virtually all motivators and hygiene factors via their guiding principles. Few organizations spend this much time or effort in crafting and living out such policies. Regarding the Theory Y approach to management, Zingerman's specifically addresses empowerment and encouragement. Staff members are an asset and managers invest in them by giving extensive training, competitive pay (for the industry), and creating an environment where staff can learn and make mistakes with minimal fear of reprimand or punishment.

Zingerman's practices the Theory Y philosophy in the following ways: They hire people so they can help them succeed, they treat staff like customers, they help employees build skills that help them at work and in life, they offer resources and training employees need, they say "thanks" often, they treat staff complaints like customer complaints, and they give immediate feedback and coaching daily.[14] Additionally, Zingerman's practices open book management, which requires significant employee training and investment. Open book management allows all employees to think like owners. Investing in employees, so they understand the financial impact of their decisions, leads to increased morale and improved decision making. Basically, workers at all levels can make effective quality improvements if they understand the financials. As a result, customers are happier. For example, a dishwasher noticed that the most thrown out food was French fries. As a result, Zingerman's was able to increase profitability by cutting the number of fries in half on an initial order while offering free refills.[15]

Another business that has been successful with a Theory Y approach to supervising is Pal's Sudden Service, a fast-food chain in the southern U.S. Known for their quality and lighting fast speed, Pal's is four times faster than other fast food competitors. Pal's only makes a mistake $\frac{1}{3600}$ orders and customers only wait 18 seconds at the order window and 12 seconds at the handout window. They also boast a much lower employee turnover rate (about $\frac{1}{3}$) than the industry average. To maintain high levels of productivity, efficiency and quality, Pal's challenges and empowers employees though continuous training and study.[16] There is a myth that low-skilled jobs/employees require managers to use a dictatorial style of supervision. However, as Pal's and Zingerman's have shown, even mundane and repetitive jobs can be made more fulfilling by investing in employees via training and coaching.

Trust—The Main Ingredient in Sustainable Leadership

Without reliable leaders, employees have no chance of being satisfied with their jobs. More specifically, employees must be able to trust their leaders. Joel Peterson, the chairman of the board at JetBlue, describes three essential elements of trust: character, competence, and authority.[17] Character refers to supervisors that employees can look up to, morally speaking. One of the benefits of promoting from within an organization is that upper level managers can get a feel for how an advancing employee behaves and makes decisions. Job-related trust is undoubtedly of importance to employees. Bosses who cut corners and do a poor job following policy set a negative example while promoting a culture of quick fixes that employees will emulate. If managers are not truthful with customers, in order to make a sale or dodge complaint resolutions, employees may imitate this behavior. When hiring from outside of an organization, it is challenging for the selection committee to see the moral aspects of a candidate. Drawing a line between the workplace morality and off-site morality of a candidate can be precarious as well. Many employers screen a candidate's social media accounts, for example, during the hiring process. But does the candidate's social media presence (online morality), positive or negative, truly translate to the workplace? And what about poor decisions that potential candidates have made in their personal lives, in the past? A prime example is politics. Should a political candidate that demonstrated poor judgment in their personal life, perhaps decades ago, be eliminated from contention for office today? Of course, the severity of the charge is at play. But does personal carelessness in a non-related work environment impact the candidate's ability to perform a job-related task? Assume the candidate was unfaithful in marriage. Does this moral indiscretion truly impact an ability to maintain a city's budget, for example? Likewise, should leaders in a company be held to a similar off-site moral standard? A 2018 study of leaders supports the notion that ethical conduct should be perceived, or judged, the same both inside and outside of the workplace.[18]

Competence is the mix of skills that leaders possess to keep a business profitable. Are they able to analyze competitors and exploit new opportunities? Do they fully know the product or service that is produced and how to make it better? Do they communicate well to staff and customers? Typically, as an employee is promoted through the ranks, she will lose some of the technical, day-to-day job skills because bigger picture skills like budgeting, forecasting, and strategizing, are demanded. The main question is "Do employees believe that this leader is competent enough to make good decisions that ensure the survivability of the company?"

The third and final element of trust is authority. When a leader speaks do the subordinates listen and follow instructions? Typically, there are power struggles in virtually every organization where few lower level employees use either political or coercive power to push back against management orders. For instance, "systematic soldering" is when a group of employees is working towards a goal and a few of the less motivated employees put pressure on the high performers to slow their efforts.[19] Regardless of a supervisor's directives, the group may not meet performance targets due to members of the group exerting a negative influence. In this case, the supervisor possesses legitimate authority, or the authority to give a direct order, to the group. However, does the group properly respond, or disobey (whether overtly or secretively), the supervisor's directive? Employees will lose motivation if the supervisors do not adequately possess, or use, their authority correctly.

Modern Worker Focus—Younger Workers Want Authenticity

When considering Theories X and Y, managers should first seek to be authentic, then look to incorporate elements of Y, if possible. Additionally, no manager should rely solely on generational stereotypes (i.e., millennials are innovative job hoppers) when crafting a leadership style. For example, one would expect the late Steve Jobs, the modern management legend who saved Apple from the brink of bankruptcy in the late 1990s through strategic restructuring, to possess a Theory Y style. Apple is one of the most innovative tech companies on the planet and it seems like leadership styles would follow suit. However, Jobs was true to his personality and possessed an autocratic, dictatorial style, being quite meticulous and micromanaging.[20] The fact that Jobs was authentic and wildly successful demonstrates a need for managers to be true to themselves first, then, focus on motivational theory. Compared to billionaire Richard Branson, founder of the Virgin Group Ltd., Job's leadership style was more aligned with Theory X while Branson is aligned with Theory Y. Branson believes in delegating authority to lower levels of management and giving workers freedom to make mistakes. The key to success for both leaders, regarding employee motivation, is that they were true to themselves first and foremost. Branson is a natural delegator while Jobs was naturally autocratic. Tim Cook, another example of an authentic leader, practices a democratic leadership style true to his personality.[21]

According to the Millennial Leadership Survey conducted by Workplace Trends in 2015, 91 percent of participants aspired to be organizational leaders and 43 percent wanted to do so in order to empower others.[22] Sixty-three percent of respondents said that they would seek to be transformational, which is a form of leadership that seeks to challenge and empower employees. Transformational leadership closely aligns with Theory Y. Interestingly, only 5 percent of survey participants said money was a motivator and only 1 percent were seeking power. In another study of millennials in the workplace, 70 percent stated that authenticity was important to them both in and outside of the workplace.[23]

Therefore, managers should be authentic, yet they should also find ways to harness a Theory Y mentality. Although not exhaustive, there are a couple of ways that managers can begin to change their mindset to Theory Y. First, give employees some discretion over their work.[24]

Undeniably, some jobs require strict adherence to rules and procedures from a safety standpoint. For example, workers who are responsible for building the brake assembly for an automobile cannot freestyle their work methods. However, giving workers input, whether at the development stage or while creating work instructions, can be of benefit. Often, managers and "smart people" develop the organization's processes and miss details that workers would catch since they perform the technical, day-to-day duties. Additionally, workers will buy into work processes if they are involved in their creation and improvement.

Second, managers, as in the Zingerman's example, can share relevant financials with their employees. This does not mean that an employer should train employees to analyze financial reports, per se, but providing basic information to employees can help them realize why certain decisions are made. In manufacturing industries, reengineering improves productivity while reducing the quantity of required workers. If an employee is haphazardly reassigned to another workstation, a morale issue can ensue. Humans are creatures of habit and relocating a well-trained employee can be traumatizing. However, if the rationale for the restructure is presented to employees, and their input is considered throughout, the workers will feel involved.

Chapter Summary

Supervisors must possess two sets of skills to be effective: technical competence and leadership. Since supervision is a hygiene factor, simply hiring inspiring leaders will not motivate employees in the long term. However, the presence of incompetent supervisors will demotivate workers. Leaders must tap into the internal drives of their employees. Supervisors should be authentic, utilize a Theory Y mentality, while building trust.

Application Questions, Chapter 4

1. Does your current organization lend itself more to a Theory X or Theory Y leadership style? Explain.

2. Can you identify employees who would thrive in a Theory Y environment? Would some prefer X? What characteristics are common amongst the X and Y employees?

3. What Zingerman's practices (i.e., open book management) would benefit your workforce and why? Which financials would be most relevant to share with employees?

4. Self-reflect and determine what your "authentic leadership" qualities look like. For example, are you naturally more of a team building or process-oriented person? How can you hone your natural talents while addressing weakness?

5. Think about leaders you have, or currently, work with, and their level of trustworthiness. Are employees happier when they work for trustworthy leaders? Explain.

5

Policy

Why Workers Want Wi-Fi

Since the development of the Two Factor theory in the mid–20th century, the way in which employees view the workplace has changed. No longer do employees live to work: laborers want to take care of personal issues while working. As jobs have transitioned from manufacturing to service-based,[1] there is less need for employees to be 100 percent on task. Compartmentalizing—the separation of work and home life, is no longer a part of American employment culture. Many jobs no longer require the clock-in and clock-out mentality. For instance, financial services professionals have busy schedules yet can multitask and check in on their families or job-related activities like stock market trends rather efficiently while working. Even manufacturing workers, like forklift drivers or assembly line operators, can quickly check in on family, news, or other interests (preferably during allotted times) and still meet the employer's production schedule. Company policy, then, needs to be addressed in a modern-day context. This chapter describes why policy is still a hygiene factor, discusses modern day policies that employees expect (diversity and work-life balance), and provides a brief overview of technological advancements that have impacted the workplace.

The Technological Revolution and Its Impact on the Workplace

The Internet, or cell phone, could be the most popular candidate for top innovation of the 20th century. Yet a box, specifically a 20'×8'×8' intermodal container, may be even more important. In the second half of the 20th century, logistics engineers started standardizing shipping containers to this formatted size, which allowed for drastic increases in shipping efficiency. Once a freighter reached a port, these containers could easily be transitioned to the back of a semi-truck or railcar.[2] Basically, the containers could be filled efficiently, providing the right size for most materials to fit. Then, unloading was minimized since the containers could be easily transferred, as a unit, to the next vehicle (semi-truck or train) in the supply chain. Containerization, as it is called, coupled with advancements in communications technology, increased the speed and ease of global logistics. Ships could carry more cargo, trucks and trains could quickly take this cargo to the next location.

One notable difference between the work environment of old and the new is that exchanges of information are processed exponentially faster. Compared to 1965, computers process information 3,500 times faster, are 90,000 times more energy efficient, and the price per transistor (processing) has become 60,000 times less expensive.[3] Because of containerization and advancements in computer and phone technology, Friedman declared in his bestselling 2005 book that: *The World Is Flat.* Essentially, the technological revolution that occurred from the 1990s through the time of his writing in 2005 enabled the earth to become flat, making it easy for companies to outsource and operate in multiple countries. Friedman begins his book by using the example of Infosys Technologies Limited, near Bangalore, India, to illustrate the flattened earth concept. Infosys could easily communicate with its global supply chain partners via virtual meetings while seamlessly coordinating activities. On the wall were eight clocks with the times in Australia, Japan, Hong Kong, Singapore, India, London, and the U.S. East and West. From 1992, when Bill Clinton was president, until 2005, U.S. citizens transitioned from landline phones, and no Internet connectivity (no email), to being "full-time" connected to the outside world via the Internet and cell phones. Businesses communications drastically improved as the mode of communication shifted from phone conversations and postal mail to email and virtual meetings. Expectations that workers, especially white-collar workers, be available around the clock, became the norm.

Today, products and services can be purchased on the fly via smartphone technology and digital banking, increasing the complexity that business owners face when tracking transactions and managing inventory. Managers must store and analyze vast amounts of data and communicate real-time business decisions. The pressure that customers have placed on business has only intensified since 2005. Customers expect businesses to respond immediately to their requests, at all hours of the day. Since U.S. consumers spend shockingly large amounts of time on their smartphones each day, there is an unspoken expectation that service representatives are continually connected. In a recent study, American millennials checked their phones less than every 12 minutes, or 84 times per day.[4] The older generations are beginning to mirror this trend. As the typical person is continually checking their phones, the expectation is that businesses will continually check their "phones."

Instantaneous notifications are undoubtedly a blessing and a curse. Although modern day technology is increasing the speed at which business is done, problems arise for employees. Being continually connected to the outside world results in more demanding work schedules. One negative consequence for white-collar employees, especially, is they are expected to communicate with global suppliers and customers at all times of the day. This makes it difficult to fully check out of work. Separating work life from home life is not a possibility for many modern workers. To further illustrate the pressure that customers put on businesses, in regard to response time, 77 percent of consumers will not wait more than six hours for an email response, 85 percent expect Facebook replies within six hours, and 64 percent of Twitter users expect customer service to respond within an hour.[5] Waiting for a response is not something customers are willing to do. Thus, the line between work and home life, for employees, is blurred.

Crafting Policy from a Work-Life Perspective

Work-life balance is defined as the ability to effectively balance both work and family roles.[6] Nearly 40 percent of workers would consider moving out of the country to achieve better work life balance,[7] yet many companies still have policies that reflect those prevalent during the prime baby boomer working years.[8] Baby boomers, or employees born between 1946 and 1964, possess a "pay your dues" mentality, which means working hard for only one employer.[9] It is a badge of honor to work long hours and come home late from work. The employer fully "owns" employees who are on the clock and personal problems are not welcomed at work. In general, baby boomers are mostly concerned with policies reflecting stability and long-term employment, i.e., retirement packages tied to years of service. They also grew up with the traditional family as the norm. Work and life were clearly separated with only one working adult.

Section II—The Foundation: Hygiene Factors

Generation Xers are more independent, when compared to baby boomers, since many grew up independently as their parent(s) worked long hours outside of the home.[10] They have experienced similar technological trends as the millennial workforce, but a bit later in their careers. Texting, email, and cell phone (flip phone) were the major communication technologies present at the beginning of their careers versus smartphones and data plans being ever present at the beginning of millennials' careers. The line between work and home life became less defined for the generation X workers and is only becoming more blurred today. Combining the advances in technology with pressures associated with roles common to nontraditional family members (i.e., dual earners or single parenting), employees want to be able to take care of personal responsibilities at work. Likewise, employers want employees to take care of work responsibilities at home. Modern workers, then, need more time to complete personal tasks while at work since they often work after hours, from home.

Workers expect to flex their schedules so they can leave work and pick up children from school, take care of sick family members, attend classes, or take care of important time sensitive tasks.[11] Typically, workers are required to work core hours and are allowed to flex around these hours. For example, an office employee may be required to be present from 10 a.m. to 2 p.m. due to heavy customer contact or meeting times. Additionally, the worker may need to log in eight hours per day but may be able to flex their schedules before or after the core hours. Perhaps the office worker performs data entry tasks in the flex hours that do not require the worker to be present at a specific time. Or the work may be able to be performed from home, which benefits both the worker (able to better manage work/life) and the employer (fewer resources consumed, i.e., utility usage). In addition to flex schedules, some companies have compressed workweek and job-sharing policies. Compressed work weeks enable workers to put in more hours in fewer days so they can have longer weekends. A four-day, 10-hour shift is an example of a compressed workweek. Job sharing, on the other hand, attempts to minimize work hours and is an arrangement that allows workers to go part-time and share a job. For example, a job that requires eight hours of labor can be split equally between two workers. The benefits to the employer, for both compressed workweeks and job sharing, are that they reduce overhead costs and these changes may lead to improved morale due to better work/life balance for employees. Compressed workweeks require less utilization of resources since the company is open fewer days per week.

Job sharing allows companies to minimize benefits (although not necessarily recommended) since workers are part-time and not full-time. Workers, in both instances, can free up time for personal use. Granted, compressed workweeks still require an equivalent amount of labor hours per week, but employees receive more days off per week.

One company that is concerned with work/life balance is Raytheon, a hi-tech cybersecurity company. Raytheon allows workers to have flexible schedules, compressed work weeks, job sharing, reduced hours, and telecommuting opportunities.[12] Human Element, an ecommerce consultant out of Ann Arbor, Michigan, believes that workers are more productive and healthier if they are able to recharge and spend time with their families outside of work. Management believes that spending too much time on work projects can be an unhealthy behavior. Additionally, the company has mandatory fun days, additional vacation days for every year worked, flexible schedules, an end-of-the-year week-long vacation, and time off on birthdays.[13] Taking work/life policy a step farther, Patagonia offers subsidized on-site childcare, leading to 100 percent of moms returning to work after maternity leave.[14]

Work-life balance not only addresses flexible scheduling but includes employees being able to take care of personal tasks while on the clock. Shopping online at work, for example, is a common employee practice. To illustrate this point, on Cyber Monday alone, more than half of workers shop online.[15] Of course, if workers are neglecting their job duties, this is a glaring issue. But in service-based jobs, workers can take care of both personal and professional tasks. Interestingly, 11 percent of employers have fired workers for online shopping during work hours. In addition, 24 percent of employers fired an employee for using the Internet on non-work-related activities and 17 percent fired employees for inappropriate social media postings. Regarding smartphone usage, workers spend an average of five hours per week on non-work- related activities.[16] Social media also consumes a considerable amount of time with conservative estimates stating that 77 percent of employees use social media while at work.[17] In 2014, one study showed that 80 percent of companies had social media policies with 70 percent of those companies disciplining workers for violating these policies.[18] Undoubtedly, employers must decide if turnover costs, opportunity costs (costs associated with policing Internet use instead of administration working on productive tasks), and morale costs are worth the effort to monitor employees' technology usage.

At the core of the work/life discussion are the ideals of the baby boomer generation: work and life are separate functions and should be treated as such. Here are some questions that operations and human resource managers should ask before crafting polices. Is the compartmentalization of work and life necessary? To what level should the employer be involved in catching "time thieves," or workers "stealing" company time to pursue personal objectives? Should employers police employees' Internet usage during work hours? Of course, inappropriate sites should be banned, especially if employees are using company resources. Does the "loss" of productivity that results from too much personal time at work outweigh the costs of reprimands and firings? Certainly, workers can spend an excessive amount of time on non-work-related matters. But do employers need workers, especially those in the service industry, to be 100 percent on task? Finally, do employees have the right to spend time on personal issues, while at work, if employers also expect these employees to be available during non-work hours? Policies that promote a healthy work/life balance are of the utmost importance to modern workers.

Policies Not Only Punitive

Employee policies are typically created so members of a firm behave in a way that minimizes litigation. In the U.S. especially, there are many laws that need to be considered when crafting policy. Employee policies need to be fair and written with the law in mind. However, human resource professionals focus too much on employee control, and rightly so. But they could also create policies that promote employee engagement. Policies can be written with the employee's welfare in mind. Instead of policies being a list of do's and don'ts to follow, policies can be created to help employees be more creative and enthusiastic about their jobs.

When crafting punitive company policy, managers should first determine if the policy is absolutely "necessary," followed by how it will be "fairly" and efficiently controlled and enforced. Following are examples of punitive policies. In the first example, it might be necessary and easily enforceable to have a "no smartphone usage policy" while employees work on a high-volume assembly line. The policy is relevant since it is easy for managers to provide the rationale that distractions cause errors and decreased productivity. Imagine trying to create controls for this policy. One idea may be for the IT department to monitor any connection to the company's Wi-Fi during worktime, minus break times.

At first glance, the policy is easy to implement, and the IT department could run a weekly report. However, monitoring the Wi-Fi connection is not efficient since it requires time for the IT department to add an additional task to their day. There are also employee privacy concerns. Undoubtedly the company has the right to monitor the connections since they provide this service, but employee morale may decline as they feel their privacy, right or wrong, has been violated. If Wi-Fi connections are discovered during worktime, the IT workers will then spend additional time communicating with production team leaders, who may have differing views and disciplinary methods regarding the policy violation, and workers could use their own data plan to work around the Wi-Fi connection. A secondary control could be implemented: supervisor monitoring. Of course, the supervisor would need to be fair when administrating this policy and continually monitoring smartphone usage can be an opportunity cost: supervisors could be making better use of their time.

The second example relates to a smartphone policy but in a different workspace. Instead of the high-volume assembly line, the workspace is one of customer service call center employees who answer random, incoming phone calls. In this scenario, calls are inconsistent, and workers can easily shift from personal phone usage to answering an incoming work-related call. Compared to the high-volume assembly line which produces many parts per minute, leaving no time for employee slack, the call center does not require 100 percent worker productivity. Would a no personal smartphone/Internet usage policy be necessary and easily controlled? Typically, office workers expect to be able to take care of personal details while working. The workspace is drastically different than the high-volume assembly line. This is not to say that taking care of personal business during working hours is an acceptable practice, just an expectation. It would also be a bit more difficult for managers to control employees who work in offices than it would be for those working on an assembly line. Is it necessary, and readily controlled, to have a no personal phone/Internet usage policy for these call center workers? Especially if they can still get their work completed on time? In this case, it may create an unnecessary burden for supervisors to monitor smartphone use if it does not affect worker productivity.

Following are two more examples of actual punitive policies that exist in different industries. The first policy example is common for automotive manufacturers. An easy way for human resource administrators to maintain employee attendance is with a 10-point scale. If an employee is absent, or late, for any reason, he earns a point. After a calendar year, points are removed. If, however, the employee earns 10 points before the end of the calendar year, he is terminated. The policy seems fair from a legal perspective in that it applies to everyone equally. Of course, there is no motivational element to this policy as it is 100 percent punitive, but it may be necessary to organize the start and end shifts. On the face, this policy is reasonable in that 10 absences or late arrivals to work in a year is generous. Of course, being late or tardy could affect performance appraisal scores but overall, employees could miss work for any reason, which seems reasonable since "life happens." The policy is also simple to administer since the automated time clock could objectively determine if an employee was tardy or absent from work. If managers followed the no-fault system as designed, the policy is fair. The policy becomes unfair, however, if it turns into a mechanism not previously stated by administration. For example, if the company uses the policy to promote work-life balance (not using it punitively), allowing workers to miss work for any reason, it should not be used to keep employees from promotions or used against them on a performance appraisal. If a worker was dealing with many family illnesses during the year, she may have missed more work than the average worker. But this should be acceptable since the policy was created for work-life balance purposes. Or, if an employee simply did not feel like going to work, and the policy allows for this behavior, the employee should not suffer a consequence. On the other hand, if the policy is communicated by management as punitive only and missing an increasing amount of days clearly impacts appraisals and promotion opportunities, management has the right to discipline. One thing to note, should managers have to decide between legitimate missed days or non-legitimate? Is this worth policing? Probably not. Automotive manufacturers typically pursue the punitive implementation of the policy. Point policies have also been used, during economic downturns such as that of 2007–2009, for layoff purposes. As demand for company vehicles minimized, companies could no longer afford to fully staff their factories. Some manufacturers decided to lay off workers who had higher amounts of points. Again, if the policy was communicated as punitive, which may have been the case, and workers were aware that using the point system could impact them in such a layoff scenario, then the policy would still be fair. However, if the policy was either not communicated in this manner, or if the policy was created to be a work/life policy, yet used for layoffs, then this would be an unfair implementation of the policy.

The next scenario is common to the service industry, in particular, health care offices. It is debatable as to whether the policy is necessary, but it is easily enforced. Workers, primarily receptionists, must be clocked in and logged into their computer several minutes before the start of their shift (7:53 a.m.). The reason for this rule is that patients may call in immediately, or just before, the office opening time (8 a.m.). Additionally, patients may arrive on time or early to their appointments. Thus, the receptionist gets paid starting at 8 a.m. but technically starts working at 7:53 a.m. One could argue that receptionists should be fully logged in and prepared by 8 a.m. sharp. However, is it necessary to be clocked and logged in at 7:53 a.m.? Or, is it fair, from a pay perspective, to punish a receptionist for logging in at 7:58 a.m.? According to the Department of Labor, it is legal to round employee's time to the nearest quarter hour.[19] Therefore, if the employee is forced to clock in seven minutes early, this time can be rounded off. The policy is easily enforceable since login and clock in times can be monitored electronically. But punishment for not working before the shift technically starts is not a legitimate practice.

The Hot Stove Rule

Although the previous examples demonstrated disciplinary policies related to attendance and how employees balance their personal and professional time at work, the "necessary" and "fair" doctrine applies to other policy areas such as promotions and performance appraisals. The "hot stove rule" is a simple analogy that managers can use to visualize the previous elements (necessary and fair).[20] First, the stove should be set to the correct temperature. The stove represents the policy being formed. If a university has a tenure and promotion policy for its faculty, is the policy necessary (set to the right temperature)? For example, if most colleges have a five- to seven-year tenure track and another university has a seven- to 10-year track, is that a necessary policy? Second, the stove should burn any cook who touches it, the same way, every time. In other words, the stove is not biased as to who it burns, "disciplining" consistently. Regarding the tenure policy, a method to make the policy consistent and fair would be to institute a committee, preferably cross-functional and diverse, to minimize bias, that evaluates tenure tracked professors who are up for promotion.

Simplified Policy Writing

One example of innovative policy writing is the *Survival Manual* created by Semco, a manufacturing company based in Sao Paulo, Brazil. Although the *Survival Manual* may technically not be a modern-day publication since it was published in Ricardo Semler's 1993 *Maverick*, few companies have been able to imitate its simplicity and positive effects. The *Survival Manual* is still used by Semco today. Written in a cartoon format, the manual is given to all Semco employees. It is a quick, fun read. Each of the 20 or so policies is succinctly written. For example, the *Factory Committees* policy illustrates a boss and subordinate in a boxing ring, with a paragraph below stating: "Employees at Semco are guaranteed representation through the Factory Committee of each business unit. Read the charter, participate, make sure your committee effectively defends your interests-which many times will not coincide with Semco's interests. We see this conflict as healthy and necessary."[21] This policy encourages workers to be informed and communicate with company leaders. It is easy to understand without the legalese. The policy is also realistic in that conflict is considered normal, addressing the fact that businesses and employees often have competing interests.

Policy Still a Hygiene Factor

Do employees get excited to come to work because of modern, pro-worker policies? No. Workers expect these policies to be in existence as they are considered the "right thing to do." This does not mean that workers do not respect or become more loyal to employers who create beneficial policies. Laws and policies are supposed to reflect the desires of the constituency in hopes of setting parameters for acceptable and encouraged behaviors. Imagine a city that has the perfect system and administration of laws, if possible. The townsfolk will adapt to this environment; they will expect it to function this way in the future. Creating this atmosphere is simply the right thing for government officials to do. Citizens will get used to these news laws; they become the new standard. At some point the excitement of the perfect legal system wears off. This is not to say that this system is not worth pursuing or that it is not valuable, but laws, like policies, do not motivate workers, especially in the long term. For example, diversity policies, which are mentioned in the *Modern Worker Focus* section below, are likely to create more loyal millennial workers but only over a five-year period. Successful policy implementation may minimize turnover in the short term, but it is only one ingredient in the Two Factor theory model. More specifically, policy is a hygiene factor.

Modern Worker Focus—Diversity Policy and Practice

As the workforce continues to become more diverse than previous generations, millennial and generation Z workers want policies that promote diversity. Modern workers are likely to be more loyal to employers who have diverse workforces and management teams.[22] Principally, modern workers want the makeup of organizations to reflect the makeup of their communities. Universities, as a result, now offer diversity and inclusion degrees. Most corporations have diversity and inclusion policies and programs. As younger workers are entering the workforce their demographic characteristics differ much more than previous generations, especially the baby boomers. Following is a list of how communities and workforces are changing. First, in a study of 18- to 34-year-olds, 62 percent in the 1960s were either married or lived with a partner in the home. Today, this percentage is less than 32 percent. Eighty percent of millennial workers today are part of dual career families compared to generation Xers at 73 percent and baby boomers at 47 percent.[23] Second, multigenerational family living is becoming more commonplace. The Pew Research Center cites diversity, especially among Asian and Hispanic families, as the source of this trend.[24]

Third, the U.S. workforce is aging. By 2030, over 20 percent of the population will be older than age 65. As a result, immigrants will continue playing a vital role in the workforce. Without immigrants there would be 18 million fewer working age adults by 2035 due to lower births amongst U.S. born parents.[25] Fourth, workers are more diverse regarding race and gender. In 1990, one-fifth of the U.S. population was non-white. By 2060, this percentage will be closer to one-third. As the workforce continues to be less "white" and "male," and modern workers value diversity, it is relevant to discuss where workplaces currently stand regarding race and gender. To begin, 17.5 percent of businesses are minority owned yet 38 percent of the population are minorities.[26] Taking a look at high ranking officials in Fortune 500 companies, 80 percent are men with 72 percent being white.[27] In a study of job applications, a researcher sent out 1,600 entry level resumes, through job search websites, to employers in large cities. Some of the black and Asian resumes were "whitened," meaning that racial clues, i.e., organizations in which the applicant volunteered, were removed, while others were not "whitened." The whitened resumes received approximately two times more callbacks. One of the more shocking findings from the study was that organizations that touted their diversity and inclusion practices were just as likely to discriminate as those that did not.[28] In regard to women in the U.S. labor force, the percentage has increased from 32 percent in 1960 to 47 percent today. Pay inequality, however, is one of the most prominent issues facing women in the workplace today. Although the median wage for women has improved to 85 percent of what men earn, 42 percent of women state they have experienced gender discrimination.[29] Fifth, perhaps the most discussed sociocultural development in the U.S. is the acknowledgment of LGBTQ+ (lesbian, gay, bisexual, transgender, and queer) rights. The percentage of American adults who identify as LGBTQ+ has increased from 3.5 percent in 2012 to 4.5 percent in 2017, which is primarily driven by millennials.[30] Furthermore, 48 percent of LGBTQ+ millennials are planning to grow their families as compared to 55 percent of non–LGTBQ+ millennials; with the gap narrowing considerably in recent years.[31] Undoubtedly, there are varying opinions regarding gay marriage with just over half of Americans in support.[32] In response to the previously mentioned trends, companies are hiring for positions such as Director for Diversity and Engagement and Chief Diversity and Inclusion Officer. Human resource managers, especially, should be aware of demographic trends to improve hiring and promotion practices.

The previous list describing how workplaces are becoming more diverse is not exhaustive and briefly describes a few major trends. For example, diversity regarding mental and physical disabilities was not addressed. The main takeaway for managers is that, if employers choose to create policies that address diversity, they must also live out these policies. As previously mentioned, companies that promote their diversity policies to the public may not actually care about diversity at all. As with any policy, workers will follow management's lead as to how to behave in the workplace; policy is secondary. Simply creating policies and posting them for all employees to see is not a sufficient way to change the practices within an organization. Leaders and employees must embrace policy changes.

One company that is making headlines for its diversity related successes is Publix Supermarkets, the largest employee-owned grocery store in the U.S. Publix has won awards such as "Best Workplaces in Retail," "Best Workplaces for Women," "Best Workplaces for Diversity," and "Best Workplaces for Millennials." These awards align with statements from their website: "Diversity is a very good thing because of fresh ideas and unique perspectives" and "Publix makes it a priority to employ and work with people from many backgrounds, cultures, abilities, and ethnicities."[33] To win Fortune's "Best Workplaces for Diversity" award, associates anonymously commented on factors such as fairness and inclusion.[34] Over the past 10 years Publix has consistently increased revenue from $24.5 billion in 2009 to $36.4 billion in 2018. Likewise, over the same time period, net profit has increased from $1.2 billion to $2.4 billion.[35] Undoubtedly Publix's workforce reflects statements about their embracement of diversity. Below is a table displaying Publix's workforce demographic profiles, including age and disabilities.[36]

Diversity at Publix

Workforce Makeup	*Employee Description*
43%	Minorities
11%	Minority Executives
33%	Minority Front-Line Managers
20%	Minority Mid-Level Managers
49%	Women
22%	Women Executives
40%	Women Front-Line Managers
24%	Women Mid-Level Managers
21%	Baby Boomers or Older
8%	Workers with Disabilities
5%	LGBTQ+

The workforce is changing, and managers must tap into the talents and perspectives of a diverse workforce. The first step that a company can take is creating a diversity and inclusion council. The council should contain representatives from all organizational levels that represent the diversity of the community and workforce. The purpose of this council is twofold. First, the council should allow workers to voice any concerns in a safe environment and have access (open door policy) to upper level management to voice concerns.[37] Publix, for example, maintains an environment that allows workers to express their opinions and annually surveys employees.[38] If a council is created, it can address concerns with managers, perhaps in quarterly meetings. The council must also have legitimate power to make necessary changes.[39] Second, the council should audit and help to create policies and procedures that promote worker wellbeing. Instead of purely top down driven policy, which may include bias, workers and the council would have a voice and say in policy matters. The heart of the council is to ensure that all workers, despite personal beliefs or demographic differences, have fair and equal treatment.

Chapter Summary

Following is an excerpt from the University of Western Australia's Code of Conduct: "The University is committed to providing an environment of equal opportunity, free from discrimination, for existing and prospective staff and students in the pursuit of their academic and professional goals and the realization of their potential to contribute to the achievement of the University's mission. This objective is supported by an employment philosophy of providing job security through ongoing employment where possible and encouraging flexible work practices that accommodate a range of needs in a diverse workforce. The University seeks to remove any barriers that may impede full access to the benefits and conditions of employment and the delivery of University services ... the University will act to ensure that its structures are free from direct or indirect discrimination on the grounds of sex, marital status or pregnancy, race, age, sexual orientation, gender identity, religious or political beliefs, impairment, family responsibility or family status."[40] Throughout this chapter policies that modern workers are concerned with, namely work-life balance and diversity, are captured in the code of conduct above. Regarding diversity, this public university states that their customers (students) and employees will not be hindered based on their demographic traits. Work-life balance is noted, within this context, as an important practice. The policy, then, is "modern." As previously mentioned in this chapter, managers must actively demonstrate that they truly support work/life and diversity in the workplace. Policies that are created for promotional purposes, i.e., recruiting, but not actually lived out, will not eliminate the presence of this hygiene factor.

Application Questions, Chapter 5

1. Which of the work-life balance methods (compressed work-week, job sharing, daycare subsidies, or flexible scheduling) could your organization realistically pursue in the next six months to a year?

2. Regarding question one, create a list of steps that needs to be followed to improve your selected work-life balance method.

3. If your company is large enough (at least 30 workers for sampling purposes), how would you create a diversity council? Who would be represented (departments, employees, suppliers, etc.)? Who would lead it and what powers would the council possess?

4. Go to the census.gov website and investigate the demographic makeup of the area surrounding your business. Demographics included are typically age, gender, race, military status, family living arrangements, Internet access, income levels, and citizens with disabilities. How does the composition of your workforce compare to the demographic makeup of your region? Fill out the table below. Of course, any demographic analysis must be nuanced. For example, perhaps one ethnicity has a higher percent of youth than another. The business, then, may need to look at ethnicity based on 18 years or older.

Demographic Profile i.e., Race	Regional Percentage i.e., 7% Hispanic	Company Percentage i.e., 4% Hispanic

Section II—The Foundation: Hygiene Factors

Demographic Profile i.e., Race	Regional Percentage i.e., 7% Hispanic	Company Percentage i.e., 4% Hispanic

5. In general, what policies can your company create, or revise, that promote employee well-being?

6

Working Conditions

Why the Legal Landscape Needs Navigating

Imagine, or remember, working conditions at the dawn of the 1960s. As Herzberg discovered that working conditions were hygiene factors, the legal landscape was completely different than today. There was no Equal Employment Opportunity Commission (EEOC), no age or disability protections, no Occupational Safety and Health Administration (OSHA), and no requirements for equal pay. Labor unions were present at 30 percent of employers, compared to less than 11 percent today.[1] Many states have also turned into Right-to-Work states, meaning employees at unionized facilities do not have to pay union dues, minimizing the power of unions. In general, the modern work environment that managers must navigate is at-will coupled with burgeoning legislation. Human resource managers are responsible for ensuring fair and legal employment practices while minimizing discrimination; especially when employees, who can technically be fired at-will, may pursue either EEOC or legal compensation for unfair terminations.

Working conditions can be viewed as a three-tiered structure (see Figure 10). At the base is legislation that impacts the workplace, titled the "Legal Obligation to a Safe and Non-Discriminatory Environment." Employers, at minimum, must meet state and federal regulations or suffer potential litigation. Second, managers can create procedures that ensure the workplace is perpetually clean and well-groomed. This section is titled a "Well Maintained Workspace." Finally, an organization can transform a workspace into a "Fun Place to Work." Some companies have gone to great lengths to create entertaining and collaborative atmospheres for their employees. The purpose of this chapter is to walk through this three-tiered working conditions structure. Major legislation that has impacted working conditions since the creation of the Two Factor theory will be addressed. The lean workplace discipline of 5s, related to the second tier, will be unpacked. At the top tier, Google,

71

amongst other companies who provide a "fun place to work," will be described. Ultimately, a case is made for working conditions being a hygiene factor.

Legislation Overview—Tier I

Working conditions have improved immensely over the years. In 1970, for instance, there were 14,000 workplace fatalities. In 2009 the workforce itself doubled in number yet workplace fatalities totaled 4,340. Additionally, workplace injuries and illnesses have declined from 11 out of 100 workers in 1972 to 3.6 out of 100 workers in 2009.[2] While

Figure 10.

this degree of improvement is impressive, the ideal number of workplace fatalities and injuries per year would be 0. Examples from modern day include settlements by TOMRA Recycling, which paid $16,000 for exposing workers to hazardous materials (2017),[3] and the United Parcel Service (UPS), which was fined $320,000 (2016) regarding a worker falling 22 feet to his death. UPS was previously cited by OSHA for not providing a safe working environment on the same jobsite.[4]

Many companies track and tout their safety records while targeting 0 injuries. But do employees get excited to work in a safe office or factory? The answer is, simply, no. Safe working conditions are expected by workers and rightfully so. However, if the workspace is not designed to minimize injury or illness, employees will be dissatisfied. In other words, working conditions are a hygiene factor. Poor working conditions lead to job dissatisfaction but improving working conditions does not lead to satisfaction. Quite often, bosses are too busy to make safety a priority. Typical bosses are just trying to survive each day, dealing with the onslaught of emails, notifications, and meetings that pile up in addition to their daily job duties. Safety, although a priority for the company at large, is often not the focal point of production managers. Some companies combat this phenomenon by hiring a safety manager or creating a safety committee. This committee (or safety manager) has representation at relevant meetings and audits the work environment for safety violations or ergonomic improvements.

Not only should managers be worried about safety legislation and maintaining a hazard-free work environment, they should also be concerned about discrimination. The law, in general, prohibits employers from discriminating based on age, race, gender, ethnicity, pregnancy, and mental or physical disabilities. Company lawsuits based on discrimination, whether settled by the EEOC or in court, can be quite costly for employers. Uber, for example, paid almost $2 million to employees because of gender and minority pay discrimination. Additionally, they were accused of harassment and creating a hostile work environment.[5] Human resource managers are tasked with maintaining fair hiring, pay, appraising, and promotion opportunities, within the legal framework. However, it is a tall task to ensure that all employees and leaders behave ethically. Although it would seem that employers today would do a good at keeping the law, in just one month (April of 2019—selected at random) EEOC settlements tallied just shy of $2 million. Settlement categories included pay, gender, disability, pregnancy, race, and age discrimination as well as sexual harassment.[6] Following is a brief overview of the major laws related to working conditions post 1960 that managers should understand prior to making employee related decisions[7]:

Year	Act	Purpose (in Brief)
1947	Taft-Hartley Act[8]	*Although this law was in place at the time of Herzberg's writing, 27 states (in total) have since gone "Right-to-Work." Employees do not have to join a union as a condition of employment.

Year	Act	Purpose (in Brief)
1963	Equal Pay	Prohibits unequal pay, gender discrimination, for jobs that require equal skill, effort, and responsibility
1964	Civil Rights Act Title VII[9]	Employer cannot discriminate based on race, color, religion, sex, and national origin
1967	Age Discrimination in Employment Act	Forbids employer to have discriminatory policies that negatively affect employees aged 40 or older
1970	Occupational Safety and Health (OSHA)[10]	OSHA administration sets and enforces standards to ensure employers have safe working conditions
1974	Employee Retirement Income Security Act (ERISA)	Protects employee retirement accounts from mismanagement (more noteworthy in the pension plan era)
1978	Pregnancy Discrimination	Prohibits employers from discriminating against pregnant women
1990	Americans with Disabilities Act (ADA)	Employers cannot discriminate based on mental or physical disability
1993	The Family and Medical Leave Act (FMLA)[11]	Employees may take up to 12 weeks of unpaid leave for the birth of a child or family health problems *There is currently a proposal, at the federal level, for a payroll tax to subsidize paid FMLA

Year	Act	Purpose (in Brief)
2001	Lilly Ledbetter Fair Pay	From the time of the last paycheck, women have 180 days to file a wage discrimination complaint, allows for compensatory and punitive damages

5s and a Clean Workspace—Tier II

It is important to note that providing employees with acceptable working conditions requires managers to attend to concerns, daily, at all tier levels (I, II, and III): it is an ongoing process. Once Tier I is tackled by management, and a safe and discriminatory free workplace becomes the norm, the next phase to address is maintenance. All processes that produce waste or create a mess should have a maintenance schedule. The schedule could be as simple as cleaning up at the end of the day to conducting monthly audits. The hospitality staff manager of a hotel, for instance, could 100 percent inspect the cleaned rooms. Regarding the stock room, maintenance staff may perform weekly checks on machinery, i.e., the washers and dryers, to ensure they are cleaned and performing at optimal levels.

To maintain a clean and visually appealing workplace, many companies have adopted the Japanese 5s methodology. The 5s model includes: seiri (sort), seiton (set in order), seiso (shine), seiketsu (standardize), and shitsuke (sustain).[12] Employees, regardless of position or department, are expected to: eliminate any unnecessary tools, parts, or instructions, neatly organize and label whatever remains, clean the work area, set regular maintenance schedules, and make this set of behaviors a part of everyday life. Undeniably, working in a consistently clean work area is beneficial from both an efficiency and safety perspective. If the workplace is properly maintained, for example, trip hazards and particle inhalation are less likely.

Unfortunately for managers, keeping a clean and well-organized workspace will not motivate employees. The lack thereof, however, will be off-putting, especially if the work environment is service based; customers interact with the facility. Certainly, a restaurant or hotel that is not well maintained beyond the minimal health and safety regulations will have high employee and customer turnover. From an injury and workers' compensation perspective, implementing a 5s plan can save an organization time and money (fewer claims). To further demonstrate that organized working conditions do not motivate, employees at Toyota Motor Corporation, a 5s proponent, were asked "what motivates you at work?" The survey, conducted through the Process Improvement Japan organization,[13] received the following responses: "accomplishment, my supervisor trusts me," "my job has a purpose," "I enjoy my work," and "recognition." Notice how all responses represent Herzberg's motivators. Not one response mentioned 5s or working conditions.

Fun Workplaces—Tier III

Imagine a company that has an exemplary work environment: 0 injuries and a well maintained 5s program. In addition, they uphold the highest standards regarding hiring and safety practices. Now, this company wants to transform their workplace into a fun and flexible atmosphere to attract and retain employees. Can this company, who will successfully address all three tiers of the Working Conditions Structure, expect more loyal and motivated employees? Again, the answer is no. This is not to say that managers should not continue improving their working conditions since it is the right thing to do. Hygiene factors, like fixing the basement wall of a house, need to be fixed and improved. But workers will not be motivated by fun, flexible, and safe working conditions. Interestingly, in a survey of 1,700 workers, only 20 percent of millennials, which is less than the baby boomers score, stated they care about work being a fun place.[14]

To illustrate how innovative working conditions are not a motivating agent, the tech industry will be examined. High tech companies are known for attracting the best and brightest millennials. The movie *The Internship*, for example, portrays two "older" generation X fictional interns who are the only non-millennial applicants at Google. This is one of the most innovative companies in the world, owning the Google Search engine, YouTube, Google Maps, Chrome, and beyond. Google's unique and innovative working conditions are often highlighted in management textbooks. The Googleplex, where their employees work, has the following frills: onsite computer experts to diagnose and fix digital problems, a swimming pool with a lifeguard on duty, employee lounges with pool tables and snack bar, top-notch hairstylists that give employees free haircuts, volleyball courts, three free gourmet meals per day, on-site play areas for employees' children, free massages, and places for dogs to play.[15] One would expect the annual turnover rate at such an amazing workplace to be minimal. Shockingly, the average Google employee tenure is just one year![16] Tech companies, in general, post similar turnover numbers while offering up premium working conditions. For instance, Square, the digital payments company whose tech is used at many retailers, has just a 2.3-year average employee tenure.[17] They also provide free meals, extended paternity and maternity leave, unlimited paid time off, and a work from home option. Again, these external perks are related to the bottom of Maslow's Pyramid (or the Employee's Pyramid) as they are hygiene factors. True motivation occurs when workers can fulfill their internal desires.

Modern Worker Focus: Telecommuting

The traditional way that "things were done," whether it be education, shopping, or working, is that a person would travel to a brick-and-mortar location to perform the said task. To work, learn, or shop, required the individual to leave her home and obtain this service or good at an outside location. Prior to innovations in communications technology, compartmentalizing one's life was the norm. Today, completing tasks in an online or virtual environment is normal. It is common for people to shop, attend school, go to church, and live (social media) online. It is no wonder, then, that workers expect employers to allow virtual work. Perhaps compartmentalization was a strength of previous generations in that "work was work" and "home life was home life," and there was nothing in-between. For better or worse, people today have become accustomed to multitasking and non-compartmentalizing. There is not always a need, then, to "go to work": "work can come to you."

Flexible scheduling is important to modern workers. The practice of telecommuting, or working remotely either from home or other location outside of work, is increasing in popularity. The number of telecommuting workers doubled from 2005 to 2015, currently at four million workers.[18] As communications technology continues to improve it is much easier for managers to allow their workers, at least in part, to complete work at home. From a working conditions perspective, on the face at least, it is easier for managers to have fewer employees on site to minimize injuries or potential personnel conflicts. Simply stated, the odds of things going wrong decrease with fewer on-site workers. One interesting statistic is that, if workers are allowed to telecommute 50 percent of the time, it saves companies approximately $11,000 annually in reduced overhead costs (less energy usage and space required).[19] It may also be easier to accommodate workers with disabilities if they are allowed to work from home. For employees, telecommuting minimizes travel, saving time and money, and has a positive environmental impact. Workers also have a better work-life balance. However, allowing workers to telecommute creates its own issues for management. Monitoring, via website tracking or audio recording, can cause privacy concerns yet managers need to track productivity. From an overtime perspective, it is difficult to track worker hours when they are not "punched-in" at the office. Workers can still get injured at home and it is nearly impossible for managers to ensure safe working conditions in an employee's home. Although telecommuting can be of benefit to businesses, there are still legal and productivity risks. One study suggests that the benefits outweigh the risks. Workers who worked from home in a two-year study were more productive, had a 50 percent less attrition rate, had fewer sick days and took less time off than the at-work group.[20]

Regarding large companies and the effectiveness of their telecommuting programs, the results drastically vary. To attract modern workers, large health care provider Aetna is a telecommuting powerhouse. Aetna was one of Forbes' most admired companies in 2018 and offers work-from-home jobs for various positions, including nursing consultation, data analysis, underwriting, and case management.[21] *The Working Mother* magazine, a proponent of mothers who want to excel at career and family, promoted Aetna and their remote jobs and benefits.[22] However, companies such as Best Buy, Yahoo, and Hewlett-Packard, have reduced or removed their telecommuting practices all together, citing a lack of collaboration and innovation that occurs on-site.[23] It would behoove managers to analyze their job descriptions and determine if there is an appropriate amount of work that can be done, with low risk, from home, as a first step towards telecommuting. Since work-life balance is a major concern for many employees and there are cost savings implications for managers, telecommuting, at least in part, should be a common employer practice.

Chapter Summary

This chapter addressed the three working condition tiers: legal and safety, maintenance, and fun. Companies that adhere to safety regulations and anti-discrimination policies create a fair work environment. Workspaces that are well-maintained benefit employees, customers, and the employer as there are less injuries, legislative costs, and costs of separations. Fun workplaces, although used to recruit talented employees, do not lead to a more faithful workforce. Maintaining acceptable working conditions should be a priority for managers but workers will not be motivated because of these efforts. Working conditions are a hygiene factor.

Application Questions, Chapter 6

1. How many of the 5s elements does your company (or department) adequately address? Create a 5s procedure with a timeline for a process or department.

2. Are your supervisors aware of the various laws mentioned in this chapter? What benefits are there to legal training?

3. What improvements can be made to your work environment? Legal? 5s? Fun/engaging?

4. Which jobs or tasks could be partially telecommuted? What policies would you need to implement to ensure that productivity and quality targets are met?

5. Perform a walkthrough at your company and write down any potential safety hazards, improper labeling, or improvement suggestions and assign a date to fix each issue.

7

Job Security

Why Rank and Yank Doesn't Motivate

One of the most glaring problems in U.S. business culture is that management performance is based on short-term, bottom-line fiscal outcomes. Instead of viewing an organization, and its employees, holistically and through a long-term lens, managers realize that bonuses are tied to monthly and quarterly financial results. Employees, then, are viewed as a means to achieve these goals. Newly minted managers tell employees that their concerns, issues, and ideas matter. But top-down pressure to financially perform is real. The well-intended manager can quickly become a crass individual. Since CEO annual bonuses are tied to financial measures such as profitability or stock price, and not indirect measures such employee turnover or innovation, lower level supervisors are pressured to achieve short-term financial results at all costs due to this trickle-down effect. Managers at all levels have little time or concern for employee well-being.[1]

The previous paragraph may be an oversimplification of management behavior, as it relates to performance, but what it describes is often the case. To further illustrate, management theorist Henry Mintzberg claims that workplaces are communities, not collections of individuals, to simply be hired and fired. Part of the Great Recession, he claims, was partly the result of a corporate focus on achieving bottom line (stock price) results at the expense of undervalued workforces.[2] The long-term health of organizations was ignored at the pursuit of profit. Undoubtedly, profitability is not a pejorative term and it is necessary for any individual or business to survive, but the "profitability at all costs" mantra can have devastating consequences. Mintzberg also believes that too much emphasis is placed on viewing executive leaders as heroes. He makes a bold assertion: the fact that corporate leaders demand such large pay and benefits packages should exclude them from the job since their focus is on self-interested pursuits and not the long-term needs of the organization. Undoubtedly, he is not making a case for a purely egalitarian pay structure, but he would question the obscene pay differences between CEOs and the workforce. In work environments where bottom line financial results are the only concern, job security becomes an issue. Short-term thinking and bottom-line driven decision-making leads to a callous work environment. Workers can be shuffled around or terminated, at-will, if it serves the immediate bottom-line.

Job Insecurity and Its Negative Effects

Job security can be broken down into two main components. The first component deals with a manager's treatment of employees. Are employees treated as a means to an end? Are employees continually fearing that any mistake will result in termination? Does management set reasonable standards for performance? At the core, the walking on eggshells feeling, the feeling of expendability, may be prevalent. The second component of job satisfaction relates to the organization's relevance and likelihood of surviving in the marketplace. Does the firm produce a product or service that is in demand? Will this firm adapt and innovate when necessary? Is the firm consistently profitable? Modern workers know how competitors are performing and have no problem switching to a more relevant employer.[3] Buffer, a social media analytics company, is aware of this trend and openly displays real-time revenues, research and development projects, fundraising, and pricing to its employees.[4]

Studies show that workers who feel expendable are more likely to develop work-related stress symptoms such as anxiety, depression, sleep disorders, back pain and digestive problems. Additionally, the halo-effect is ever present regarding job security. The halo-effect is when a person identifies one negative trait or factor (in this case the lack of job security) and subconsciously allows this negative perception to transfer to other unrelated factors.[5] Workers who feel insecure about their jobs, then, also negatively view the quality of other Two Factor elements such as responsibility, the job itself, recognition, interpersonal relationships, and quality of supervision.[6] In other words, the foundation of the Two Factor "house" is cracked and a hygiene factor is present: job insecurity. The purpose of this chapter is to explain the modern-day context of the job security hygiene factor. This chapter begins with a brief historical and economic overview, describing how the pendulum has swung in favor of employee performance over lifelong employment and job security. In addition, the pros and cons of the popular relative performance appraisal will be discussed in its relation to job security.

Job Security Today

In the U.S., job security has declined over the past 25 years.[7] Job security and lifelong employment were important for traditionalists and baby boomers, the workers of Herzberg's day. Globalization was not as powerful a force to contend with, or harness, for U.S. employers. Unionization was evermore present, and seniority was the ticket to wage increases and bonuses. Thus, workers had less reason to job hop. Additionally, it was difficult for employers to fire low-performing workers since managements' decisions were checked by union leadership. A common struggle legislatively in the mid–20th century, and no less important today, was the balancing of power between employers and unions. Should the union, or the employer, have more power? As unions have lost much power and membership since then, and collective bargaining is not the norm, a better question today would be framed at the individual level: Should the employee or the employer have more power in their working relationship? Of course, a business has the legitimate right to hire and fire, but do they have a duty to provide a respectable level of job security? Well established employers, especially large corporations, can accumulate more resources than individuals, or new entrepreneurs, by issuing stocks and bonds or various investments not available to the common person. Typically, businesses have more resources than employees and they are said to have the work relationship advantage. At-will contracts, which are technically two-sided since the employee can quit for any reason or the employer can terminate for any reason, undoubtedly provide a greater advantage for the employer. If both parties had equal power, employees could fluidly switch between jobs, if fired, for commensurate pay. There would be a lineup of companies willing to hire said employees on the spot. Since it is difficult to start up a new business and compete with the oligopolies of the world, at-will is more "impartial" at the small business level. Smaller employers with minimal resources would face a similar hardship regarding employee separations. It would be challenging to find replacement workers and maintain adequate pay levels, especially if there are limited resources, available to the small business. Regardless of the at-will doctrine, employers of all sizes benefit by providing stable employment for their workers. Employees are less likely to quit their jobs if job security is present,[8] leading to fewer separation and hiring costs.

Today, senior workers are often viewed as a liability, not an asset. Part of this mentality is fiscal and the other is cultural. From a purely short-term, budgetary perspective, older employees who have been with the company for many years are more costly than new hires. Although age discrimination in employment is technically illegal, companies often find ways to fire or entice older workers to quit, especially during economic downturns.[9] Older employees typically have higher salaries, expensive benefits, i.e., fully vested 401k and life insurance, and file more health insurance claims than younger workers.[10] From a cultural perspective, western cultures like the U.S. are guilty of not holistically valuing people, especially in regard to age. Similar to how bottom-line financial results drive companies, youth and vibrancy drives western culture. The goal is to stay forever young. Youth equates to relevance. Companies often follow suit with this mentality. In Greek and Native American cultures, contrastingly, elders are valued for their life experience and wisdom, passing down information and stories to younger generations.[11] Based on Native American culture, U.S. office furniture manufacturing company Herman Miller has preserved its "water carrier" policy, which dignifies their senior workers. Employees who have served for 20-plus years become water carriers. These long-term employees are considered invaluable to the company as they connect past experiences and learning moments to the present, teaching newer workers. Essentially, water carriers are mentors that maintain and share the collective wisdom of the organization. Water carriers' names are enshrined on a sculpture for all employees to see.[12]

Loyal employees, regardless of their respective costs, should be considered an asset, not a liability. The term "asset" can be portrayed positively or negatively. Asset, from a negative perspective, is synonymous with the company "owning" the employee, exploiting their upper-handed advantage. Positively speaking, which is the intent here, employees are valuable resources. These resources are not owned, per se, but are necessary ingredients for a company's success. They are a part of the organization and not merely a cost to be minimized. A company should protect the employees' job, and their well-being, as if they are protecting the brand's image and identity.

One of the problems that occurs when U.S. companies consider their employees to be assets, negatively speaking, is they can simply hire and fire, or in the words of Frederick Taylor, continue to find the "one-best" person for the job. An extreme propensity towards performance, over endurance (long-term employment) can result in high turnover rates. A microcosm of this extreme performance orientation would be professional athletics. Players are routinely traded, and coaches are fired for not winning, in the short term. Likewise, players and coaches feel no need to be loyal to their organization. They often look for the next best opportunity while working for their current employer. Applied to more common businesses, owners who are not loyal to employees should expect no loyalty in return. Often, employers would rather hire more talented employees from outside of the firm than developing loyal employees already in their midst. On balance, disloyalty is not all on the employer as employees also seek better opportunities elsewhere. Similar to professional athletics, modern workers and companies do not expect long-term employment. This trend is happening abroad as well. Companies in Japan, who are noted for their lifetime employment policies, have declined to less than 9 percent who promote lifetime employment.[13]

The Seniority vs. Performance Mindset

Should workers be rewarded for their years of service, or should the emphasis be on how well they perform their jobs? The easy answer is both. It is a manager's dream to discover a loyal employee who excels at their work. High productivity and low turnover are metrics that companies cannot choose to ignore. Depending on the type of job or work environment, laborers will have a preference towards seniority or performance. For example, in automotive sales, performance would be highly valued. If worker A outsells worker B, regardless of seniority, she will want adequate commission. Of course, managers would be thrilled if a top performer also worked for the company long term, but only if productivity was consistent and noteworthy. Jobs that require a craft or trade skill, such as academics, plumbers, or playwrights, prefer seniority-based pay over performance-based pay.[14]

So how does the seniority versus performance mindset relate to job security? The following examination of European culture is demonstrative. In a study that investigated job security in two distinct regions of Switzerland: the region that valued seniority (French influence), compared to the region that valued performance (German influence), was more likely to react negatively to potential job loss. However, both regions showed lower job satisfaction and higher turnover (quit) intentions if job insecurity was present. In the higher performance-based culture (German influence), losing job features was more negatively impactful than to the seniority based (French) culture. However, the threat of losing job features impacted both cultures' likelihood of quitting their jobs.[15]

If this study is used as a representation of the shift from seniority-based-pay, in the U.S., to that of performance-based-pay, the study intuitively makes sense. In a high-performance culture like the U.S. (similar to Germany), job loss would be considered a bit more normal for those with a performance mindset. Those who value seniority would have worse reactions to job loss as they expect job security in exchange for years of service. The performance mindset also reflects the job-hopping (at-will) attitude of modern workers. The workers owe no loyalty to an organization in the long term. Having noted these differences in attitudes, it is important to note that workers possessing both mindsets still view job insecurity negatively and are more likely to quit, or be less satisfied, at work, if employers do not secure employment.

Relative Performance Appraisals

U.S. business culture, with its emphasis on performance over seniority, has lent itself to relative performance evaluations. Typically, a company will use either a relative or absolute appraisal system. Absolute appraisals, with the graphic-ratings scale being a common form, tie performance to compensation. For example, a manager will measure an employee's performance based on some set of criteria such as quality and quantity of work, or dependability. The supervisors rate the employee on some scale, i.e., 1–10, and may give a brief rationale for their scoring. The employee, then, is being evaluated based on an objective standard.

Relative appraisals differ from absolute because they compare the performance of employees to one another. Instead of an objective measure that remains constant over time, the "best employee's performance" is set as the new standard. Imagine a classroom where an "A" grade is based on the best student's performance, not a standard. Therefore, there is no objective standard for quality of work, it changes over time based on the work of the best employee, or in the classroom example, the student. Following is a study that demonstrates the relative performance appraisal concept. In a group of 32 nurses, managers' scores were used to identify the top performers. Categories included quality of work, quantity of work, timeliness of work, problem solving, interpersonal relationships, behavior, management and leadership skills (if applicable), and professional development. At this point the study appears to be "absolute," but, these categories are not graded to a common standard since they change based on the top performer's score. Thus, the top performer's scores were identified and set as the high bar. Then, low performers were labeled "question marks," mid-level performers were labeled "potential stars" and high performers were labeled "superstars." Specific percentage increases that lower performers needed to achieve, in order to become "superstars" or "potential stars" were noted. The purpose of this ranking system, then, was to set a benchmark for performance based on the best employees' performance.[16] Again, this benchmark would change over time as employees' performance changes.

Rank and Yank—Extreme Relative Performance Management

To demonstrate how aggressive relative performance appraisals can be, Jack Welch's Rank and Yank policy from the 1990s will be explored. Under Jack Welch, one of the most famous modern-day managers, General Electric (GE) increased its value from $13 billion to over several hundred billion dollars and GE became the world's largest company.[17] Job security, from an organizational relevance standpoint, would be virtually unmatched by any other employer. GE was profitable and relevant in the marketplace. However, to achieve this level of success (in part), Welch implemented the infamous Rank and Yank system. Welch was brutal with employees and insisted that 10 percent of the workforce be fired annually.[18] Essentially, the bottom performers were discharged each year, which created a competitive yet cutthroat work environment. The assumptions of the Rank and Yank system were that a small percentage of employees would either be exceptional or extremely underperforming, while most would be average. The GE Rank and Yank curve was dubbed the "vitality curve," similar to a bell curve in descriptive statistics. Corporations like Microsoft and Ford also adopted this system and curve. However, Microsoft ditched this system as it resulted in less cooperation and innovation. GE, Ford, and Microsoft dealt with lawsuits citing age and race discrimination.[19]

In general, there are some pros and cons of a forced-ranking system like Rank and Yank. Weeding out poor performers improves morale since hard workers have less slack to pick up. Managers have an easier time meeting productivity targets and fewer work hours are needed per day, thus reducing expenses. Setting the bar high for employees minimizes mediocrity and creates a culture of progress. However, such a system creates a hostile environment where nobody wants to be labeled the "worst" employee. In an "only the strong survive" atmosphere, employees may feel more pressure to cut corners or behave unethically if it improves their performance numbers. Not only is discrimination an issue but there are many rater biases of which managers are not even aware when evaluating employees. For example, similarity bias occurs when people "like" others that are similar to themselves, regarding personality, interests, or demographics. In the extreme form, managers play favorites, perhaps subconsciously, and evaluate those they like higher than those they do not. Or distance bias occurs when actions taken recently are given more weight than those that are months older.[20] If forced rankings happen every year, managers may weight recent efforts higher than those from earlier in the year. These are only two examples of many biases that exist. Most managers do not even consider or are unaware of these biases.

Modern Worker Focus: Employee as Owner

One trend that should not be overlooked regarding employee rights and job security is "co-determination," or power sharing. In the U.S., corporations are governed by boards of directors who hire the CEO, approve budgets, and craft strategy.[21] Boards of directors are elected by stockholders. The corporate structure, in general, flows from top to bottom: executive leadership (CEO, president, and vice presidents), mid-level managers (directors, regional managers), followed by lower-level managers (team leaders and supervisors).[22] Employees do not get to vote for board members unless they own stock themselves. Therefore, important company decisions are made without employee involvement. The main goal of upper management and the board is to reward the stockholders for their investment by increasing the stock price. So, is there a way for employees to have a compelling voice while living at the bottom of the corporate pyramid? Enter co-determination, a German practice, and law, which requires 50 percent of corporate board seats to be elected by employees. In Germany, the employer/employee relationship is viewed more as a power-with, instead of a power-over, relationship. Co-determination gives employees power and representation regarding a firm's decision making. Elizabeth Warren, a democratic presidential candidate for the 2020 election, has called for co-determination in the U.S., wanting up to 40 percent of corporate boards to be elected by employees.[23]

Co-determination is a method for giving employees a voice, but it is not representative of direct ownership of a firm. Employee stock option plans (ESOPs) allow employees to earn shares or buy at a discount. Thus, they get to vote on members of the board of directors since they own shares. King Arthur Flour, a company who is all in on the ESOP plan, has been 100 percent employee owned since 2004. During one bad month, management openly addressed its stockholders (employees) and clearly explained the issues at hand: rising flour prices coupled with a large cancelled order resulted in a sharp decrease in sales.[24] Since employees were involved in the decision making process and had a say in how the company was run, employees of all ages typically did not quit, with many reaching the 20 year employment mark. ESOPs are risky, however, if the company were to fold. Mutual funds, in which most 401k plans are invested, diversify investments over many companies to minimize risk. If one company in the portfolio collapses the entire investment is not lost. With an ESOP, if a company like King Arthur Flour's stock prices drop, or far worse, bottom out, employees can lose their entire retirement savings. Although this book does not necessarily advocate for ESOPs or co-determination, these practices are gaining in popularity. The "power-with," as compared to the "power-over" mentality, is important to modern workers. Workers who have a direct say in how their jobs are impacted by managerial decisions will have higher levels of job security.

Chapter Summary

The purpose of this chapter was to describe the two components of the job security hygiene factor: organizational relevance and the ease of which employees are expendable. Employees who feel that their jobs are not secure are likely to have work-related stress symptoms. Turnover should also be expected at companies who do not promote job security. Employers today have shifted their job security policies from seniority-based pay to performance-based pay. Companies must be careful to minimize bias when evaluating employee performance. Finally, modern employees expect policies that allow them to have a say in how the company is run.

Application Questions, Chapter 7

1. Do some research regarding rater-error bias. Which errors are supervisors likely to make when giving performance appraisals?

2. In regard to question 1, what type of training can be conducted to standardize how supervisors complete employee performance appraisals?

3. In what way can your company give employees a voice? Or are there ways to better inform employees regarding management decisions?

4. Is there any value to the relative performance appraisal method? What problems can occur when employees are compared to one another?

5. In what ways do your competitors better manage job security?

SECTION III

The House:
Motivators

8

Interpersonal Relationships and Recognition

Why Cliques Persist Post–High School

When a graduate reminisces about her high school experience, most likely her relationships with peers, good or bad, come to mind. School can be a miserable experience for those who were bullied whereas it can be nostalgic for those who had a tight-knit group of friends. But are students motivated to go to school because of their friends? Or do their functional friendships just make school more tolerable? Considering Two Factor theory, these friendships would be considered a hygiene factor. A student who is bullied, for instance, will not like school, yet the presence of friendship will not motivate a student to excel at school. Students who want to fulfill internal drives such as achievement, while engaging in positive social interactions with friends and teachers, will undoubtedly like school. Healthy relationships are a basic expectation in any environment. The absence of healthy relationships (i.e., a bully) leads to dissatisfaction. Therefore, interpersonal relationships, represented by high school friendships in this instance, are a hygiene factor.

"Interpersonal relationships" is one of the most contentious hygiene factors. Perhaps semantics are at play, depending on how "relationship" is defined. Herzberg's definition focuses on the "interactions" between coworkers. How employees treat each other, then, is what is meant by interpersonal "relationships." Maslow's "social" needs, which would closely align with interpersonal relationships, differs in that it represents belonging and affection, not necessarily interactions. Belonging to a team, society, or fitting in with a group, then, would be the essence of social needs. Undoubtedly, relationships are complicated and an individual's needs for community differ. Introverts are energized, for instance, through quiet time and reflection compared to extroverts who

93

are energized through social stimuli.[1] This is not to say that introverts do not like being around people but certain types of jobs, or interactions, may be more appealing to introverts. Interpersonal relationships, or affiliation needs, are in the center of the employee's pyramid (as referenced in earlier chapters). From a Two Factor perspective, interpersonal relationships are a hygiene factor since employees would not derive job satisfaction through positive interactions with fellow employees. These positive, professional interactions are a basic societal expectation. Dysfunctional relationships at work, though, will lead to dissatisfaction.

Recognition, a motivator according to Herzberg, is related to interpersonal interactions. Acts of praise (recognition) from leaders and colleagues are not always clearly or consistently disseminated. Frankly, supervisors have bias as they weight certain employee actions and behaviors as more favorable, or less favorable, than others. Additionally, workers who are closer to their supervisors, regarding work unit or personal friendship, are more likely to get noticed and recognized. The same biases are present when evaluating coworkers and acknowledging their performance. Therefore, the hygiene factor, interpersonal relationships, is connected to the motivator, recognition, in the work context. This chapter will define the four types of recognition that are relevant to employers. Leader-Member Exchange Theory, which describes the common clique phenomenon, is described, leading to recommendations for improving employee interactions and recognition policy. Finally, innovative companies that systematically allocate recognition and connect it with interpersonal relationships, are presented.

The Importance of Recognition

In the modern era it appears that employers do not fully understand how impactful recognition is to the employee psyche. To illustrate, a study conducted by the Work Human Research Institute reported that 92 percent of workers believed that continual recognition made them feel more appreciated at work and 85 percent said recognition was related to their job satisfaction. However, only 40 percent of the employees had been recognized by their leaders in the previous year.[2] As mentioned in the chapter of this text on salary, the Boston Consulting Group surveyed over 200,000 people from around the world and discovered that the most important factor related to employee happiness was recognition. Likewise, the Universal Dual-Factor Survey (UDS), which is included at the end of this book, was tested at a mid-sized bank in the southeastern U.S. and recognition emerged as the most salient predictor of job satisfaction.[3]

In a study of 1,831 Spanish workers, researchers discovered that employees who felt their supervisors and coworkers recognized their work had increased levels of psychological functioning (i.e., self-esteem) and overall wellbeing.[4] The employees were asked to respond to two statements: "My supervisors consider me a valuable worker" and "My coworkers value my work." What is interesting about these statements is that they focus on the intangible. The workers believed, internally, that their work was valued. This does not mean that tangible rewards, such as plaques or gifts, do not serve a function. The key takeaway is that the workers who believed they were valued, or recognized, felt better about themselves and their organization. Another interesting finding from this study is that coworker recognition was more impactful than supervisor recognition; although both were meaningful. From the previous studies, recognition is one of the most important factors to consider for managers who are trying to improve the satisfaction and wellbeing of their workers.

Recognition Effected by LMX—Vertical Relationships

Leader-Member Exchange (LMX) theory "examines the quality of relationships between leaders and followers."[5] Leaders naturally develop an inner circle, the "in-group," leaving the remaining followers in the "out-group" category. These in and out groups exist at all organizational levels. Team leaders, mid-level managers and executive leaders will naturally have their own in and out groups. Similar to cliques in high school, leaders will socialize more with their in-group (close friends) while sharing basic, arms-length exchanges with the out-group (acquaintances). Exchanges with the in-group are much more personal whereas out-group exchanges are trivial. The in-group is best described as "trusted assistants" whereas the out-group would be "helping-hands." Regarding recognition, studies show that in-groups are given higher performance appraisal evaluation scores than out-groups.[6] These employees advance faster in their career, are less likely to quit, and perform "better" than out-group members. In a study of 640 manufacturing associates in the U.K., LMX relationships were indicative of employees' perceived recognition and rewards.[7] These high quality, social relationships, were related to recognition at both the senior management and line management levels. Moreover, employees who had positive LMX relationships with management were less likely to get worn out, have better relationships with colleagues, and have positive views of their workload and working conditions.

High quality, LMX relationships, are also related to transformational leadership practices.[8] Employees who experience transformational leadership have positive attitudes and behaviors and are less likely to quit, have more creativity, and outperform coworkers. Transformational leaders invest in the development of their workers, primarily through inspiration and paying attention to their needs.[9] Thus, the leader will act in a transformational manner with their in-group. The out-group, on the other hand, will experience transactional leadership. Transactional leaders exchange rewards for productivity. Like the previously mentioned Theory X and Y (transformational representing Y and transactional representing X), transactional leaders communicate with the out-group in a non-personal way.

Transformational leaders, theoretically, are concerned about the personal wellbeing of their followers, helping them to reach their full potential. Being "others focused," then, is a core principle of transformational leadership. Transactional leadership, on the other hand, uses economic exchanges, i.e., salary, to get followers to achieve goals. Both parties "need something" and exchange some action for a return. For example, a manager needs to have 200 parts made per hour and the employee needs a salary. Thus, transactional managers have a quid pro quo mindset: "I give salary, you give work." Since no relationship is 100 percent transformational, perhaps, a continuum could better represent the idea. On one end is a full emotional investment in the employee's wellbeing from the leader. The leader gives his all to see the employee succeed. On the other end of the continuum is fully arms-length, transactional exchanges. The employee encounters no personal interactions from his boss. Instead, he simply comes to work to receive a paycheck, expecting nothing more from management. Social exchanges, on the transactional end, with the boss, are entirely work related. See Figure 11 below for a visual depiction of the in-group/out-group experience.

Undoubtedly people, in general, can only mentally and emotionally handle a few close friendships. The time that it takes to nurture and cultivate close relationships is a limited resource. Company leaders and

In-Group Experience	Out-Group Experience
Transformational Leadership	Transactional Leadership
⬇	⬇
High Quality LMX Relationships based on Personal Wellbeing	Low Quality LMX Relationships based on Job Performance
⬇	⬇
Employee Feels Valued	Employee Feels Expendable

Figure 11.

supervisors are no different in this regard. Similar to a Facebook friends list, only a select few, of hundreds of "friends," will be truly trusted confidantes. Most contacts on the friends list would be best placed into the acquaintance zone. And rightfully so. Likewise, managers, naturally, will only have a few insiders that they trust to share personal information. However, this inner circle will become apparent to outsiders. One study suggests that outsiders are more likely to be envious of the inner circle members and the high-quality LMX (transformational) relationship.[10]

Leaders must realize that in-groups and out-groups will naturally exist in any organization. It is a good management practice to minimize the magnitude of differences between both groups. Knowing they exist, managers can make focused efforts to communicate with out-group members beyond the basic, inconsequential exchanges that often take place. The in-group relationships should be kept in check, especially during work hours, to minimize favoritism, or the appearance thereof. Additionally, understanding that in-group members are more likely to be recognized, promoted, and evaluated, due to their in-group membership status, should be considered and attempts to minimize bias during these processes should be undertaken.

Horizontal Interpersonal Relationships

Interpersonal relationships involve two main categories: boss to employee (vertical) and employee to employee (horizontal). Like high and low quality LMX boss-to-employee relationships, employees will create cliques, or in and out groups, among themselves. Thus, not only should bosses/leaders be concerned about the in-groups and out-groups they create but also the in and out groups employees create. Out-groups, at large, feel ostracized and excluded from the organization.

While it is important to improve intra (within a team or department) and inter (between a team or department) group communications and relationships, one thing to remember is that human beings tend to have self-serving bias accompanied by fundamental attribution error (FAE).[11] Self-serving bias is when individuals believe their own internal factors, such as aptitude or ability, are the reason for their success, while failures are blamed on external circumstances. For example, if this individual is promoted, he may believe his advancement is due to his hard work and know-how. If, on the other hand, he is passed over for the promotion, he may believe that his coworker received the promotion due to favoritism. Fundamental attribution error is when a person underestimates the influence of negative factors when judging the behavior of another person. For example, a coworker struggling to meet deadlines may be considered lazy instead of having an external issue, such as a family illness, with which to contend. Or a coworker who is late to work may considered to be slothful when the real reason she was late was due to a flat tire on the way into work. Some common examples of how self-serving bias and attribution errors impact the workplace are as follows: "Our department is much more competent than other departments," "Alex is always gossiping about other workers" (as I fail to realize that I am gossiping about Alex), "Other people are treated better than me because they have connections," and so on. Regardless of how much effort managers exert to improve boss-to-employee and employee-to-employee relationships, they will never fully be able to negate self-serving bias and FAE.

At the departmental level, employees may bond with their group in a way that is unhealthy to the organization at large. The department becomes their in-group. Goals created by upper level management, for the betterment of the company, may not be effectively administered by each department as they may have their own conflicting goals.[12] A common example is the departmental budget. If administration determines that each department receives a certain budget for the fiscal year, each departmental manager may spend their entire budgets, even if it is not necessary. The purpose for doing so is that administration will not reduce their respective budgets the following year if the departments seems to need all the available funding. Although all departments cutting costs, while not using their entire budgets would help the bottom line of the firm, members within each department feel the need to "fight" for resources. Each department, then, becomes an adversary to the others in this fight.

Improving LMX Relationships Across the Board

Regarding both employee-to-employee and boss-to-employee relationships, there are some proactive steps that can be taken to minimize the negative effects of cliques. First, organizations can organize events that get employees involved beyond their typical work situations. One of the most common examples is the annual company/family picnic. Although these are not a bad idea, they are too infrequent of a stand-alone activity. Festering interpersonal problems are not likely to be resolved in this setting. Second, some companies get involved with non-profit work or health-related events, like local 5k competitions, weight loss challenges, or collecting donations for the local Food Bank. Employees may work together on projects related to these events beyond normal work hours which provides an opportunity for communication and bonding. Regardless of the activity, the idea is that employees can get to know one another better if the organization provides opportunities during, or beyond, the typical workday. Third, offsite retreats, another common team-building exercise, feature games or activities that force workers to interact with those outside of their inner circle. A third-party, or the specialist hosting the retreat, leads the team-building exercises and can be a non-biased agent of change. However, retreats are expensive and work hours are sacrificed in the hopes of morale building. If the retreat occurs during non-work hours, employees may choose not to attend. Fourth, managers can hire a consultant to come into the workplace, instead of a retreat, to conduct experiential activities like personality grouping. The consultant will administer a personality survey (for instance) individually, then, group employees together by similar personality types. The exercise helps employees to better understand and effectively interact with one another. To illustrate, employees who are "investigative types" can discuss their similarities while also understanding how different types, such as "enterprising" or "dominating," differ. Fifth, simple practices, such as managers (or employees) purposefully sitting with out-group employees at lunch, stopping by employees' workstations to check-in, or rotating seats/members for meetings can also help improve interpersonal relationships.[13]

Developing Recognition Policy: When and What to Recognize

There are four types of workplace recognition. The most relevant to the job itself is recognition for quality of work. The second type recognizes employees for their organizational contributions beyond the job. The remaining two types of recognition focus on personal accomplishments and contributions to society.[14] Regarding the first type of recognition, quality of work, the main question that arises is "How should quality of work be recognized?" Is a regularly scheduled compliment to each employee sufficient? A supervisor who says "you did excellent work today" undoubtedly has a positive impact on the employee. Often, compliments are given haphazardly. Typically, managers do not schedule recognition opportunities into their schedules as they see no immediate effect on profitability. Unfortunately, recognition or praise, when given, is unevenly distributed to the in-group.

When it comes to annual performance appraisals, employees systematically are given recognition (or discipline). During the appraisal a manager may score the associate high on the quality of work measure. She may even get a "keep up the good work" comment. End of the year awards ceremonies are also a common, systematic device for distributing recognition. Fellow employees, or customers, vote for employees who demonstrate exemplary performance, in turn, a reward such as a plaque or gift card is publicly handed to the winners. The main issue with awards ceremonies is that only a handful of workers win, leaving the remaining employees feeling unappreciated. Similar to students who vote on their favorite teacher or fans who vote for their favorite professional athlete, these kinds of awards are subject to favoritism and bias. Students, for example, may not vote for the best teacher, functionally or academically speaking, but the one whose personality they like best. Athletes are often selected for all-star games based on their popularity, more so than skill. Likewise, employees may win awards due to likability or close LMX relationships instead of actual performance. Undoubtedly, an employee may possess both high quality LMX relationships and stellar performance, but the in-group members are most likely to win awards. This is not to say that awards ceremonies should be foregone but objective measures should be implemented to minimize bias in the selection process. Overall, infrequent recognition methods such as performance appraisals and awards ceremonies are not enough to make an employee feel like they matter in the workplace. Nor are random, infrequent compliments. This is not to say that appraisals and annual awards ceremonies are inherently bad, but they are insufficient for providing the recognition that associates need.

The second type of recognition notices undertakings beyond direct job requirements. A prime example of this type of recognition is that universities highlight the academic publications of their faculty on their website and in alumni magazines. Both the university (relevance and credibility) as well as the employee (recognition) benefit from this type of recognition. The third type of recognition focuses on personal success outside of work. Some companies publish monthly newsletters or place monitors in common areas (i.e., breakrooms) that display current company news. Congratulating employees on the birth of a child, a wedding, or the completion of a college degree would be examples of personal success stories that a company can share. New employees can also be highlighted in a "get-to-know-them" format with their accolades and personal history described. The fourth recognition method, which is important to modern workers, is the active promotion of employees' societal contributions. PNC Bank, for instance, allows employees to spend up to 40 paid hours per year volunteering. Employee social contributions are then recognized on their website.[15] PNC benefits as they can demonstrate their concern for the community. Employees benefit since they are publicly recognized.

The County of San Bernardino Department of Behavioral Health is an organization that addresses all four types of recognition. Ceremonies are conducted to recognize employee of the month (Type 1), newly licensed staff (Type 3), employees who were exceptional contributors to projects (Type 2 and Type 4), public service (Type 4), years of service (Type 1 and Type 2), and educational achievements (Type 3). Additionally, periodic/random rewards are given for outstanding employee performance including notes placed on an "I Saw You" board, memos, and emails.[16]

Recognition Frequency

How often should managers recognize their subordinates? What should the recognition look like? Should management simply say "thank you" once a week or give an employee of the month award? Should praise be reserved for the best performers? Who or what measures determine peak performance? Finding the optimal frequency (meaning "just the right amount") and appropriate rewards for employee recognition is a difficult task for managers. According to Lorea Seidel, director of human resources at Southern Methodist University, recognition has a shelf life of one week (based on a Gallup poll)![17] Although it is not recommended to buy thank you cards in bulk and distribute them to employees with each paycheck, the idea that praise should be distributed often is important. Tying in desirable behaviors with the impact to the organization is also important. Employees, then, can see how positive behaviors affect the organization at large.

Most likely, employees of different departments receive varying levels of recognition from their direct supervisors. Team leaders in one department are likely to recognize more often and appraise higher than team leaders in other departments. Or, from shift to shift, leadership styles and recognition frequency may differ. This is known as rater-error, which can be described as consistently "under-rating" or "over-rating." In the case of recognition, it could be described as "over-praising" or "under-praising." This concept can be applied to life in general, i.e., parenting styles, schools (teaching styles) and so on. Culturally speaking, it is important to note that, depending on how individualistic a culture is, employees may want to be recognized as a team (high collectivist cultures) instead of being recognized for individual successes (high individualistic cultures). Additionally, certain types of jobs are more prone to recognition than others. Accountants, for example, are expected to keep the books in order. Like a hygiene factor, few managers get excited that their accountants are maintaining the finances. It would be more likely for a salesperson to be praised than an accountant, since a sale is more exciting and directly tied to revenue generation.

Modern Worker Focus: eXp Reality Innovating the Real Estate Landscape

One company that is harnessing modern technology to drive growth, through purposeful recognition and relationship building, is eXp Realty. eXp is a cloud-based real estate brokerage that has over 16,000 agents, growing 145 percent annually.[18] In the traditional broker-agent model, agents are technically independent contractors who work for the broker. Upon the sale of a home or business, the agent would split their commission with the broker 50/50. Other agents who work for the broker are competing for the same clients. Thus, agents in the broker's office are competitors. Although there may be cordiality in the office, there is no incentive for each agent to help the others.

eXp Realty is modernizing the real estate industry. First, the traditional brick-and-morter, broker-agent model has been torn down. eXp has taken their business to the cloud and provides a platform for their agents to conduct business. Instead of the "Blockbuster" or "taxi" model, eXp is using a "Netflix" or "Uber" model. The cost savings that derive from not owning traditional physical office spaces is distributed back to the agents. Many agents earn 80 percent commission, instead of 50 percent, and can even keep up to 100 percent in a given year.[19] Second, eXp offers their agents a chance of ownership since their stock is traded on NASDAQ. In the traditional model the agents do not own the company. Specific milestones, once met by each agent, result in stock rewards. The ICON Agent Award, a difficult but obtainable annual milestone, rewards agents with $16,000 worth of stock.[20] To win this award, the agent must give back to other agents via training or mentoring. Third, and perhaps most important regarding recognition and interpersonal relationships, is the revenue sharing program. Traditional brokers do not share profits with realtors. eXp rewards teamwork in that agents who recruit other agents earn a capped amount of income from their recruit's sales. Agents, then, earn commissions through both their direct sales and indirect sales from their network of recruited agents. No longer are agents competitors. Agents benefit when their "coworkers" are selling as there are more profits to share back with the company. Essentially, eXp has taken the multi-level marketing concept and applied it to the real estate industry. Finally, the passive income that agents earn from their network allows them to retire from real estate while earning residual income from their network's sales. Agents are also likely to recruit millennial workers since their longevity at eXp will translate into more passive income in retirement.

eXp has created an environment where agents want their coworkers to succeed. The compensation system rewards employees for helping others. Recognition is common in this environment as agents have an incentive to praise other agents for their hard work. Instead of direct competition, agents want their coworkers recruiting and selling. A recruit is not a competitor. In regard to formal recognition, eXp issues stock to agents instead of a plaque or other non-monetary reward.

Chapter Summary

This chapter explained how recognition and interpersonal relationships are connected. In-group members are more likely to receive promotions, recognition, and rewards. Managers should be aware that low quality LMX relationships are likely to exist in out-groups, resulting in their feeling unappreciated. Since recognition is one of the most salient predictors of job satisfaction, it should be distributed evenly and systematically.

Application Questions, Chapter 8

1. Identify members of your in and out groups. What characteristics do your in-group members possess? For instance, do they share similar interests to you? Are they in the same department? Similar beliefs?

2. Note conversations that you have with in-group members this week. Do they contain elements of transformation, high quality LMX? Describe them here.

3. Note conversations that you have with out-group members this week. Do they go beyond basic, arm's length transactional exchanges? Describe them here.

4. How often do you recognize your workers? What simple steps can you take to systematically recognize your workers?

5. In what ways can you standardize recognition in your organization so that most supervisors recognize subordinates fairly and consistently?

9

Achievement

Why "Culture Officer" Is a Legitimate Job Title

One unfortunate consequence of industrialization is the neglect of worker spirituality. "Spirituality," in this instance, is not synonymous with "religion," per se, but "purpose." For efficiency and productivity's sake, workers are often compartmentalized and work seemingly meaningless tasks. Employees want to find value in their work, yet they cannot often state their employer's mission statement, much less if their job makes a meaningful impact on others. The goal of making more and better widgets per day, to earn extra pay, is not a purposeful exercise to an employee in the long term. Regardless of profession, doing a job for its own sake or for incentives like pay, does not satisfy the worker's internal desire for meaningful work.

One way to make work more meaningful is for the business to have a relatable mission and culture. The organization should have a purpose beyond simply making and selling a product or service. Life insurance salespersons will not be satisfied, long term, based on the amount of commission they can earn per sale. There needs to be a greater purpose, not only in the job itself, but also within the company. Leaders can craft a culture that goes beyond the "sale." Leaders who make "excelling at customer service" their priority could share up-to-date stories of how their products have improved customers' lives and reward employees based on how they helped the customer. The "sale," then, gains meaning as the salespersons believe they are making customers' lives better.

Culture can be defined as the shared beliefs of stakeholders regarding what makes the organization special.[1] Culture, essentially, is the personality and the norms of the organization, and they evolve over time. Often, managers neglect to shape the culture of an organization. If upper management does not intentionally define and craft the culture, employees will create their own, often, with disastrous results. If the personality of the organization is not tended to, managers will arrive at work one morning realizing that their pessimistic employees, however small the percentage, have created a toxic culture. Managers need to be aware that workers need purpose and an empowering work environment to derive meaning from work. Workers need to believe they are making a positive difference to themselves, their customers, and society at large. Turnover due to poor culture fit costs employers approximately 50 percent of workers' annual salaries.[2] Creating and maintaining organizational culture has become a priority for numerous companies today. Many are now hiring chief culture officers.[3] This chapter describes how the "achievement" motivating factor can be addressed by improving company culture. According to Herzberg, achievement is the employees' belief that they can make meaningful contributions at work. This chapter concludes by demonstrating how the CSR Pyramid, a subset of culture, can make jobs more meaningful to modern workers.

Developing a Positive Culture

The culture of the organization can add value to the employee's experience at work. The culture provides a sense of "who we are" for employees. It goes a step beyond "what we do" or the mission. The mission of the company, though, is the foundation of culture. Employees who work for a company with a relatable mission and culture feel a sense of achievement and meaning.[4] In turn, the wellbeing of the organization is improved since employees feel as if their work matters. Positive culture is linked to higher levels of employee commitment and retention.[5]

There are five steps to creating and sustaining culture: Define the organization's mission and vision based on the desired culture, hire personnel who fit the culture, appraise employee performance in light of culture, promote leaders who exhibit the culture, and continually assess and adjust policies and procedures to enhance the culture. See the Culture Feedback Loop below (partially derived from Fortini-Campbell's Four Aspects of Culture model).[6] It is important to note that the feedback loop below is a reinforcing loop. Each phase must be purposefully and continually managed to ensure that the desired culture is ingrained into employees and demonstrated to customers. If the loop is left unchecked by upper management/human resources, the culture will deteriorate.

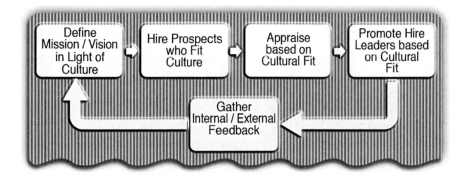

Figure 12.

Define Mission/Vision Considering Culture

The foundation of any culture is the mission/vision statements of a company. The mission statement explains why the company exists. For example, Toyota North America's (N.A.) mission statement is "To attract and attain customers with high-valued products and services and the most satisfying ownership experience in America." Toyota N.A., then, does not simply manufacture automobiles but they attempt to do so by implementing industry leading quality control. The mission statement, albeit implicitly, provides a foundation for the culture of quality that Toyota N.A. promotes.

To set a bold destination for the future of the company executives often craft a vision statement. The vision statement flows from the mission statement. Toyota N.A.'s vision is "To be the most successful and respected car company in America."[7] In a nutshell, Toyota N.A. seeks to make high-quality products, in turn, leading to success in the U.S. market. Toyota's focus on quality has led the automaker to become one of the largest sellers of automobiles in the world while dominating Consumer Report's rankings for quality and reliability.[8]

Hire Prospects Who Fit Culture

Once the company has created a relevant mission statement, employees should be hired who believe that the mission can be achieved. When recruiting new employees, many human resource managers are guilty of simply trying to fill the open position. This may not be their fault as upper level managers habitually pressure human resources to fill the job opening and "move on." Thus, a job description is created based on the required skills needed for the job and the recruiting begins. The sole focus of the hiring process, then, is to find a recruit who has the qualifying credentials and skills as quickly as possible. One key ingredient that is often forgotten, however, is cultural fit. Getting the right people on the "bus" requires effort and resolve. For example, the Mayo Clinic screens applicant doctors based on how well they will focus on patients. Although important, pedigree is not the most important criterion during their hiring phase. Interview questions are purposefully created to see if the applicant states that her most important accomplishments are patient related, rather than, individually driven. Applicant doctors who demonstrate a willingness to help patients at any cost are given hiring preference.[9]

Using recruiting methods that attract talent who fit in with the organization's culture should be the first step of the hiring process. To reduce the number of applicants who will not fit the culture, some organizations only place a job posting on their website to attract prospects who already have an interest in the organization. If a larger net needs to be cast, i.e., a recruiting website, it is imperative for the organization to clearly state the type of applicant (how they need to fit the culture) that is being sought in addition to skill level. Once the recruiting is completed, the second step is to select candidates based on cultural fit. If candidates' cover letters do not address how they will help the company fulfill its mission and/or promote its culture, for example, they should be discarded. A case needs to be made as to why the candidate would be a good fit. Although it is tempting to only hire for experience or skill, cultural fit is just as, if not more, important.

The question that is likely to arise from a longstanding company is "What if we currently have a poor culture and morale?" In this instance, the company is not starting fresh and hiring employees for the first time. Rather, managers may have neglected the culture, over time, and arrived at a point where they feel hopeless to make positive changes. Interestingly, poor attitudes are not just a problem in low skilled environments, like a factory, although that is often the stereotype. Virtually all organizations are susceptible to toxic attitudes and poor culture. To fix or "find" the culture is not easy. Changing the hiring policy to hire for cultural fit is a good first step to improving the company's culture as a whole. Regarding the "weeds," or poor-attitude employees currently working for the company, it is not always possible to start firing at-will. Legal issues, for example, may emerge from employees who feel like they were unjustly terminated. Instead of firing, one method to improve employee attitudes is to purposefully organize employees. Instead of placing employees in teams because of knowledge or skill, attitude placement is important. Employees who have a consistently positive attitude, the "zoysia plugs" can be placed near the toxic employees, the "weeds."[10] Zoysia grass is nice and thick and can withstand changes in temperature.[11] The plugs, once planted, eventually come together to form lush turf. Like the workplace, zoysia plugs (positive attitude employees) take time to overcome the weeds. The idea is that a purposefully cultivated landscape, over time, will result in a healthy workplace culture.

Appraise Based on Culture Fit

Similar to hiring for skill first, and culture fit second, or not at all, employees are typically evaluated based on productivity first, then, with concern (or no concern) for culture fit. Performance appraising should be a purpose-driven process with cultural improvement as the focus. Most often appraisals are generic and do not serve a purpose beyond deciding if a raise is warranted. Undoubtedly, systematically evaluating and documenting employee performance is a necessity. Unfortunately, it is common for employers to use non-purposeful phrasing when appraising. For example, a common appraisal form would evaluate workers on criteria such as performance, attendance, dependability, and attitude; perhaps, on a scale from 1 to 5. However, these criteria are quite subjective. Should each appraiser go with gut feel when evaluating? Are there certain standards for each criterion that must be met? What is the difference between a 4/5 and 5/5 grade for performance, etc.? In addition, do these criteria encourage employees to improve the organization's culture? A performance appraisal for a Toyota manufacturer, in theory, would contain many quality performance criteria based on standards that can be objectively measured. The appraisal could contain other criteria as well not based on quality, but much of the appraisal should deal with criteria related to culture. Improving performance, then, implies an improvement to the organization's culture.

Promote/Hire Leaders Based on Culture Fit

Employees should be appraised based on their performance related to culture. Promoting employees to leadership positions should also be done with culture in mind. All too often, the hiring and promotion processes, are focused on finding the most talented fit skill wise, which undoubtedly is a benefit to the company. In the long term, though, finding leaders who fit and promote the culture is more important. If a company is struggling to improve their culture look no farther than the leadership. Leaders who do not openly live the culture should not expect the same from employees. Following are a few ways in which leaders can maintain the culture:

    a. Set a positive example for employees to follow while exhibiting the culture (i.e., a culture of quality should be apparent in the leader's work and attitude)

    b. Place artifacts around the facility that symbolize the culture so there is a perpetual reminder

    c. Mention the mission/culture, in some form, at meetings and how the purpose of the meeting relates to the mission/culture

    d. Monitor employee performance considering the culture.

Gather Internal/External Feedback

To evaluate the organization's culture, the simplest method is to survey both employees and customers. The customers should "feel" the culture when they interact with the business. Zappos, a common example of a strong workplace culture, hopes to "Deliver 'WOW' through service."[12] A customer, then, if asked about their shopping experience at Zappos, should mention a high-quality customer service experience. Like customers, employees should be aware of the greater purpose (culture) for which they serve and be able to describe it to friends and family. Managers can also talk to employees and customers to get a sense of their cultural engagement. However, both employees and customers may be more open to sharing their feelings on a confidential survey. Employees or customers may not want to directly hurt a manager's feelings by telling them a hard truth. Company culture should be systematically evaluated by managers.

The Culture Feedback Loop in Action: Dutch Bros. Coffee

The following example illustrates a company that addresses each phase of the Culture Feedback Loop, Dutch Bros. Coffee. Dutch Bros. is a large coffee drive thru chain known for their exceptional customer service. To provide a sense of purpose they clearly state on their website, "Coffee is what we do, but it is not who we are: we are in the relationship business."[13] Dutch Bros.' mission is represented by three core values: speed, quality, and service. After hiring employees based on extroversion and optimism criteria, employees become a part of the "Dutch Mafia" and are given the "bro-ista" title.[14] Employees are expected to build relationships with customers, memorize their preferences, and are allowed to give away free drinks to customers who are falling on hard times. To further illustrate how Dutch Bros. lives their mission, they give away over one million drinks and donate over $2 million a year, including donations to study muscular dystrophy, in part due to cofounder Dane who died in 2009 from Lou Gehrig's disease.

Training is critical to Dutch Bros. franchises. Employees train for a month to ensure that the culture is instilled and preserved. "No bad attitudes allowed" and "there is zero tolerance for employees who don't promote the culture" are phrases common to Dutch Bros. Franchises are only sold to employees who have absorbed and lived the culture over at least three-year period.[15] Travis Boersma, the cofounder AKA the "Big Kahuna," leads the organization with a surfer-like attitude, wearing a backwards baseball cap and casual attire. One franchisee claimed that she would work for "Trav" for free. She also knows and hugs customers, which is a norm because of the culture. To perpetuate a healthy culture, franchisors take care of franchisee payroll and update their facilities as needed. Franchisees can then focus on the culture at their respective locations. Essentially, corporate lives the culture by treating franchisees like customers. Although Travis may seem relaxed, he is relentless in maintaining the culture. Travis puts employees and franchisees on notice that they should be "all in" on promoting a customer relationship culture.[16] Based on feedback from customers, employees, etc., Dutch Bros. corporate buys out franchisees who cannot promote the culture. The previous Dutch Bros. example illustrates how a company can make a difference in the lives of their workers by building and sustaining a relevant company culture. Next, the CSR Pyramid, another method for fulfilling workers' achievement needs, will be described.

Making Work Meaningful Via the CSR Pyramid

At the top of Maslow's Hierarchy of Needs is self-actualization. Perhaps not fully individualistic, a human being is motivated to achieve one's sense of calling. Like Two Factor theory, the focus of Maslow's theory is primarily on the individual, yet a part of self-actualizing can include improving society. A person can both reach their own potential while helping society reach its potential. Similarly, a job can provide a deeper sense of meaning if the community in which the business operates, or beyond, is purposefully considered and improved as a result of its operations. The business, then, can self-actualize in a societal sense. Known today as corporate social responsibility (CSR), organizations can take a holistic approach to understanding how their actions affect all stakeholders. Capital One, for example, discovered that CSR efforts (promoting employee volunteerism) has improved both recruiting and retention in younger workers.[17] CSR can be a component of culture if leaders make it a priority. As companies expand, they have an ethical obligation to promote a healthy corporate culture, partially composed of the CSR mindset.[18]

In the 1960s, Milton Friedman, one of the most popular free market economists, stated the following: "There is one and only one social responsibility of business-to use its resources and engage in activities designed to increase its profits so long as it stays within the rules of the game, which is to say, engages in open and free competition without deception or fraud."[19] At the core of this statement, known as the Friedman Doctrine, is the belief that earnings that are spent on social issues or philanthropic endeavors are paid at the expense of investors, employees, or the customer. A corporation that donates millions of dollars to a charity does so at the expense of employee raises, lower prices of finished goods, or dividends. For example, workers who invest a portion of their salary into a 401k are mostly concerned that the monthly returns are increasing. Since their retirement plan is heavily invested in corporations, increases in stock prices are the sole concern for the employee. If any portion of the corporation's returns are invested in CSR, in the short term at least, the stock price or dividend may be negatively affected. In this context, employees investing for retirement would want corporations to follow Friedman's prescription.

Perhaps, though, corporations who invest in philanthropic efforts and utilize resources to solve community issues could improve profitability via improved public image. In a study of companies listed on the Bucharest Stock Exchange, there is a positive relationship between corporate financial performance and CSR efforts.[20] Regarding millennials, 90 percent would switch to a more CSR focused brand if available, 70 percent would pay more for a product produced by a CSR engaged company and 62 percent would take a pay cut to work at a socially responsible company.[21] On the face, then, shuffling funds to purse social responsible initiatives may reduce profitability in the short term. There is a case to be made, though, for the long-term benefits of CSR: increases in sales and the retainment of modern workers.

Unfortunately, many businesses abuse the Friedman Doctrine and take his statement to an extreme, which leads to short term thinking and a lack of focus on society. A company could outsource production to a country with lax environmental and human rights regulations, for example, to reduce costs, while staying within the "rules of the game." Unocal stayed within the rules of the game when it worked with the Myanmar government to build pipelines within the country.[22] At the time, the militaristic dictatorship was known for their lack of human rights protections. Human rights groups claim that the government used involuntary labor practices, forcibly removed citizens who lived in the path of the pipeline, and even murdered those who would not work on the pipeline.[23] Perhaps Unocal was unaware of the potential for these types of serious allegations but it was common knowledge that human rights abuses were likely. Undoubtedly, there are companies in existence today who navigate the laws to increase profitability, at the expense of society.

Most examples of the Friedman Doctrine gone wrong are less extreme than the previously mentioned Unocal case. Consider household cleaning agents, for instance. It is often cheaper to produce poisonous cleaners as they are cheaper to manufacture, and they are legal. Undoubtedly, many of the cleaners directly harm the environment and can cause harm to those who use them. Window cleaner typically contains ammonia, bleach is often used as a disinfectant and contains chemical sodium hypochlorite, dishwashing detergents include phosphate, and antibacterial cleaners contain pesticides, to name a few.[24] As a result of the abundance of cleaning agents in the home, the Poison Control Center created a national database and hotline for the public in the 1970s and 1980s.[25] Many families posted the poison control phone number in their kitchen just in case their children consumed any of these products. Consumers may have been aware of these hazards, but the products were, and still are, less costly than competing healthier products. Today, there are many companies that make poison and chemical free kitchen products that are not harmful to the environment or their users. Thus, the poison control contact information is not as necessary as in the 1980s. The main question that arises is "Why didn't household cleaner manufacturers take the initiative to remove chemicals from their products in the 1980s and beyond?" and "Why do companies still produce hazardous products?" Perhaps, the Friedman Doctrine explains this. Customers have free will to buy whatever they want. Is it a company's job to tell them what to buy if they are not breaking any laws, and more importantly, turning a profit? Profit, in general, is undoubtedly a good thing as it is needed to pay workers, a company's bills, and so on. And following the laws, if they are just, is a good thing. But is it acceptable, now, with the vast number of scientific databases and knowledge, to continue making such harmful products?

Enter the CSR Pyramid, a simple model that helps managers develop a more holistic mindset concerning how their business should operate in today's society. The CSR Pyramid is a simple model with economic responsibilities forming the base, followed by legal, ethical, and philanthropic responsibilities. See Figure 13 below:

The foundation of the pyramid is representative of the Friedman Doctrine. The most important section is a firm's economic responsibilities. Without profitability, a company cannot survive. Within the law, then, a firm should maximize profitability for its shareholders. An employer who creates jobs and valuable products and services positively impacts society. Not breaking laws is also necessary from both ethical and survival perspectives. For instance, a company will be fined for

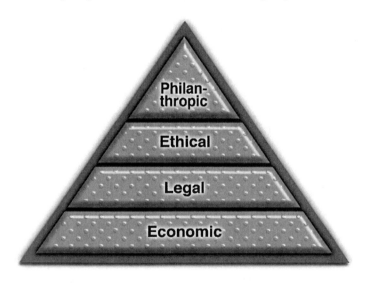

Figure 13.

violating safety regulations, minimum wage requirements, and so on. Additionally, employees, from a hygiene factor perspective, expect the company to keep the law and consistently achieve profitability. Employees do not get excited by their employer's safety record or their ability to keep profitability in the black.

Undeniably, there are multiple economic factors and laws to consider when doing business. These two sections of the pyramid deserve the most time and attention. Competing within the rules of the game is challenging, to say the least. But is simply keeping the law while creating a valuable product or service enough? The next section of the pyramid dictates that managers must consider the ethical implications of their decisions. The top two sections are much more subjective in that managers should try to figure out the "right thing to do." The ethics section is probably the most challenging to address. Most people learn how society functions and simply learn "right and wrong" based on what people in their region consider to be ethical.[26] In a global context, ethical actions in one culture may not be acceptable in another. Often the law is considered the ethical line not to cross yet there are countless examples of following laws in various parts of the world that are deemed unethical by others. "Law" and "ethics" are not synonymous terms. In many cases the law is simply the minimal level of acceptable behavior established by society. Consider wages, for instance. Competition typically dictates the wages that a company will offer. But is a livable, or competitive wage, the right thing to do? Assume that society determines that $20 per hour is livable, yet the company can only afford $14 per hour. Should the company provide fewer jobs at $20 per hour or more jobs at $14? What should the company pay employees in other countries where the minimum and livable wage is lower? Regarding the product or service that the company manufactures, a smartphone, for instance, how long should the product last? The longer it lasts the more it costs to produce, yet if consumers typically change phones on three-year cycles, should the phone last much longer than three years? Considering the cleaning agents examples above, must a company avoid manufacturing poisonous products if they are properly labeled and the chemicals are legal? If the product became less profitable by switching to an environmentally safe formula, and employees and stockholders are affected, should the change happen? There are countless examples of ethical decisions that companies must make daily. Most decisions require ethical consideration since committing an action requires the neglect of other potential actions.

At the top of the CSR Pyramid sits philanthropy, or direct contributions to society. Philanthropy consists of monetary donations, volunteering, or focused efforts to help the community. This is the smallest section since the main focus of a business is fulfilling their mission to achieve profitability. It is important to note that, as a company gets larger and more prosperous, society expects them to fully address, and excel at, all responsibilities within the CSR Pyramid. A consumer would expect a large cap multinational corporation to behave ethically across borders (many corporations hire executive ethics officers), engage in philanthropic activities (especially large donations), pay employees well, etc. Small companies will have a much harder time excelling at all levels of the CSR Pyramid,[27] yet they can still address each level, just with fewer resources.

The Universality of the CSR Pyramid

Can the CSR Pyramid be applied to most companies? Consider a payday loans company. Payday loans are controversial in that they have extremely high interest rates since the loan is expected to be paid off in the short term (on pay day). Payday loan providers create jobs and follow the law. Perhaps some give back to the community through philanthropy. However, the ethical section of the pyramid is the contention. Typically, these types of loans target the poor and those who are not financially savvy. Since the targeted borrowers may be desperate to meet their current debt obligations, they may be enticed to take out the loan. If they are unable to pay off the loan immediately, which is often the case, the interest rate causes the principal amount owed to spiral out of control. If borrowers make payments of the minimum amount, they may never be able to pay off the loan. Payday loans are considered by many to be predatory. Few would argue that short term loans should have higher interest rates than long term loans. But excessive interest rates are the main problem, especially if they are revolving (interest accumulates daily). In the payday loan company's defense, nobody technically forced the borrower to take out the loan. But is it ethical to advertise and tempt those who are in dire straits? Often, the cycle of borrowing is not broken in this situation which leads to the financial ruin of the borrower.

OppLoans, a payday loan company based out of Chicago, Illinois, is attempting to be socially responsible compared to other payday lenders. Working up the CSR Pyramid, OppLoans provides lower interest rates than competitors, offers many employee perks such as benefits, free gym memberships, and subsidized lunches, and they have an A+ rating from the Better Business Bureau.[28] One could say that offering lower interests rates is ethical compared to other payday loan originators. However, the interest rate can still reach almost 200 percent. Compared to other payday loans, which have 400 percent interest, OppLoans is more reasonable. Philanthropically, OppLoans provides free financial training to their borrowers and identifies other lenders (i.e., credit unions) that may be of service to the borrower. In a tainted industry, OppLoans is still using the CSR Pyramid to promote social responsibility.

Modern Worker Focus: The CSR Pyramid and Alaffia

Once small, but growing company, that is attracting modern workers and customers is Alaffia. Based out of the Washington state, Alaffia means "peace and well-being." Alaffia produces fair trade natural bathroom products such as shampoos and conditioners, body wash, soaps, scrubs, and deodorant.[29] The owners met in Togo, Africa; an impoverished nation. They fell in love with the region and developed a cooperative that empowered women. Shea tree nuts are native in this ecosystem as they are a key ingredient in Allafia's products. Women of the region harvest the nuts and craft them into refined butter. Then, the butter becomes the key ingredient in Alaffia's product lines. Alaffia utilizes the social enterprise model, meaning their primary focus is selling products in hopes of enriching society, and, more specifically, Togo.[30]

Alaffia addresses each step of the CSR Pyramid. First, at the economic level, Alaffia pays a fair price (approximately 20 percent over the market price) for the cooperative's Shea butter. The result of this transaction is a salary of cooperative members (women) being four times higher than average wages in the region. Instead of exploiting the region for its cheap labor, Alaffia wants their suppliers to be successful, both personally and professionally. Climbing past the legal level of the CSR Pyramid, since Alaffia is undoubtedly going above and beyond legal requirements regarding wages, working conditions, and following importing laws, is the ethical level. The products Alaffia creates are non-genetically modified, chemical free (no carcinogens or heavy metals for example) and contain environmentally safe ingredients, which are sold in sustainable packaging.[31] As previously stated, many companies have, and still produce, household products that are hazardous to consumers and the environment. At the top of the CSR Pyramid is philanthropy. Alaffia purposefully gives back to the Togo region, far beyond buying Shea butter. Alaffia invests in empowerment projects such as providing maternal care, education, eyeglasses, and bikes: leading to a more environmentally and economically sustainable community.

Chapter Summary

Regardless of the industry, managers can help employees meet their achievement needs by creating a purposeful culture. Modern day employees want their work to be meaningful. Moreover, they want to work for companies and buy products that promote the wellbeing of society. Tools that managers can use to provide meaningful work experiences are the Culture Feedback Loop and the CSR Pyramid.

Application Questions, Chapter 9

1. If an employee asked why their job matters, how would you respond?

2. Define your company's culture. What policies promote the culture, and which need improvement? For instance, do performance appraisals address the culture?

3. Use the Culture Feedback Loop to create a plan for improving your organizational culture.

4. Identify your "Zoysia" plug employees. How can they be better utilized to improve workplace culture?

5. What are some simply ways your company can improve its CSR image?

10

Work Itself + Responsibility

*Why the Division of Labor
Created Bored Workers*

Modern workers are bored. In part, the boredom derives from a lack of importance. Jobs were much more meaningful prior to the Industrial Revolution; before the advent of modern machinery, assembly lines, and job standardization. To illustrate, Adam Smith, a Scottish political economist, stated in his 1775 book the *Wealth of Nations*, that workers in a pin factory could produce 48,000 pins per day if jobs were specialized. Workers, then, were more productive if they only performed the same, repeated task, throughout the workday. If the work was not specialized, and each worker performed every task from start to finish, they could only produce 20 pins per day.[1] One of the trade-offs for this exponential increase in productivity was that dividing the work into simplified tasks led to worker boredom and fatigue. Instead of being responsible for all the steps in an assembly, which is a meaningful exercise, only completing a small step of the process became the norm, leading to isolated tasks. Pumping out many parts per hour became the focus of managers at the expense of the employee psyche. According to Herzberg, the work itself and responsibility are motivators. Pre-industrial jobs naturally required many skills, making the work itself meaningful. Managers today must find ways to make specialized jobs more meaningful. This chapter defines the Job Characteristics Model and prescribes it as a method for making modern jobs important to workers. A comparison of pre-industrial jobs and modern jobs is delineated. Finally, modern examples of employers using elements of the Job Characteristics Model are illustrated.

Why Pre-Industrial Farmers and Apprentices Had Meaningful Work

The Job Characteristics Model (JCM) describes the five components of a job that make it meaningful: skill variety, task identity, task significance, autonomy, and feedback. The following is paraphrase of the JCM component definitions. "Skill variety represents opportunities for employees to learn different skills or use their talents. Task identity describes how the work and employee efforts affect the finished product or service. Task significance is a bit broader than task identity in that it describes how the work impacts others (i.e., society) in a meaningful way. Autonomy is the amount of freedom a worker has regarding her schedule and methods of performing the job. Finally, feedback is the extent to which workers are informed about their effectiveness at work."[2] Apprenticeships and farm work contained all elements of the JCM as described in the following paragraphs.

Prior to the industrialization of the U.S., and in Adam Smith's day, most workers were either apprentices in the skilled trades, or farmers. Apprenticeships worked, and still work well, in the skilled trades professions. Essentially, a master would take on an apprentice with the goal of turning him into a master, at some future point in time. Silversmithing, for example, is the art and practice of forming steel into objects such as coffee pots, goblets, sauce boats, and cutlery, through heating, molding, cutting, and hammering. Fine dining utensils crafted by silversmiths were quite exquisite and required high level artistry and design skills.[3] A master would have possessed the skill necessary to produce one of these high-level utensils whereas an apprentice would not. Apprentices would have started their careers by first performing basic day-to-day duties around the shop while slowly learning the profession. Making a bowl would have been a reasonable task for an apprentice. Silversmith apprentices would learn both horizontal and vertical skills.

Horizontal skills are used in the employee's current position but can also be of benefit after being promoted. For example, learning how to read blueprints, maintain equipment, or the physics of heating and fashioning silver, would be horizontal skills. They are skills that are needed to become an expert at a specific task. Vertical skills, on the other hand, allowed the apprentice to move up the "corporate ladder," or in this case, to one day become the owner of the smithery.[4] Budgeting, scheduling, and supervising are vertical skills.

10. Work Itself + Responsibility

What made apprenticeships unique, from a job satisfaction viewpoint, was that they naturally included motivators. For example, as apprentices reached certain milestones, skill wise, they were promoted and recognized for their accomplishments. Apprentices became experts at their job making it hard for others to replicate their work. The apprentices undoubtedly made a noticeable contribution to their community as the fruits of their labor could easily be seen in their town. It is not hard to see how all the motivators: recognition, growth, the work itself, responsibility, and achievement, were inherent in the apprentice system. Considering the JCM, apprentices, in general, were given continual feedback as to whether their work was at an acceptable level. They were experts at the various requirements of their jobs (skill variety), building their items from start to finish (task identity). They saw their work being used in the community (task significance). As they matured, they were given more responsibly over their duties (autonomy). Like the pin factory workers who put the pins together, start to finish, the apprentices had meaningful jobs.

One modern day career that still uses the apprenticeship system is the electrician. Apprentices spend approximately five years in the classroom while working alongside master electricians, for up to 10,000 hours. Once they reach this milestone, they become a journeyman. Like the silversmiths of old, electricians can see, directly, how their expertise makes a positive contribution to society.[5] Their work can be seen in their "town." They can gain both horizontal and vertical skills on the job. Apprenticeships, however, are not too common today.

Unfortunately, as scientific management and the factory work environment became the norm in the industrialized U.S., apprenticeships diminished. According to C.D. Wright, the president of Clark College in 1908, most academics believed that the apprenticeship system was dead.[6] Managers during the Industrial Revolution were mostly focused on creating efficient processes. Repetition and endurance were the skills that were most in demand. Instead of valuing craftsmanship, highly valued workers in an industrialized economy could produce the most mass-produced goods. As work processes became standardized, employee boredom and fatigue became rife in industry. Employees were not intellectually challenged and managers "motivated" by focusing on hygiene factors. The work itself, for example, lost its value to workers. Quantity became greater than quality.

Farm workers, like apprentices of old, experienced meaningful employment. Working dusk to dawn, farmers tended to many tasks (skill variety) such as taking care of livestock, planting, maintaining, and harvesting crops, performing maintenance on farm equipment, and managing predators. Workers were not micromanaged and had many responsibilities (autonomy). Each job they performed was directly impactful (task identity) since not feeding livestock or watering crops would lead to their demise. The work performed on the farm fed the family or community (task significance). Finally, the quality and yield of the harvested crops or meat was immediately noticeable (feedback). Although this is a bird's eye view of farm life, the point is that the job was naturally meaningful to workers. As jobs became specialized, they lost their meaning. During the Industrial Revolution, factory workers only worked on one part of an assembly line and repeatedly performed remedial tasks. They no longer were connected to the outcome of their product. Supervisors micromanaged and primarily focused on productivity. The Luddites in England became so disenfranchised by factory life and the mundaneness of their work that they revolted by smashing machinery to halt production.[7] Certainly, it was a culture shock leaving the farm and transitioning into relatively meaningless work. The modern-day work environment is not much different in this regard. College students specialize in a certain field, i.e., accounting and often do not see how their work directly impacts others. Students choose careers based on income but not their significance. Employees are compartmentalized instead of performing many tasks as in the agrarian age. Feedback is given inconsistently, sometimes annually, and workers often do not make decisions regarding their daily tasks. Specialization has its benefits, namely increased productivity and workers become experts at a minute portion of a job, but, boredom and fatigue are an unfortunate consequence.

Modern Job Characteristics Model Examples

Semco, a manufacturing company out of Brazil, was previously mentioned for their innovative approach to policy writing. In the late 1980s and early 1990s, executives from corporations such as IBM, General Motors, Goodyear, Siemens, and Nestle traveled to Semco to witness firsthand what a fully empowered workforce looked like. The labor union at Semco realized that managers had employees' best interests in mind. Because of this, the union broke tradition by creating less specialized contracts. Most unions negotiate strict rules so that employees do not have to work beyond their prescribed job duties. Semco's positive relationship with the union, coupled with an empowerment culture, enabled the JCM to be utilized in a unionized environment.

A review of the JCM reveals how Semco addressed all five of its components. First, Semco ensured that employees at all levels worked on a variety of skills. Their workforce, including janitors, laborers, and managers, were trained on how to read balance sheets and cash flow statements.[8] Lower level employees also participated in redesigning products, purchasing contracts, and marketing strategies. Since no receptionists worked at Semco, managers would handle secretarial duties in addition to their normal leadership tasks. Second, worker autonomy and responsibility were addressed by allowing employees to set their own production quotas and salaries. Since open-book management was practiced, all employees were able to see what their coworkers were earning; keeping productivity and salary in check. Third and fourth, task identity and significance occurred as employees designed their own workstations, allowing the team to assemble all components of a product. Each employee was skilled enough to perform multiple tasks, both directly and indirectly, related to their specific job duties. For instance, employees could also drive a forklift to supply the workstation with components, which led to knowledge of production control and warehousing. A team would assemble an entire product, such as an entire cooling unit system (task identity) while performing interrelated tasks such as purchasing components and supplying warehouse materials (task significance). Finally, Semco revolutionized the feedback process. Instead of bureaucratic, top down feedback, employees evaluated their managers every six months and results were posted. Essentially, employees could fire bad bosses.

Undoubtedly, not all companies will be able to emulate Semco's practices. It took over 12 years for Semco to implement and sustain these policies, yet companies can consider how Semco used the JCM to create meaningful jobs. A good first step for managers is to determine which of their own JCM components need immediate improvement. For instance, nursing is a high turnover profession. Managers could use the JCM to identify not only why nurses are hard to retain but also how to make improvements. One study uncovered that three of the most important aspects of improving nursing retention were autonomy, job variety, and peer feedback.[9] Companies need to be concerned with all JCM components, but there are most likely some glaring issues (like the previous nursing study) that can be prioritized. Utilizing the JCM also requires leaders to adopt the Theory Y mindset, as did Ricardo Semler of Semco. Modern workers prefer Theory Y minded leaders. Essentially, making the job more meaningful while giving more control to subordinates, the JCM assumes they want more responsibility over their work. If workers preferred minimal responsibility and enjoyed completing routine tasks, the JCM would not be effective.

In the subsequent paragraphs, modern examples of the JCM in practice will be illustrated.

Autonomy/Responsibility

Autonomy, from the JCM, is similar to Herzberg's responsibility motivator. Both terms refer to employees having control over their work. At Asana, a team-based software company, employees at both junior and senior levels can make decisions that directly impact their jobs.[10] Employees set their own schedules and their hours at work are not tracked. Employees are evaluated by how effectively they meet goals, usually set four months in advance. They also have unlimited time off if their goals are met. Among tech companies, Asana is in the top 1 percent for employee satisfaction.[11]

Skill Variety and Task Identity

One of the easiest ways to improve task identity and skill variety is job rotation. Employees who perform different tasks throughout the day are less bored. Task identity focuses on how employees' tasks impact the entire product. Thus, rotating an employee through different tasks throughout the day helps to minimize boredom while increasing task identity. For example, assume that an assembly line employee drills two holes into a steel plate. If this is the only task the worker performs throughout the day, he will easily burnout for two reasons: redundancy (boredom) and lack of purpose. Repeatedly drilling the same holes will not provide the worker with a sense of accomplishment. If the worker rotates jobs every two hours though, he will see how the drilling process affects other processes, and eventually, the entire product assembly. At a Japanese bank, researchers discovered that mortgage processors were more productive when they learned, and worked, on each of the 17 distinct tasks such as data entry, conducting credit checks, and scanning applications, instead of only working on one, repeated task. The researchers also pointed out that Pal's Sudden Service fast food employees rotate jobs every day to minimize boredom and increase engagement.[12]

Task Significance

Task significance is probably the most overlooked JCM component when employee training is concerned. The primary focus of training is teaching an employee how to correctly perform a task. But how does the work that the employee does on a day to day basis affect other employees, customers, and even more broadly, society? A first step to improving task significance is to treat the succeeding workstation as the first "customer." Using this mindset, a factory worker's immediate customer is the next process, not the family who buys the product from a retailer. This often holds true in the service industries as well but there are often fewer subsequent processes that act as customers. A dishwasher's immediate customer would be the chefs, whose customer would be the patron. A mechanic's immediate customer would be the manager of the garage, then, the end-user who is paying for the service. Both are important to serve from a task significance point of view. In manufacturing, the immediate customer is the next process. To demonstrate a "next process as customer" success story, a study was conducted at a vegetable harvester in the western U.S. Productivity increased by 7 percent as workers began receiving feedback from their internal customers[13] (not the end user). In other words, "customers" from the next process began interacting with employees from previous processes.

To further illustrate, a childcare (service industry) worker's immediate customer would be the child. Although the parent is technically the end user (customer) who pays for the childcare, the first step to improving significance is for managers to demonstrate why certain practices must be followed to benefit the immediate customer. For example, when childcare workers are trained to certain policies (i.e., safety, teaching, nutrition, etc.) the rationale as to why it benefits the immediate customer (child in this case) should be provided. Although the end user is important, the internal customers should be first considered, then, the end user and beyond (society). It is not hard to see how a childcare worker's daily decisions and actions impact the immediate customer (the child), the parent, and society at large. Using a broad brush, across industries, employees should know how their work impacts all potential customers, from the immediate customer to society. From a supply chain perspective, employees should know how their actions affect all customers, not just the original equipment manufacturer and end user.

Feedback

One of the most difficult aspects of management is providing critical feedback to employees. Similar to how losses experienced by gamblers are more impactful on their psyche than winning, negative comments weigh on employees minds more so than their enjoyment from positive feedback.[14] As a good business practice, managers should provide both critical and positive feedback immediately, not only at set performance review dates. Colorcon, a firm specializing in pharmaceutical film coating and formulation development, ditched the annual performance appraisal system altogether. Instead, supervisors give immediate feedback to employees in hopes of quickly developing their performance. Weekly bonuses are tied to the employee's own goals as well.[15] Employees do not have to guess how their supervisor feels about their work quality, and the company benefits by becoming more agile. Workers always know how they are performing. They do not have to wait until an annual review to see how their daily behaviors are perceived by managers.

Modern Worker Focus—Using Technology to Provide Feedback

According to Gallup, millennials require more and consistent feedback than previous generations. In part, this is due to technological advances providing an upbringing of interconnectedness.[16] From a schooling perspective, this is easy to see. Generation Xer parents only received teacher feedback at parent teacher conferences and through semi-annual report cards. Today, parents receive weekly, if not daily, updates from teachers. Grades are current and accessible.

One company that has transitioned through multiple generations in the workforce is General Electric (GE). In response to the feedback needs of their millennial workers, GE has overthrown their outdated annual performance review system by providing immediate employee feedback via an app. This is not to say that GE does not perform annual reviews, but they are no longer the primary method for delivering feedback. Annual performance appraisals, then, have become informal. GE has created a feedback app that accepts voice and text inputs, attached documents, and handwritten notes, providing up-to-minute feedback to employees. Since using the app, GE has become more agile. After abandoning the traditional feedback system, productivity increased fivefold within one year![17] Supervisors also shifted their focus to both positive and negative feedback, now called "Continue Insights" and "Consider Insights," respectively. Basically, Continue Insights focuses on praising behaviors employees should continue, whereas Consider Insights provides constructive criticism.[18]

Regarding negative feedback, or constructive criticism, a foodservice distributor was able to harness voice technology to reduce errors from 2.44/1000 to .94/1000. In this study, the distributor discovered that immediate feedback could decrease mistakes. Forklift operators would use the hands-free headset to speak in the order numbers and quantities they were picking/stocking. The computer system did not allow for a misplaced item unless the operator spoke an override code into the headset. This system was able to improve quality while providing critical feedback to employees.[19] Undoubtedly, both negative and positive feedback should be communicated with employees efficiently, not waiting on quarterly, six month, or annual performance appraisals.

Chapter Summary

As work transitioned from the farm to the factory, specialization ensued. Worker boredom and fatigue resulted after this transition. Apprenticeships and farm jobs were much more meaningful than jobs today. Modern workers often have no idea how their work impacts other processes or their communities. Today, managers can use the Job Characteristics Model as a template for creating more engaging jobs. Employees who experience autonomy, task identity, task significance, skill variety, and immediate feedback, will find their work to be more meaningful.

Application Questions, Chapter 10

1. Consider the following comment: "Millennials need continual feedback and generation Xers and baby boomers do not." Is this true? Or has management theory finally caught up to employee needs?

2. Consider skill variety, autonomy, task identity, task significance, and feedback. First, from left to right, list the characteristic that you believe is lacking the most in a specific job. In other words, making improvements to this characteristic will give you noticeable results. For instance, skill variety is the most lacking and feedback is the least lacking in the table below (left to right). List ways/methods that can be implemented to improve these job characteristics for specific jobs at your facility.

Job Title

Skill Variety	Autonomy	Task Identity	Task Significance	Feedback

3. Consider some ways in which management at your company can provide more frequent, meaningful feedback to employees.

11

Growth

Why Maslow Is Still Magnificent

After decades in the spotlight Maslow's Hierarchy of Needs is still the go-to motivational model for schoolteachers and organizational psychologists. There is much truth in this simple, yet relatable, model. Sitting at the top of Maslow's hierarchy is self-actualization. This section is also the smallest of the pyramid. Some individuals never achieve self-actualization since it the most elusive and the hardest to reach. Self-actualization is the "fulfillment of one's greatest potential."[1] Some people struggle all their lives to figure out their purpose or calling. Others claim that a person can "create" his or her own purpose; "finding" one's purpose is not necessary. Thus, it is hard to determine if a person has a true calling (especially regarding career), how to discover it, and what to do with it if it is detected. Regardless of one's thoughts on the matter, the employer plays a vital role in this search for self-discovery as people spend a considerable amount of their lives at work. Herzberg tapped into the self-actualization concept, albeit indirectly. Growth, a motivator according to Herzberg, is the ability to receive a change in status or learn new skills. The lacking ingredient in Herzberg's definition though, is that learning new skills and changing positions within a company only matters if the employee is on a path to self-actualization. The purpose of this chapter is to demonstrate how managers can align company and individual goals so that both can self-actualize. The human resource development and personality fit concepts will be described and applied as methods for addressing the growth motivator.

Human Resource Development and Self-Actualization

This chapter will primarily focus on human resource (HR) managers and the impact they have on employee growth, yet all managers should be aware of how important the growth motivator is to employees. What is interesting about HR departments is that they are completely separated from operations. The workers, then, only see HR representatives if they are summoned, and it is usually a nerve-racking experience. It is common for employees to not even know what their human resource representatives look like. Typically, HR managers are hired by firms to maintain legal compliance: creating and communicating policies, using appropriate disciplinary methods, and administering pay and benefits. Their focus, then, is how to keep the company out of potential litigation. Employees realize the HR managers have the company's best interest at heart. This is HR's job and this practice is known as human resource management (HRM).

HRM, not HRL (human resource leadership), is prevalent at most companies. Managers, in general, differ from leaders in that they are focused on processes and productivity. Similar to how a production manager keeps the assembly lines running and employees on task, HRM ensures employees are properly trained and compliant with policy. A relevant analogy for the duties associated with HRM is "keeping the ship afloat." In other words, production managers and human resource managers keep the company in business by meeting production quotas within the legal environment. The company does not sink. Of course, following laws and producing respectable products are necessary manager responsibilities. But the intentional leadership aspect is missing. Managers, like employees, in general, just try to survive the various demands of the workday, and they lose sight of the bigger picture: self-actualization. To further illustrate how companies are plagued with the HRM mindset, the following is a human resource manager job description from the Indeed job search website.

Human Resource Manager

Required Knowledge, Skills, and Abilities
- Ability to speak in a public forum
- Ability to lead projects and supervise
- Strong IT skills
- Ability to prioritize tasks, work under pressure, and solve problems
- Knowledge of local and state laws
- Knowledge of recruitment trends
- Knowledge of staffing and employment practices

11. Growth

Responsibilities

- Lead oversight of human resource policies
- Develop and implement rollout strategies for policy updates
- Lead enterprise wide relations projects and trainings
- Lead investigation and resolutions of complaints
- Improve managers' abilities to evaluate employee performance and handle conflicts
- Identify employee relations trends
- Serve as expert in handling disciplinary issues[2]

There is nothing inherently wrong with this job description. HR managers must possess these skills. And implementing training and improving employee performance are mentioned. However, what often happens is that HR managers will get lost in the day-to-day demands of the company, keeping the ship afloat. Ultimately, HR representatives, who focus on the skills, abilities, and responsibilities presented in the above job description, will probably be focused on short term issues. Even the training and performance improvement duties that were mentioned in the job description will be viewed with a short term, annual review measured, lens. There will be no clear career path that will be implemented or long-term employee development plan of employees that is meaningful. Career paths require managers to provide milestones that employees can achieve regarding acquired competencies, their fit with the culture, and their accumulation of more responsibilities.[3] Training is typically associated with completing a specific job or task whereas development is related to long-term career development.

What is noticeable about the human resource manager job description above is that it mostly focuses on management practices. There is no call to organizational transformation. Most likely, human resource managers hired by this firm will be physically separated, in secluded offices, from where the employees conduct their work. How much improvement in morale could a company expect if HR representatives were purposefully engaged, visible, and promoting employee growth, instead of being secluded in a separate office? Imagine that the HR office was placed in the middle of the factory instead of an outside facility. Enter the human resource development (HRD) mindset.

The purpose of HRD is to merge the ambitions of individuals with those of the company. Maslow stated that, ideally, "the task is no longer separate from self ... but rather employees identify with their task so strongly that you cannot define their real self without including that task."[4] In the context of Peter Senge's bestselling book about creating a learning organization, which emphasizes employee growth and development, he includes this Maslow quotation. More specifically, Senge states that, for an organization to continue to develop, employees must continually want to learn and gain skills in a work atmosphere that provides a shared vision. Like HRD, personal goals should be aligned with the vision and goals of the organization. Therefore, both the organization and the employee work towards self-actualizing. HR representatives play an active role in organization and individual development.

There are four components of HRD. The first two components are concerned with short-term performance, titled: individual development and performance management. Individual development focuses on improving skills and training related to one's current job. Performance management is essentially an appraisal system that ensures that employees have the right skills to do their current jobs.[5] In the long term, the organization and employee come closer to self-actualizing through policies geared towards career development and organizational development and these final two components are titled as such. Companies that are concerned with career development create paths for employee advancement and relevant training such as mentoring, resource development centers, and career counseling. This component is most related to Herzberg's growth motivator. Organizational development, the second long-term component, occurs when the business becomes more cohesive and employees continue learning new skills, purposefully evolving with the direction of the business. Employees learn skills that benefit not only themselves but the company's strategy.

From a bird's eye view, HR should create policies that promote effective onboarding. Employees should be appropriately trained to their jobs, and skills they need to gain should be listed and measured. Employees ought to be aware of how they impact the culture, captured by the performance appraisal system. Additionally, a path to both short and long-term success should be provided. Often, HR managers only fill supervisory positions with applicants from outside of the firm. The message is clear to lower level employees: "we do not believe that you have the skills, nor do we want to take the time or energy to improve your skills, so that you are promotable." Of course, there may be severe skill or attitude deficiencies present within the organization that HR cannot fully fix. In most cases, though, the supervisory skills of lower level employees can be improved if career planning and training are available.

Finally, the goals and strategy of an organization can be addressed through HRD. Organizational performance can be improved if the employee skills that are measured, both from a career and individual development standpoint, help them make relevant job-related decisions. For instance, if a customer service employee dreams of becoming a store manager, the training he receives, both in and outside of work (i.e., higher education), should focus on skills that will improve company performance. Examples include financial, operations management, and leadership training. Many companies haphazardly offer tuition reimbursement as a perk. It is important to tie learning into actual workplace improvements. If an employee wants to learn statistics to improve her knowledge of process control, and takes a class for instance, is there an effort to ensure these skills can be applied immediately to processes? Isolated learning will not produce results. Immediate application is necessary to build recently developed skills.

Human Resource Development (HRD) vs. Human Resource Management (HRM)

When HRM and HRD are compared, their differences are apparent. The purpose of HRM is to help the company accomplish its current objectives and determine which skills are necessary for employees to complete the tasks at hand. HRM belongs in the hygiene factor category. HRM does not motivate employees but the lack of effective HRM leads to job dissatisfaction. Employees expect to be trained correctly and essential functions, such as payroll or the tracking of paid time off, to be done without error. They also expect fair disciplinary policies and so on. They do not get excited when a paycheck is correctly calculated. If a paycheck is not correct though or if discipline is not distributed evenly amongst associates, employees will be dissatisfied. Undoubtedly, HRM is important, yet HRM cannot motivate employees. The ultimate of goal of HRD, on the other hand, is high-performance for both the worker and employer (self-actualizing).[6] HRD, then, functions as a motivator. At the core, HRD proactively aligns employee skills with the skills needed of the organization in hopes of creating high-performance, now, and in the future. HRM is reactive in that it primarily attempts to provide for the day-to-day needs of the firm.[7] At the core, the focus of HRD is transformational whereas HRM is transactional.[8]

One reason that businesses outsource their HR departments is that they are deemed to only work on HRM tasks. Supporting functions, such as accounting and HR, do not add direct value to a product or service. They are necessary functions but most likely to be outsourced. Payroll, benefits administration, legal compliance training, and recruiting and background checks, are prime tasks for outsourcing.[9] From a growth perspective, HR should be viewed as an encourager of employee and organizational development. Payroll, benefits, etc., although important, should be viewed as something HR "does" but not what defines their "purpose."

REI—HRD in Action

Recreational Equipment Inc. (REI) is a top-quality outdoor gear and apparel company whose mission is to "inspire, educate and outfit for a lifetime of outdoor adventure and stewardship." REI has adapted to the needs of their members, and consumers, since 1938, and they currently do an exceptional job hiring and selling to millennials. For instance, they currently sell used products and they rent gear. The director stated that younger shoppers are concerned about sustainability (as is REI according to their mission) and often prefer renting to owning.[10] From their inception, REI has been a member-driven co-op. Seventy percent of their annual profits are either distributed to members as dividends, profit sharing and retirement as well as a portion being donated to environmentally focused nonprofits.[11]

Regarding HRD, and its four components (individual development, performance management, career development and organizational development), REI coherently addresses each component. First, from an individual development perspective, REI hires employees who fit, both in skills and interests, with the purpose and culture of the company. The story of REI and their unrelenting focus on taking care of the environment are shared with potential new hires. Regarding employees, their transportation costs to and from work are partially subsidized, if they take public transportation to work, minimizing carbon emissions. Tuition reimbursement is provided, although, learning is not directly tied to HRD. REI provides health care to all workers, both part-time and full-time.[12] They also reward employees who bike to work. Moving into the second component, performance management, which attempts to improve both the individual and the organization through employee development, REI spends a considerable amount of effort on training. In the first two weeks, new employees are paired with veteran mentors to not only learn the ins and outs of their jobs but also to work on environmentally focused community service projects. On their first day, employees work through real scenarios that are likely to occur at work as well as engage in an environmental project like waterway cleaning. A perk for the sales team is that they receive a five-day training at corporate headquarters.

Regarding the third component, career development, employees are given personal action career kits by the human resources department. Included are individualized plans for advancement in the company including planning tools for growth and goal setting opportunities/frequency with management. REI provides a nine-month manager training program for interested applicants. Finally, REI promotes the fourth component, organizational development, through open book management. Employees are privy to the company's financials to ensure they feel like real members of the co-op. Employees often work with upper management, including the CEO, on outdoor projects. REI provides frequent townhall meetings so employees can get any questions answered, making them more engaged and productive. Awards distributed by REI are to employees who espouse values related to the mission. Unsurprisingly, the rewards consist of outdoor related events for the winners. The results of REI's focus on HRD: 62 percent employee retention in a 29 percent retention retail industry.

Modern Work Focus: PJ Fit, Drive and Skill Alignment

Part of the self-actualization process is matching employee personality to the work. People not only want to discover "what it is they are supposed to do?" in life, they also want to know "what they are supposed to do?" for a career. Reducing these questions to a concise statement results in the following: Employees want to work jobs that they naturally enjoy, helping to fulfill their purpose in life. For instance, employees working in the high turnover hotel industry were less likely to quit, or burnout, if they possessed an "agreeable" personality.[13] They had the "right" personality for the job. Supporting this notion is Personality-Job (PJ Fit) Theory.[14] Holland created the RAISEC Typology to demonstrate how individuals had natural vocational preferences. The assumption is that employees are less likely to quit, and are more likely to enjoy, jobs that match their personalities. Saberr, a software company that exists to help teams improve performance, has consulted for large companies such as Siemens, Unilever, and GE Healthcare.[15] Through a personality app, employees are able to see how their personality relates/differs from coworkers so they can better understand each other, which may lead to better interpersonal relationships and improved productivity.

Regarding the RAISEC Typology, the U.S. Department of Labor, Employment, and Training Administration has created the O*Net Resource Center. O*Net provides a free "Interest Profiler" assessment, online, that allows the user to see what their RAISEC type is and what jobs are common to this type.[16] The RAISEC types are realistic, artistic, investigative, social, enterprising, and conventional.[17] For instance, conventional jobs often deal with data analysis and have clearly written rules and procedures whereas enterprising jobs typically involve working with others, risk taking, and decision making. More information is available, and personality testing can be completed, via the O*Net website.

An example of how PJ Fit plays out in colleges is when students change their majors. Although the student may possess a certain skill required of their major, the program of study does not match their personality. Take engineering for instance. A student may enjoy math (skill) but she may not enjoy the engineering profession. Students excel in school if they possess both the talent (skill) and the personality, meaning, they like the subject and can do the work. Additionally, their motivational drive, partly influenced by aligning a major with personality and skills, will determine how productive and effective they are in their studies. Motivation is often the most difficult factor for employers, or in the instance of higher education academic advisors, to determine during the hiring process. Personality and skill assessments are common, and many exist for employers to use. However, it is important for employers to note that simply aligning employee skills and personality to a job may not yield higher productivity. Motivation, which can be partially improved by this alignment, still depends on the employee's own initiative. Hopefully, PJ Fit, coupled with skill alignment, will influence the employee's motivation.

Modern workers should be aware of the various personality assessments that employers will use in the hiring and developing phases of employment. Likewise, managers should be aware of the strengths, and perhaps more importantly, the pitfalls, of personality testing. It is estimated that upwards of 62 percent of companies use personality testing in one form or another.[18] One problem with testing is that too many similar candidates may be hired into a department. For instance, the most common personality type for accountants is ISTJ: introverted, sensing, thinking, and judging.[19] According to the Myers and Briggs Foundation website, persons who possess this type of personality are "quiet, serious, earn success by thoroughness and dependability. Practical, matter of fact, realistic, and responsible. Decide logically what should be done and work toward it steadily, regardless of distractions. Take pleasure in making everything orderly and organized—their work, their home, their life. Value traditions and loyalty."[20] Although the ISTJ type may be drawn to accounting this leads to a homogenous group personality. Managers should be aware that simply hiring for this type will not necessarily produce results as internal drive and skill are also important. The ISTJ type may be more prone to like the accounting profession but it is also not a guarantee. Additionally, employees applying for positions should be aware that employers may be looking for a specific personality type.

Chapter Summary

Maslow and Herzberg realized that employees want to continually grow in both their work and lives. The employer plays a role in helping employees self-actualize and mature. If employees do not feel like they are growing in their profession, they will not seek long term employment. Human resource professionals are often pushed to the outskirts of the organization as they focus on maintaining policy in hopes of minimizing lawsuits. Human resource development, a motivator, requires human resource management, a hygiene factor, to succeed. HRD seeks ways to help employees grow in their careers, aligning the goals of the individual and the organization.

Application Questions, Chapter 11

1. Are there simple steps you can take to help employees grow? For example, could implementing goals, at the discretion of the employee, be a part of the appraisal process?

2. Does your organization have a career planning center or provide a clear path for promotion? What improvements can be made to career planning at your company?

Section III—The House: Motivators

3. Review how REI addresses the four components of HRD. In the table below, list ways (in black) in which your company addresses each component. In red, list ways that each section can be improved.

Individual Development	Performance Management
Career Development	Organizational Development

4. In what ways can personality testing be used to better the fit of worker and job at your facility? Or are there ways, currently, in which personality testing is being used in a nonconstructive way?

SECTION IV

Measuring Employee Job Satisfaction

12

The Universal Dual-Factor Survey (UDS)

The Universal Dual-Factor Survey (UDS) is based on Herzberg's Two Factor theory. It includes both motivator and hygiene factor categories and the following facets of job satisfaction: recognition, the work itself, achievement, growth, responsibility, policy, supervision, relationships, working conditions, salary, benefits, and job security. See the appendix for notes regarding the reliability of the UDS. This chapter will introduce the UDS, describe how to administer the survey, and provide a rationale for its construction.

Figure 14: The Universal Dual Factor Survey (UDS)

Think of your current job. How much do you agree with each statement?

Statement	Disagree Strongly	Disagree a Little	Neutral	Agree a Little	Agree Strongly
Job Satisfaction					
Overall, I am satisfied with my job.					
I feel good about my job, in general.					
Recognition					
I am a valued employee.					
I am recognized for my hard work.					
The Work Itself					
I am energized by tasks I complete each day.					

Section IV—Measuring Employee Job Satisfaction

Statement	Disagree Strongly	Disagree a Little	Neutral	Agree a Little	Agree Strongly
My daily job duties are enjoyable.					
*I am bored by my daily responsibilities.					
Achievement					
My job gives me a sense of achievement.					
My work has a major impact on other people.					
Growth					
I have been, or can be, promoted.					
My job allows me to grow as a person.					
Responsibility					
I frequently make important decisions.					
I have authority over my work.					
Policy					
Our company has fair rules.					
Things are done the right way around here.					
Supervision/Management					
I get along well with my supervisors/leaders.					
*Supervisors have no people skills.					
I like working for my leaders.					
Relationships					
I fit in well with most of my team members.					

12. The Universal Dual-Factor Survey (UDS)

Statement	Disagree Strongly	Disagree a Little	Neutral	Agree a Little	Agree Strongly
I like working alongside my fellow employees.					
Working Conditions					
I have the right tools to do my job.					
I have adequate work-space.					
My work environment is acceptable.					
Salary					
My wages are competi-tive.					
I am happy with my pay-check each week.					
*I am not paid enough.					
Benefits					
I am happy with my ben-efits.					
*I am not satisfied with my benefits package.					
Job Security					
My company does its best to make sure I have a job.					
*I am worried about my job security.					
My employer wants me to succeed at my work.					
*I am easily replaceable.					

Note the job security facet has not been tested for reliability. See the Appendix.

The UDS can be used in its form above or the facets may be removed (see Figure 15 below). Additionally, the statements (i.e., I am happy with my benefits) can be randomized if the facets headings (i.e., job security) are removed. Statements may also be removed or added. However, the reliability (see next chapter for more information) may be

143

diminished, or perhaps improved, if statements are added, or removed. The key is to identify statements that are the most relevant to your organization. If statements are added, make sure to not ask leading questions. In other words, the statements should be clear, simple, and should not trigger a worker's potential bias.[1] **It is extremely important to note that statements containing an asterisk need to be reverse scored.** The asterisk should be removed prior to administering the survey to employees. Instructions for reverse scoring are in the following chapter.

Figure 15: The UDS Without Facets

Statement	Disagree Strongly	Disagree a Little	Neutral	Agree a Little	Agree Strongly
Overall, I am satisfied with my job.					
I feel good about my job, in general.					
I am a valued employee.					
I am recognized for my hard work.					
I am energized by tasks I complete each day.					
My daily job duties are enjoyable.					
*I am bored by my daily responsibilities.					
My job gives me a sense of achievement.					
My work has a major impact on other people.					
I have been, or can be, promoted.					
My job allows me to grow as a person.					
I frequently make important decisions.					
I have authority over my work.					

12. The Universal Dual-Factor Survey (UDS)

Statement	Disagree Strongly	Disagree a Little	Neutral	Agree a Little	Agree Strongly
Our company has fair rules.					
Things are done the right way around here.					
I get along well with my supervisors/leaders.					
*Supervisors have no people skills.					
I like working for my leaders.					
I fit in well with most of my team members.					
I like working alongside my fellow employees.					
I have the right tools to do my job.					
I have adequate work-space.					
My work environment is acceptable.					
My wages are compet-itive.					
I am happy with my pay-check each week.					
*I am not paid enough.					
I am happy with my ben-efits.					
*I am not satisfied with my benefits package.					
My company does its best to make sure I have a job.					
*I am worried about my job security.					
My employer wants me to succeed at my work.					
*I am easily replaceable.					

An asterisk means that the responses to the phrase need to be reverse scored.

Survey Development and Rationale

The UDS is a short form survey that allows managers to quickly assess which facets their employees are satisfied with and which need improvement. The term "facets" in this case means the motivation or hygiene factors such as benefits or recognition. Each facet contains two-to-four statements.

The chief rationale for the UDS being a short form survey is that shorter surveys result in higher response rates and lower incomplete rates. In general, when participants are asked to complete a survey, a questionnaire that has only a few required responses is far more appealing than a lengthy and time-consuming questionnaire. Additionally, survey fatigue (when participants get bored and do not finish the survey) is more likely to set in on long form surveys. The trade off, though, is that long form surveys are typically more reliable than short form surveys. Reliability will be discussed, in more detail, in the following chapter.

There are two general methods available for managers to understand the satisfaction of their workforce: interviews and surveys. Interview responses are what led Herzberg to create Two Factor theory. Herzberg asked two broad questions to 200 engineers and accountants: "Give a time you felt exceptionally good about your job" and "Describe a sequence of events that resulted in negative feelings about your job."[2]

Interviews are a good way for employees to discuss their true feelings. Employees will provide guarded responses, however, if they believe that comments regarding supervisors, etc., may be used against them, directly or indirectly. Often a third party will conduct interviews to ensure the anonymity of the workers. There are two major drawbacks to interviews. First, they are time consuming and expensive. Letting employees vent about issues (or hopefully giving positive feedback) and recording responses/transcription takes a lot of effort. If a third party is involved, the time that it takes to transcribe, and conduct interviews, often outweighs the cost of sending out a survey. The interviewer can get much deeper responses interviewing, than with a survey, but analyzing and coding responses can be difficult and time consuming. Second, finding an interviewer, especially internally, that employees are comfortable enough with to let their guard down and give truthful responses, is difficult, if not impossible. Imagine an interviewer asking this question: "What is the biggest challenge in your workday?" If it is the employee's supervisor, how likely is it for him to divulge this information? Even if there is a disclosure that states "responses cannot be used against the employee" an employee will not risk retaliation. Again, a third party can be hired to conduct the interviews, but employees may still be guarded since they are describing their issues to an outsider. The pro of interviews, then, are that they can lead to robust and deep responses. The cons are that the process is time consuming and the responses are likely to be filtered as to not offend management.

The second approach to understanding employee job satisfaction is the survey method. The main reason for using the survey approach is that results are easier to generalize. If enough surveys are collected, and the sample is not too biased, the scores participants respond with can give a good overall impression of worker attitudes. Short form surveys, like the UDS, are used to minimize fatigue and increase participation. If employees see hundreds of questions on a survey, they will be less likely to participate. Thus, the UDS short form is designed to boost the response rate, but it may not give as robust responses as a long form survey or interviews. Any research method has its strengths and weaknesses. Another strength of the UDS is that questions can be easily entered into Excel for analysis. The UDS may also be administered via paper and pencil method or through an online survey platform like Qualtrics. It is important that employee responses remain anonymous. The paper and pencil method may help to boost the response rate if employees can complete it at a convenient time during work hours. Online methods have a feeling of "big brother" watching, although the responses can be kept anonymous. Online surveys make it easy to extract the data and save into an Excel document. Paper and pencil methods will require a manual data entry.

Administering the Survey

Following are a few suggestions for issuing the survey to employees. First, the human resource department should administer the survey. Additionally, employees should be notified in some form or fashion (i.e., a statement accompanying the survey) of the survey's intent. Second, as previously stated, it is imperative that survey participant responses remain anonymous. Workers should be able to freely express themselves without fear of retribution. Bias will also be reduced if responses are anonymous, and ethically speaking, employees should be free to not participate or quit at any time. If an online format is used, emailing a link to employees is a simple method for survey dissemination. Qualtrics, for example, can keep responses completely anonymous as the survey and responses are completed in the "cloud." It is recommended to offer an incentive to encourage survey participation, i.e., a gift card distributed at random, to increase the amount of completed surveys. Another dissemination method, which may help boost the response rate, is the paper and pencil method. A form can be distributed to employees and they can place the completed surveys into a sealed envelope. The benefit is that no training is required to learn additional software. Regardless of the method used, controls must be put in place to ensure that the data collection method is secure. Regarding the sealed envelope, employees should be able to place responses in an envelope without supervisors watching. The envelope must also be secured so only an impartial administrator has access. If using online software, administrators should use high quality passwords. Also, employees should only be able to complete one survey (not multiple). The final issue that may occur is employees only filling out part of the survey. Managers will need to determine if the entire survey should be discarded if it is not fully completed.

Demographic Information

Most surveys begin with the participant answering a few demographic questions. Based on the size of the company, managers must be deliberate in how they collect this information. The main question to ask is "Is the demographic information truly necessary to collect?" For example, is age an important factor? If age is important, it is best to bracket age into large groups, i.e., less than or greater than 30 years old. If the survey asks the employee to respond with her age, or only gives five-year increments (for example), the anonymity will be reduced as there will only be a handful of workers in a certain age range. Or if gender, age, department, and race are asked, it would be easy for managers to start pinpointing who is responding to the survey. Always included a "prefer not to respond" option and only collect demographic information that is necessary.

Chapter Summary

The UDS is a short form survey designed to boost response rates and minimize fatigue. The survey can be disseminated using online software or via the paper and pencil method. Responses to the UDS must be kept anonymous. Once collected, the responses can be entered into Excel for further analysis. It is extremely important to note which responses need to be reverse scored.

13

Analyzing and Displaying
Survey Results

The purpose of this chapter is to layout out a simple, step-by-step process, to analyze and visualize the results of the Universal Dual Factor Survey (UDS). These steps may also be applied to other management projects that use the survey method. The purpose of visualizing responses is twofold: to help managers make more informed decisions and to help managers effectively communicate results to employees. Data sets are much easier to digest if visualized (charts and graphs).

When considering a data analysis project, such as analyzing the UDS results, it is important to understand the foundational elements of the survey. The Harvard Business Review noted that projects, such as job satisfaction improvements, often fail not due to the statistical analysis but from managers not being able to explain the results in a simple manner. Or, management does not understand the theory upon which the data is collected.[1] Therefore, it is imperative that managers understand the Two Factor theory, as well as the motivators and hygiene factors mentioned in previous chapters, prior to surveying workers, analyzing, displaying, and communicating results. A common software that most businesses and nonprofits utilize is Microsoft Excel. Excel is easy to use and quickly calculates statistics. It also efficiently creates charts and graphs. Additionally, once a practitioner understands how to analyze data in Excel, advanced software packages, like SAS or Tableau, are easy to transition to since the core of the analysis is the same. Excel includes a free Data Analysis Tool Pak Add-In that improves the efficiency of statistical calculations.

The following steps can be used to visualize survey results: Choose a relevant data collection method and software package (Excel in this instance), organize the data into a spreadsheet, reverse score as necessary, calculate the descriptive statistics, and visualize the central tendency of each facet with a radar chart.

Install Microsoft Excel Data Analysis Tool Pak

Following are the simple steps to add in the analysis Tool Pak for most computers. If using an Apple computer, follow similar steps but perform a simple Internet search for "How to Add Data Analysis Tool Pak for Excel Apple." The Tool Pak functions a bit differently for Apple products.

First, install the data analysis Tool Pak in Excel: this tool-pack is free, easy to install, and will perform statistical analysis quickly. To begin, Click File > Click Options > Click Add-Ins > Click Analysis Tool Pak > Click Go > Click Analysis Tool Pak > Click OK. Once the Tool Pak is installed, click Data at the top of the main screen. Make sure "Data Analysis" is displayed on the top right side of the screen. For more information, go to Youtube and search for "Data Analysis Tool Pak Excel."

Organize the Spreadsheet and Code Responses

The first step after the data collection process is to organize the values in a spreadsheet. First, create a column titled "Employee Number." Since surveys are anonymous, simply add a column (Column A) and label each employee as 1, 2, 3, etc. If a paper and pencil version of the survey was used, write the Employee Number on each survey as well. Labeling each survey makes it easier for reviewing and double-checking later.

In Column B and beyond, enter the demographic values, if any were collected. It is important to give employees the option to not answer demographic questions as they may feel uncomfortable sharing personal details. Column B, for instance, could be "Race." Employees could select from the following list: "1=Hispanic, 2=American Indian or Alaskan Native, 3=Asian, 4=Black or African American, 5=Native Hawaiian or Other Pacific Islander, 6=White, 7=Two or More Races, 8=I prefer not to answer this question." These race categories were derived from the U.S. 2010 census. Putting numbers in place of responses is known as coding (not to be confused with computer programming code). Simply stated, coding takes a qualitative (worded) response, such as race (i.e. white), and assigns a numerical value. Again, only collect demographic information if absolutely necessary. Typically, the entire data sheet will be coded. So far, the spreadsheet would look like the following image.

Spreadsheet Image 1:
Setting Up the Worksheet Part I

Column A	Column B	Column C	Column D
Employee Number	*Race*	*Question 1*	*Question 2*
1	3	5	4
2	6	4	5
3	4	4	4

Reverse Scoring Items

Most surveys will require certain responses to be reverse scored. On the UDS, the scale is from 1 (disagree strongly) to 5 (agree strongly). Certain statements/questions that employees will respond to will be positively worded and others will be negatively worded. For example, the phrase "my wages are competitive" is a positively written statement. This means that an employee who scored this item as a 5 feels that his employer is paying a great wage. In contrast, consider the phrase, "I am not paid enough." This phrase has a negative connotation. If an employee scores this item as a 1, what is he saying? Is he saying that he is not paid enough? No. A score of 1 means that he strongly disagrees with the statement. To make the score represent the positive phrasing, the score needs to be reversed, or flipped. When flipping a score, imagine the phrase changing to positive wording such as: "I AM paid enough." To flip the score on a scale that uses a 1-5 scoring system (a Likert scaled survey), simply subtract the initial response from 6. So, 6-1=5. In other words, the employee who strongly disagreed with the "I am not paid enough" statement is actually saying that he strongly agrees that "he is paid enough." The employee is quite satisfied with his pay, thus, he disagreed with the negative statement/phrasing.

Once negative scores are reversed, it is easier to graph and analyze the responses. Another way to reverse score is to simply flip the score instead of subtracting it from 6 (for 5-point Likert scaled items only). Using a Likert scale, on a negatively worded phrase, take the response score and give its opposite. So, a score of 1=5, 2=4, 3=3, 4=2, and 5=1. To illustrate with one more example, if an employee scores the negatively worded phrase "I am not paid enough" with a 4, this means he agrees with the statement: "he is not paid enough." To reverse score this item, either use: 6-4=2, or, flip the 4 to its opposite, 2.

See the example spreadsheet below for Question 18. The statement that employees answered was: "I am not paid enough." Since this is a negatively worded statement, the scores need to be reversed. A score of 5 should be changed to 1 and so on for all responses under the Question 18 heading.

Spreadsheet Image 2:
Setting Up the Worksheet Part II

Employee Number	Question 18	Question 18 Reverse Scored
1	5	1
2	1	5
3	2	4

It cannot be overstated how important reverse scoring is to the visualization process. If items are not reverse scored as required, the charts and graphs to follow will be inaccurate.

Calculate Descriptive Statistics

Using the Data Analysis feature (see the beginning of this chapter for installation instructions), click "Data Analysis," select "Descriptive Statistics," then click "OK." For whatever column that needs to be analyzed, highlight the values as "input." Click the "Input Range" cell, then, highlight the column. If the column title, such as "Question 14," is to be included in the output, click the "Labels in First Row" box. Then, click "Summary Statistics." Then, "OK." The output will look like the following table.

Spreadsheet Image 3:
Descriptive Statistics Output

Question 14	
Mean	3.377358
Standard Error	0.11721
Median	4
Mode	4
Standard Deviation	1.20675
Sample Variance	1.456244
Kurtosis	-1.2156
Skewness	-0.17011
Range	4
Minimum	1
Maximum	5
Sum	358
Count	106

Note—Excel output only displays the first mode if there are more than one

Assume that Question 14 asked if employees felt like they fit in well with their coworkers. The central tendency, or, where the responses tend to gather, in this case, is 3.38 (mean), or 4 (median and mode). Since a survey score of 3 implies a neutral position, 4 implies that employees "agree a little," and 5 implies that employees "agree strongly," the central tendency from this output shows a slightly favorable result. Employees feel at least neutral, or slightly agree, that they fit in with their coworkers. Typically, the mean score will be used for the upcoming radar chart but median and mode also reflect the central tendency.

Regarding the dispersion of the data for Question 14, the standard deviation is 1.21 and the range is 4. The standard deviation refers to how spread out the data is from the center (mean). Most likely, if the manager randomly selected an employee, this employee would feel like she fit in with her coworkers with a score of 3.37 +/- 1.21, or, 2.16 – 4.58. In other words, the typical employee is going to feel OK-to-good about fitting in with coworkers. The range, however, shows that some employees feel a 1 on this question and others 5. Therefore, there are some employees, albeit not the norm, who fully fit in or do not fit in at all. On average, though, the fitting in feeling will only be slightly above average.

Rank Ordering and Visualizing the Facets

Once the spreadsheet is organized and the descriptive statistics for each column are calculated, compute the facet scores. Each facet, i.e. "The Work Itself," consists of a subset of questions. The Work Itself facet contains the following three questions/statements: "I am energized by tasks I complete each day" (mean=4.9), "My daily job duties are enjoyable" (mean=4.7), and the corrected reverse scored statement, "I am bored by my daily responsibilities" (mean=4.8). Then, the facet mean (the mean of the means) should be calculated. In this case, the facet mean, or the Work Itself score, is (4.9 + 4.7 + 4.8) / 3 = 4.8.

Spreadsheet Image 4:
Rank Ordering Facets

Rank Order	Facet	Survey Score
1	Work Itself	4.8
2	Achievement	4.7
3	Relationships	4.2
4	Benefits	4.2
5	Responsibility	4.1
6	Salary	4.1
7	Job Satisfaction	4.0
8	Supervision	4.0
9	Growth	3.9
10	Job Security	3.9

Rank Order	Facet	Survey Score
11	Recognition	3.8
12	Working Conditions	3.8
13	Policy	3.0

A few thoughts immediately come to mind upon reviewing the image above. First, recognition, one of the most significant predictors of job satisfaction, is ranked 11th. This is a problem. Employees do not feel recognized. Next, the employees seem to enjoy their work since the work itself and achievement are ranked number 1 and 2, respectively. Growth, though, is not highly scored. At a quick glance, it seems that employees enjoy their immediate job duties. However, they may not see many opportunities for advancement and are seldom recognized for their achievements. Policy is by far the worst scored facet.

Radar Charts

Once the facets are rank ordered as seen above, Excel can easily create a radar chart to visualize the table. Highlight the facets and survey scores (not the rank order), then click "Insert," then "Recommended Charts," then, "Radar", then "OK." See Excel Image 1 below for the radar chart output.

Excel Image 1: Radar Chart Output

The radar chart below is easy to read. The further the dark line gets to the edge of the chart, or, the closer to 5.0, the better the rating from employees. Policy is clearly the lowest rated facet and the work itself and achievement are the highest rated facets.

Reliability—Especially Important If Managers Add or Remove Questions

It is important to note that, if managers alter the survey in any way,

Job Satisfaction

Excel Image 1.

the reliability may be diminished. Each facet has previously been tested for reliability, also known as internal consistency. To picture what reliability looks like, consider the Job Security hygiene factor on the UDS. Job Security is comprised of four statements: "My company does its best to make sure I have a job," "I am worried about my job security" (a reverse scored statement), "My employer wants me to succeed at my work," and "I am easily replaceable" (a reverse scored statement). All four statements, when answered together, should represent Job Security.

To determine if the Job Security facet is reliable, the Cronbach's alpha must be calculated: this calculation is beyond the scope of this book. What is essential to know is that the Cronbach's alpha shows how related the statements are as a group (facet).[2] If statements are removed and/or added to the survey, the reliability will be impacted and the facet may be weakened. Therefore, caution should be used if the survey is altered. See the appendix for more information regarding survey reliability.

Chapter Summary

Properly formatting the Excel sheet and analyzing the data is a time consuming and involved process. First, make sure all reverse scoring is completed for relevant responses. Then, calculate descriptive statistics to describe the means of each facet (or individual statements). Radar charts can be used to visualize the central tendency of the facets. It is also easy to train employees to interpret radar charts. The next chapter describes one more tool that will help management visualize survey results and set job satisfaction improvement goals.

14

The Motivation-Hygiene Grid

Once the UDS survey is completed and the spreadsheet is properly set up (see previous chapter), the final step is to visualize how satisfied employees are via the Motivation-Hygiene Factor Grid. This grid can be completed in addition to the previously recommended charts, i.e., radar chart and histogram, or it can be completed on its own, depending on the level of analysis desired by management. This step is quite simple in that only one point needs to be plotted. **Take the average of all hygiene factor totals and the average of all motivation factor totals from the survey.** The hygiene average of totals should be placed on the x-axis and the average of all motivator factor totals should be placed on the y-axis. Then, plot the intersection. A sample grid is placed below.

The low hygiene and motivating factors threshold, depicted by the intersection of the dotted lines, was set at point (4,4). The rationale is that a centered score would be (3,3), or average. Nothing is exceptional about a 3 out of 5 score. The dot, in this example, is placed at (3.7, 4.2), meaning that the average total score for motivators was 4.2 (high) and the hygiene factors average total score was 3.7 (low). These are also known as the grand averages. This grid provides a quick picture as to whether a company is properly addressing hygiene and motivating factors.

The Four Possible Combinations

There are four possible combinations of hygiene/motivation factors that exist.[1] The best combination possible is located in the upper right quadrant: High Motivation and High Hygiene. Employees, in general, will have both their internal and external needs provided for by the employer. Theoretically speaking, turnover intentions would be minimal and attitudes about the company would be positive. On the far, lower right side of the grid is High Hygiene and Low Motivators. Employees

Motivation/Hygiene Grid

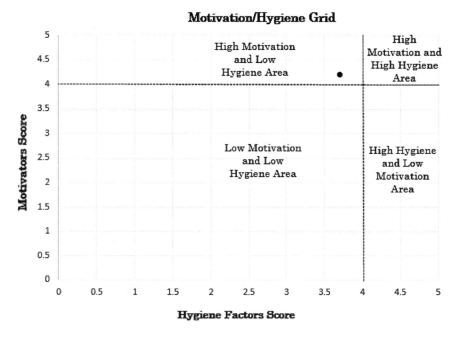

Image 16.

would have their basic needs met, leading to few complaints. However, they will feel indifferent about the company. Since hygiene factors do not motivate, employees will not be motivated, yet they will not be dissatisfied either. On the upper left side of the grid is High Motivation and Low Hygiene. The company takes care of meeting the internal desires of the employees yet does not provide enough of the foundational elements for long-term employment to be likely. This is like a homeowner who buys a beautiful house only to realize the foundation is cracked and leaking. Finally, the worst quadrant is Low Motivation and Low Hygiene. The employer does not excel at meeting the internal and external needs of employees and should expect a high turnover rate.

Cost/Benefit Analysis

After job satisfaction has been assessed within the company, a cost-benefit analysis should be completed. The goal of management should be to move employee scores into the High Motivation and High Hygiene area of the grid. It is not often financially feasible, however, to make investments to improve each hygiene and motivating factor. A cost/benefit analysis allows leaders to weigh the pros and cons of making an investment into a factor. For instance, consider the supervision factor. Assume that supervision was scored 2.9 out of 5 by employees. Undoubtedly this factor needs improvement. Perhaps, after further investigation, supervisors scored poorly on the UDS phrase "supervisors have no people skills." If this issue is to be fixed, what are the costs and benefits to do so? Excel (or a sheet of paper) can be used to create a two-sided table. One column can be labeled "costs" and the other "benefits." To begin, simply list as many costs and benefits as can be imagined. For example, on the costs side could be training costs (seminars), supervisor morale costs (addressing this deficiency with supervisors), and appraisal costs (fixing the appraisal system so supervisors are judged on this dimension). Benefits could include improved employee morale, less employee turnover, and improved company culture. Notice how both cost and benefits listed are not yet measurable. It is difficult to put a dollar figure on each cost and benefit, but it is a necessary next step. The cost of a training seminar would be easy to calculate. It would be a bit more challenging to implement annual performance reviews to include the "people skill" dimension but a cost could be calculated for the time necessary to perform and rework the appraisal system. More challenging yet would be calculating the benefit of improved morale. It would take some statistical skill to analyze before and after supervisory "people skill" improvements and any links to productivity.

Chapter Summary

This chapter is brief by design. A thorough analysis of the data set can be time consuming. The Motivation-Hygiene Factor Grid provides a quick and simple method for visualizing how robustly a company promotes job satisfaction. The only steps required are to calculate the grand means of both the hygiene and motivating factor scores and plotting them on a scatterplot (grid). An ambitious organization will attempt to move employee scores, over time, into the upper right, High Motivation and High Hygiene area.

15

Cautions, Caveats
and Contemplations

No journal article or nonfiction book would be complete without a limitations section. There is a tendency for readers of journals or books to trust the author's expertise and consider the ideas presented in the text as fact. Authors or researchers cannot fully understand all of the variables present in a situation nor control for all variables, much less describe a situation in its entirety. Interestingly, one study discovered that two-thirds of journal articles mentioned limitations, meaning one-third did not include this most important section.[2] Especially in the social sciences, where studies are often conducted in uncontrolled settings, clearly described limitations are of the utmost importance.

Limitations, though, do not make a study worthless. Future studies can build off of previous studies to capture more variables in different settings. Simply stated, each study is unique and generalizability is often a concern. Readers should be careful, then, as to how they apply the prescriptions of a study. To deal with the "too many variables" problem, models are created to simplify reality. Take personality for example. There are countless personality tests, many of which have been studied by researchers in various settings such as the Myers-Briggs Type Indicator, the Big Five Model, or the DiSC assessment. Often, the personality traits from these tests will be used to predict job satisfaction. Studies often conflict with each other and produce different results, yet common themes will emerge. For illustration, researchers compared many of the conflicting studies regarding the Big Five Model of personality, also known as a meta-analysis, to determine if a relationship between personality and job satisfaction emerged. The results were that emotional stability, conscientiousness, and extroversion traits correlated with job satisfaction most of the time.[3] Not all studies agreed but most were aligned. The individual studies were useful, but not exhaustive to all situations.

In a "pure science" experiment, such as in a laboratory, scientists still have difficulty accounting for every possible variable, yet chemical "A" mixed with chemical "B" will result in an explosion, in most circumstances. All studies, even those conducted in laboratories, have limitations, but common themes emerge. Practitioners should proceed with caution when implementing policy based upon a study's prescriptions. When considering the social sciences, in this case motivating workers, human beings differ in their personalities, motivation levels, energy, and so on. Likewise, all work environments differ regarding management presence, type of product or service created, coworker attitudes; the list goes on. Two Factor theory should be used as a guide, its prescriptions should improve job satisfaction in many instances. But it is a model, with limitations, and it may not necessarily cause all workers' levels of job satisfaction to improve.

Mental Models: A Necessary Limitation

The primary limitation of this book is that a model, in this case Two Factor, was used to depict job satisfaction and its facets. Models simplify reality, minimizing various intricacies. For instance, Maslow's Hierarchy of Needs is still being taught in schools as it is a useful tool to understand how human motivation works. It is a popular theory, but it has its detractors. One critic claims that Maslow oversimplifies reality since human beings do not always follow a progression from survival needs to self-actualizing needs,[4] yet CEOs like Chip Conley have used the hierarchy to develop policies that produce real results as seen in the opening chapter of this book. Models help break down complex concepts into a manageable picture. They are a useful tool for conceptualization purposes as many students and employees are visual learners.

Models are necessary for decision making purposes, whether at work or in daily life. Consider, for a moment, what a "human being" actually "is." What does it mean to "be" or to "exist"? What is a person? How does consciousness exist? Are humans more than just a combination of physical elements and do they have a soul? Can a human being exert free-will or does he simply "make pre-determined decisions" based purely on chemical processes in the brain related to survival needs? These are just a few, of countless questions, that exist when trying to define a human being, much less attempting to determine motivating factors in a work environment. As a mental exercise, imagine a friend or relative. What comes to mind? How do they look or typically behave? Now, try to fully understand the composition of the person. It is impossible to fully describe this individual in their totality. Certainly, a person has physical features, a unique personality, a certain level of cognitive functioning, and so on. But is it fully possible to capture the entire essence of a person through a thought experiment or written definition? It is not. Thus, a model, or image, is made to simplify the meaning of the idea, in this case: "person." It is a necessary simplification.

How can motivation be fully understood if persons are not fully understood? It is important to note that human beings are not simply like rats in a box, trying to avoid shocks, while pulling a lever to achieve a cheese reward, as in B.F. Skinner's experiments in the mid–20th century. Human beings are not fully predictable nor understandable. Therefore, no theory can fully address human motivation and describe which "lever they will pull at any given time." If this were the case, economists, for example, could simply make an economy recession proof by pulling "levers," such as raising/lowering interest rates or the money supply, at the right time. The problem is that the behavior of people is never fully predictable, yet there is an element of predictability. To illustrate, the more expensive that plane tickets become, the less flights people will make. Not always (not fully predictable), but in general (somewhat predictable). This is the essence of Two Factor theory. Improving each motivator or hygiene factor will have positive results, in general, but not in every single situation. Having mentioned the limitation of using a model to depict reality, studies exist throughout this text that demonstrate the legitimacy of the motivator/hygiene phenomenon.

The Pureness of the Factors

There is debate as to the pureness of each factor. For example, can salary, at least in part, be a motivator? This factor may have more of a hygiene composition but that does not mean it is solely a hygiene factor. There may also be certain situations where salary presents itself as a hygiene factor and others where it is a motivator. Consider an individual earning minimum wage who is trying to support a family. Frequent increases to salary will most likely motivate this worker. Once the worker reaches a certain milestone, perhaps $75,000 per year, and the basic needs of the family are met, increases to salary will most likely have fewer positive impacts on the employee's attitude. The worker will undoubtedly have a favorable opinion of raises but their effect will lessen. The salary will become a hygiene factor. Any salary increase not in line with employees' expectations will demotivate workers.

The Quantitative Approach and the UDS

Regarding Two Factor theory, studies over the past few decades that used a qualitative approach (interviews) best supported the theory. Quantitative studies (surveys) showed mixed results. As stated above, studies, especially in the social sciences, often conflict with one another. However, patterns often emerge in the literature. Qualitative research, in general, leads to deeper, more thorough responses. Quantitative studies, though, may be generalizable to a population. The UDS is a short form survey whose purpose is to increase response and completion rates due to its brevity and simplicity, in hopes of generalizing to the company's workforce. To obtain a more robust analysis of personnel job satisfaction, a mixed method, containing both quantitative and qualitative methods, should be used. However, such a method is more time consuming and expensive.

Conciseness, Generalizations and Subjectivity

This book was written so that managers can clearly, yet quickly, understand the Two Factor theory, in a modern context, so they can begin making improvements in the workplace. Thus, the book is not the length of a college textbook, although it is longer than popular press management books. This text could go much farther in depth, or provide many more examples, of motivation in the workplace. However, busy managers need to be able to efficiently understand the factors to be studied then use tools like the UDS to complete their study. To make this text more concise, broad generalizations are often made. Managers must realize that each workplace is unique. Therefore, some examples will be more relatable to certain industries than others. This volume contains a respectable mix of popular press articles, like *Forbes*, and journal articles, and rides a fine line between a scholarly book (peer reviewed) and a popular press business book.

Additionally, the examples used to describe the motivators and hygiene factors in this text are somewhat subjective. For example, the empowerment offered by Zingerman's owners, mentioned in the supervision chapter, could have also been used in the responsibility chapter. There is an overlap, in this instance, between Theory Y leadership and employee empowerment. Nonetheless, the examples, regardless of which chapter they were placed, are relevant and useful.

Motivational Theory Limited to the Non-Toxic

This text focuses on motivating workers. One assumption of motivational theory is that workers want to be motivated. Managers who possess a Theory Y philosophy, as mentioned in prior chapters, believe that workers want to be challenged and excel in their work. In other words, the assumption is that employees care about their jobs beyond earning a paycheck. Perhaps, this philosophy is correct, in general. However, a small percentage of people are simply toxic. Toxic workers, or those who behave in a way harmful to the organization such as participating in continuous gossip and slander, exhibiting an attitude of malice and incivility, or who damage company property, have psychiatric problems beyond what a company's leaders can effectively address. Some companies have elected to outsource counselors for employees' mental health by covering fees.[5] Typically, though, counselors are mainly provided to help employees cope with stress or other life challenges, not diagnose deep seated psychological issues. One study discovered that it is more beneficial to avoid hiring a toxic worker than hiring a superstar.[6] If the right people are not on the bus, or in this instance the wrong/toxic employees are hired, motivational theory will be ineffective.

Focus on Non-Entrepreneurial Workers

This text primarily focuses on workers who are not entrepreneurial. Realtors who share an office, for example, are competitors. In-office competitor sales helps the office, but the realtor loses an individual sale. Of course, positive relationships with coworkers in this setting are important to help the overall office culture but getting along well with their coworkers is not a top priority for realtors.[7] Consider a doctor's office. Nurses, receptionists, lab technicians, and the doctors all benefit from more patients as the office flourishes. No individual "sales" are lost in this environment. This text is more relatable to work environments that are not entrepreneurial.

No Advancement Motivator

Both the UDS survey and the text do not include the advancement facet. According to Herzberg, employees who already received a promotion could experience this motivator. Therefore, most employees, regardless of work setting, will not have had a promotion as only a small percentage of the workforce are typically promoted to leadership positions. If the UDS is administered and advancement statements are included, it would minimize the anonymity of the participants. For example, if an employee responded to questions regarding a promotion, it would be easy for upper management to figure out who completed the survey. Usually, employee satisfaction surveys are given to lower level employees and not low, mid, or upper level managers. Additionally, including questions for only employees who have advanced in the organization would add unnecessary questions for those who have not, while perhaps negatively impacting future responses. For instance, if an employee was asked about advancement, and he selected "does not apply," this may bring up feelings of resentment if he was passed over for a promotion. Respondents may be irritated for the remainder of the survey and respond negatively to future questions. Survey fatigue is always a concern for administrators and adding extra statements for this motivating factor would not be worth the risk of fatigue. Growth potential addresses the possibility for advancement, thus, acting as a proxy.

Chapter Summary

This chapter addressed some of the limitations of this book. Nonfiction works, including studies, have limitations as all variables cannot be captured or controlled. Regardless of any limitations, this book provides a robust framework for managers to use to improve employee job satisfaction.

Conclusion

The Motivated Worker is concisely written for both managers and employees. Many workers today are miserable at work but cannot pinpoint the reasons as to why. Managers are so busy tackling day-to-day issues that they are often neglectful of their employees' wellbeing. Both managers and workers can quickly dive into the ideas of the text and make meaningful changes to improve morale in the workplace. Laborers have an unrelenting need for their jobs to be meaningful since they spend a good portion of their lives at work. Managers would be wise to tap into this internal desire. Happy workers are not created by increasing the presence of external factors like wages or job security. Rather, internal drives such as recognition or the job itself, if properly addressed by leadership, can motivate employees. Managers benefit from more engagement, employees taking on additional responsibility, lower turnover, and improved company culture.

This text is based upon the vintage Two Factor theory framework with the goal of increasing job satisfaction in the labor force. Worker motivation can be broken down into two categories: motivators and hygiene factors. Although the focus is primarily on the millennial generation entering the workforce, this book describes how Two Factor theory has been applied in the past, and how it should be applied in a present-day context, impacting all generations in the workforce. Dozens of examples are illustrated from today's leading employers and are bolstered by peer-reviewed research. Managers are shown how to efficiently assess their workers' current level of job satisfaction using the Two Factor model, with an accompanying Universal Dual Factor Survey. Finally, managers are shown how to improve employee job satisfaction.

Appendix:
UDS Reliability

This purpose of this section is to discuss the internal consistency, or reliability, of the Universal Dual Factor Survey (UDS). Surveys that are reliable have a Cronbach's alpha of .65 (some argue a .60 threshold) or greater for each facet.[1] For example, the following three statements are supposed to represent the working conditions facet: "I have the right tools to do my job," "I have adequate work space," and "My work environment is acceptable." If the alpha is .65 or greater as recommended above, the statements, together, are considered to represent the facet.

To test the consistency of the UDS, three pilot studies were conducted of adult graduate students at a small college in the southeastern U.S. Then, low alpha questions were removed and/or revised. Finally, 106 employees at a bank in the southeastern U.S. were surveyed and the alphas are presented in the table below.[2] Note that the proposed job security statements from the UDS were not tested. All other facets are reliable.

Facet	Question Count	Alpha
Job Satisfaction	n=2	.76
Recognition	n=2	.78
The Work Itself	n=3	.75
Achievement	n=2	.65
Growth	n=2	.65
Responsibility	n=2	.71
Policy	n=2	.65
Supervision	n=3	.67
Relationships	n=2	.76
Working Conditions	n=3	.73

Appendix

Facet	Question Count	Alpha
Salary	n=3	.80
Benefits	n=2	.70
	Total Question Count	**Alpha**
Totals	n=28	.72

Chapter Notes

Preface

1. Kelly, J. (2019, October 25). *More than half of U.S. workers are unhappy in their jobs: Here's why and what needs to be done now.* Retrieved from https://www.forbes.com/sites/jackkelly/2019/10/25/more-than-half-of-us-workers-are-unhappy-in-their-jobs-heres-why-and-what-needs-to-be-done-now/#66b286520247

2. Bassett-Jones, N., & Lloyd, G. C. (2005). Does Herzberg's motivation theory have staying power? *Journal of Management Development, 24*(10), 929–943.

3. Lalwani, S., & Lalwani, S. J. (2017). Relevance of Herzberg's hygiene theory in today's context: An analysis of motivators and hygiene factors in present scenario in Indian context. *Singaporean Journal of Business Economics and Management Studies, 5*(7), 19–25.

Introduction

1. Pangaribuan, C. H., Wijaya, F. H., Djamil, A. B., Hidayat, D, & Putra, O. P. B. (2020). An analysis on the importance of motivation to transfer learning in VUCA environments. *Management Science Letters, 2,* 271

2. Aguiar do Monte, P. (2012). Job dissatisfaction and labour turnover: Evidence from Brazil. *International Journal of Human Resource Management, 23*(8), 1717–1735.

3. Hsieh, J.S. (2016). Spurious or true? An exploration of antecedents and simultaneity of job performance and job satisfaction across the sectors. *Public Personnel Management, 45*(1), 90–118. doi:10.1177/0091026015624714

4. Ravenelle, A. J. (2019). "We're not Uber": Control, autonomy and entrepreneurship in the gig economy. *Conference Papers—American Sociological Association, 1*–31.

5. Ortiz, M. (2012). Traditionalists to millennials. *Rdh, 32*(10), 26–29.

6. E. H., S., A., W., & B., P. (2016). Big city millennial workers in Indonesia and factors affecting their commitment to the organization. *Pertanika Journal of Social Sciences & Humanities, 2447*–57.

7. Martin, C. C. (2008). Getting high on Gen Y: How to engage the entitlement generation. *Career Planning & Adult Development Journal, 24*(3), 19–22.

8. Ertas, N. (2015). Turnover intentions and work motivations of millennial employees in federal service. *Public Personnel Management, 44*(3), 401–423.

9. Bromwich, J. E. (2018, January 31). *We asked generation z to pick a name. It wasn't generation z.* Retrieved from https://www.nytimes.com/2018/01/31/style/generation-z-name.html

10. Jenkins, R. (2017, August 21). *This is how similar generation z will be to millennials: A different generation entering the workforce, but they will share many similarities to millennials. Here are nine similarities between generation z and millennials.* Retrieved from https://www.inc.com/ryan-jenkins/this-is-how-similar-generation-z-will-be-to-millen.html

11. Wronski, L., & Cohen, J. (2019, July 26). *A third of U.S. workers seriously considered quitting their job in the last 3 months. Here's why.* Retrieved from https://www.cnbc.com/2019/07/16/third-of-us-workers-considered-quitting-their-job-in-last-3-months.html

12. Robbins, S. P, & Judge, T. A. (2012). *Organizational behavior* (15th ed.). Upper Saddle River, NJ: Prentice Hall.

Chapter 1

1. Ricci, T. (2012). *Frank Bunker Gilbreth: Biography.* Retrieved from https://www.asme.org/engineering-topics/articles/construction-and-building/frank-bunker-gilbreth

2. Kidwell, R. E., & Scherer, P. M. (2001). Layoffs and their ethical implications under scientific management, quality management and open-book management. *Journal of Business Ethics, 29*(1/2), 113–124.

3. Reshef, Y. *Fredrick Winslow Taylor (1865–1915): Principles of scientific management.* Retrieved from https://web.stanford.edu/class/sts175/NewFiles/Taylorism

4. Wren, D. A., & Bedeian, A. G. (2009). *The evolution of management thought* (6th ed). John Wiley & Sons, Inc.: USA.

5. Wren, D. A., & Bedeian, A. G. (2009). *The evolution of management thought* (6th ed). John Wiley & Sons, Inc.: USA.

6. Newman, M. A. & Guy, M. E. (1998). Taylor's triangle, Follett's web. *Administrative Theory & Praxis, 20*(3), 287–297.

7. Simms, M. (2009). Insights from a Management Prophet: Mary Parker Follett on Social Entrepreneurship. *Business & Society Review (00453609), 114*(3), 349–363.

8. Kiechel III, W. (2012). The management century. *Harvard Business Review, 90*(11), 62–75.

9. Oakleaf, L. (2016). *Elton Mayo and the Hawthorne experiments: Jacob Robertson and Garrett Carothers.* Retrieved from https://oer.missouriwestern.edu/rsm424/chapter/elton-mayo-and-the-hawthorne-experiments/

10. Kremer W., & Hammond, C. (2013, September 1). *Abraham Maslow and the pyramid that beguiled business.* Retrieved from http://www.bbc.com/news/magazine-23902918

11. Khalili, O. (2010). *How to grow your business by giving your employees a calling-with Chip Conley.* Retrieved from http://causecapitalism.com/how-to-grow-your-business-by-giving-your-employees-a-calling-with-chip-conley/

12. Rajput, N., Bali, R. & Kesharwani, S. (2013). Does motivational strategies and issues differ across generations: An analytical study. *Global Journal of Enterprise Information System, 5*(1), 2–10.

13. Bromwich, J. E. (2018, January 31). *We asked generation z to pick a name. It wasn't generation z.* Retrieved from https://www.nytimes.com/2018/01/31/style/generation-z-name.html

14. Wiedmer, T. (2015). Generations do differ: Best practices in leading traditionalists, boomers, and generations X, Y, and Z. *Delta Kappa Gamma Bulletin, 82*(1), 51–58.

15. 1940s.org. (2013, May 8). From the 1940s decade—famous firsts and inventions. Retrieved from http://1940s.org/from-the-1940s-decade-famous-firsts/

16. Sheetz, M. (2017, August 4). *Technology killing off corporate America: Average life span of companies under 20 years.* Retrieved from https://www.cnbc.com/2017/08/24/technology-killing-off-corporations-average-lifespan-of-company-under-20-years.html

17. Landrum, S. (2017, November 10). *Millennials aren't afraid to change jobs, and here's why.* Retrieved from https://www.forbes.com/sites/sarahlandrum/2017/11/10/millennials-arent-afraid-to-change-jobs-and-heres-why/#1a59086219a5

18. David, F. R., & David, F. R. (2017). *Strategic management: A competitive advantage approach-Concepts and cases.* USA: Pearson.

Chapter 2

1. Herzberg, F., Mausner, B., & Snyderman, B.B. (1959). *The motivation to work.* New York, NY: John Wiley & Sons, Inc.

2. Herzberg, F. (1966). *Work and the nature of man.* The World Publishing Company: Cleveland, OH.

3. Herzberg, F., Mausner, B., & Snyderman, B.B. (1959). *The motivation to work.* New York, NY: John Wiley & Sons, Inc.

4. Herzberg, F. (1966). *Work and the nature of man.* New York, NY: The World Publishing Company.

5. Herzberg, F., Mausner, B., & Snyderman, B.B. (1959). *The motivation to work.* New York, NY: John Wiley & Sons, Inc.

6. Chib, M., & Anand, P. V. (2018). Understanding the impact of culture on job satisfaction, work motivation, work engagement, affect balance, emotional intelligence and happiness. *International Journal of Social Sciences Review,* 6(10), 1991–2001.

7. Bureau of Labor Statistics. (2006, August 3). *100 years of U.S. consumer spending: Data for the nation, New York City, and Boston.* Retrieved from https://www.bls.gov/opub/uscs/

8. Bureau of Labor Statistics. (2016, August 30). *Consumer expenditures—2015.* Retrieved from https://www.bls.gov/news.release/cesan.nr0.htm

9. Pew Research Center. (2015, June 18). *The rise in dual income households.* Retrieved from http://www.pewresearch.org/ft_dual-income-households-1960–2012-2/

10. Federal Reserve Bank of St. Lous. (2017). Real gross domestic product per capita. Retrieved from https://fred.stlouisfed.org/series/A939RX0Q048SBEA

11. Halkos, E. (2015). *Employee discount and purchase programs—a smart employee benefits strategy.* Retrieved from http://www.corporatewellnessmagazine.com/voluntary-benefits/discount-purchase-programs/

Chapter 3

1. Pringle, C. D., DuBose, P. B., & Yankey, M.D. (2010). Personality characteristics and choice of academic major: Are traditional stereotypes obsolete? *College Student Journal,* 44(1), 131–142.

2. Gomez-Mejia, L. R., Balkin, D. B., & Cardy, R. L. (2012). *Managing human resources.* USA: Pearson.

3. Hunt, J. (2017). *Nurturing children's natural love of learning.* Retrieve from http://www.naturalchild.org/jan_hunt/unschooling.html

4. Long, G. I. (2013). *Differences between union and nonunion compensation, 2001–2011.* Retrieved from https://www.bls.gov/opub/mlr/2013/04/art2full.pdf

5. Smerek, R. E., & Peterson, M. (2006). Examining Herzberg's theory: Improving job satisfaction among non-academic employees at a university. *Research in Higher Education,* 48(2), 229–250.

6. Twarog, J. (2018). *Mandatory, permissive, & illegal subjects of bargaining.* Retrieved from https://www.local1222.org/index.cfm?zone=/unionactive/view_article.cfm&HomeID=42683

7. Kim, S. (2008). *The auto industry's forgotten legacy. Diversity.* Retrieved from http://content.time.com/time/nation/article/0,8599,1865121,00.html

8. Raff, D. M. G., & Summers, L. H. (1987). Did Henry Ford pay efficiency wages? *Journal of Labor Economics,* 5(4), 57–86.

9. Curators of the University of University of Missouri. (2017). *Prices and wages by decade: 1910–1919.* Retrieved from https://libraryguides.missouri.edu/pricesandwages/1910–1919#occupation

10. UAW. (2015, October 13). *UAW history.* Retrieved from https://uaw.org/solidarity-magazine/uaw-history/

11. Bureau of Labor Statistics. (2014). *Southeast information office: Occupational employment and wages in Memphis-May 2014.* Retrieved from https://www.bls.gov/regions/southeast/news-release/2015/occupationalemploymentandwages_memphis_20150722.htm

12. Greenhouse, S. (2014, February 10). *Labor battle at Kellogg plant in Memphis drags on.* Retrieved from https://www.nytimes.com/2014/02/11/business/kellogg-workers-in-4th-month-of-lockout-in-memphis.html

13. Zak, P. J. (2017). *The neuroscience of trust.* Retrieved from https://hbr.org/2017/01/the-neuroscience-of-trust

14. Global Rich List. (2018). *Income: Global rich list.* Retrieved from http://www.globalrichlist.com/#na

15. Hill, C. W. L., & Hult, G. T. M. (2015). *Global business today* (9th ed.). McGraw-Hill: New York, NY.

16. The World Bank. (2016). *GDP per capita, PPP (current international $).* Retrieved from https://data.worldbank.org/indicator/NY.GDP.PCAP.PP.CD

17. Morgan, J. (2014, December 15). *The top 10 factors for on-the-job employee*

happiness. Retrieved from https://www. forbes.com/sites/jacobmorgan/2014/12/15/the-top-10-factors-for-on-the-job-employee-happiness/#7a9a52e25afa

18. Evans, L., & Olumide-Aluko, F. (2010). Teacher job satisfaction in developing countries: A critique of Herzberg's Two- Factor theory applied to the Nigerian Context. *International Studies in Educational Administration (Commonwealth Council For Educational Administration & Management [CCEAM]), 38*(2), 73–85.

19. Singh, R. (2016). The impact of intrinsic and extrinsic motivators on employee engagement in information organizations. *Journal of Education for Library & Information Science, 57*(2), 197–206.

20. Tatsuse, T., & Sekine, M. (2010). Explaining global job satisfaction by facets of job satisfaction: The Japanese civil servants study. *Environmental Health and Preventative Medicine, 16*(2), 133–137.

21. Herzberg, F. (1966). *Work and the nature of man.* The World Publishing Company: Cleveland, OH.

22. Patton, M. (2016, February 29). *U.S. role in global economy declines nearly 50%.* Retrieved from https://www.forbes.com/sites/mikepatton/2016/02/29/u-s-role-in-global-economy-declines-nearly-50/#5996bc015e9e

23. Bureau of Labor Statistics. (2017, December 15). *Employer costs for employee compensation.* Retrieved from https://www.bls.gov/news.release/pdf/ecec.pdf

24. Gomez-Mejia, L. R., Balkin, D. B., & Cardy, R. L. (2012). *Managing human resources.* USA: Pearson.

25. Bureau of Labor Statistics. (2017, December 18). *Employer costs for employee compensation for the regions-September 2017.* Retrieved from https://www.bls.gov/regions/southwest/news-release/employercostsforemployeecompensation_regions.htm

26. Kane, J. (2012, October 22). *Health costs: How the U.S. compares with other countries.* Retrieved from https://www.pbs.org/newshour/health/health-costs-how-the-us-compares-with-other-countries

27. Deahl, J. (2016, October 6). *Countries around the world beat U.S. on paid maternal leave.* Retrieved from https://www.npr.org/2016/10/06/495839588/countries-around-the-world-beat-the-us-on-paid-parental-leaveparental-leave

28. CNN Money. (2018). *Ultimate guide to retirement: Just how common are defined benefit plans?* Retrieved from http://money.cnn.com/retirement/guide/pensions_basics.moneymag/index7.htm

29. Works, R. (2016). Trends in employer costs for defined benefit plans. *Beyond the Numbers: Pay and Benefits 5*(2), 1–9.

30. NBC News. (2010, November 10). *France raises retirement age despite protests.* Retrieved from http://www.nbcnews.com/id/40103988/ns/world_news-europe/t/france-raises-retirement-age-despite-protests/#.Wo74F-dG0dU

31. United States Department of Labor. (2018, January 1). *Changes in basic minimum wages in non-farm employment under state law: Selected years 1968 to 2017.* Retrieved from https://www.dol.gov/whd/state/stateMinWageHis.htm

32. Davidson, P. (2016, November 10). *Fast food workers strike, seeking $15 wage, political muscle.* Retrieved from https://www.usatoday.com/story/money/2015/11/10/fast-food-strikes-begin/75482782/

33. Cabell, B. (1997, August 20). *It's official: Teamsters end UPS strike.* Retrieved from http://www.cnn.com/U.S./9708/20/ups.update.early/

34. Long, H. (2018, October 5). *Amazon's $15 minimum wage doesn't end debate over whether it's creating good jobs.* Retrieved from https://www.washingtonpost.com/business/economy/amazons-15-minimum-wage-doesnt-end-debate-over-whether-its-creating-good-jobs/2018/10/05/b1da23a0-c802–11e8–9b1c-a90f1daae309_story.html?noredirect=on&utm_term=.74e5c99c4400

35. Olsen, E.J. (2014, July 21). *Zingerman's co-founder to be honored at White House event.* Retrieved from http://www.zingermanscommunity.com/2014/07/zingermans-co-founder-to-be-honored-at-white-house-event/

36. Glassdoor.com. (2018). *Zingerman's salaries.* Retrieved from https://www.glassdoor.com/Salary/Zingermans-Salaries-E270584.htm

37. Burlingham, B. (2016, October 20). *Decades later, the owners of Ann Arbor's iconic Zingerman's are still at odds over expansion.* Retrieved from https://www.forbes.com/sites/boburling ham/2016/10/20/what-price-growth/#1d 5c475f32e8

38. The Economic Times. (2018). *Definition of 'Equity Theory.'* Retrieved from https://economictimes.indiatimes.com/ definition/equity-theory

39. Bureau of Labor Statistics. (2018). *Consumer Price Index.* Retrieved from https://www.bls.gov/cpi/questions-and-answers.htm#Question_2

Chapter 4

1. Kruse, K. (2012, October 16). *100 best quotes on leadership.* Retrieved from https://www.forbes.com/sites/kevink ruse/2012/10/16/quotes-on-leadership/# 7c1a4a382feb

2. French Jr., J. R. P., & Raven, B. (1959). *The bases of social power.* Retrieved from http://web.mit.edu/curhan/www/ docs/Articles/15341_Readings/Power/ French_&_Raven_Studies_Social_Power_ ch9_pp150–167.pdf

3. Maxwell, J. C. (2011). *The 360 degree leader: Developing your influence from anywhere in the organization.* Nashville, TN: Thomas Nelson.

4. Wilkie, D. (2015, October 21). *If 1 in 3 workers wants to quit, HR had better figure out why.* Retrieved from https://www. shrm.org/resourcesandtools/hr-topics/ employee-relations/pages/many-employ ees-plan-to-quit.aspx

5. Robbins, S. P., DeCenzo, D. A., & Coulter, M. A. (2014). *Fundamentals of management: Essential concepts and applications* (9th ed.). USA: Pearson.

6. Windhorst, B., & McMenamin, D. (2016, January 23). *Long time coming: End comes for David Blatt's bumpy Cavs tenure.* Retrieved from http://www.espn.com/ nba/story/_/id/14629892/nba-final-unrav eling-david-blatt

7. Robbins, S. P. (1998). Organizational behavior: Concepts, controversies, applications. (8th ed.). Upper Saddle River, NJ: Prentice Hall.

8. Eschner, K. (2016, December 1). *One hundred and three years ago today, Henry Ford introduced the assembly line: His workers hated it.* Retrieved from http:// www.smithsonianmag.com/smart-news/ one-hundred-and-three-years-ago-today-henry-ford-introduced-assembly-line-his-workers-hated-it-180961267/

9. Varghese, S. (2010, November 3). *Henry Ford, William Sarnoff and leadership today.* Retrieved from https:// www.forbes.com/2010/11/03/ford-sar noff-mayo-harvard-leadership-manag ing-varghese.html

10. Robbins, S. P. (1998). Organizational behavior: Concepts, controversies, applications. (8th ed.). Upper Saddle River, NJ: Prentice Hall.

11. Murray, A. (2017, January 10). *Are millennial leaders different?* Retrieved from http://fortune.com/2017/01/10/ are-millennial-leaders-different/

12. Frank, K. (2016, February 10). *The 6 responsibilities of a Zingerman's servant leader.* Retrieved from http://www.zing train.com/webinars/6-responsibilities-zin germans-servant-leader

13. Zingerman's Community of Businesses. (2018). *Mission and guiding principles.* Retrieved from http://www. zingermanscommunity.com/about-us/ mission-guiding-principles/

14. Weinzweig, A. (2000). *Servant leadership.* Retrieved from http://www. zingtrain.com/content/servant-leadership

15. Zingtrain. (2018). *Why open book management is an excellent way to run a business!* Retrieved from http://www. zingtrain.com/content/why-open-book-management-excellent-way-run-business

16. Taylor, B. (2016, January 26). *How one fast-food chain keeps its turnover rates absurdly low.* Retrieved from https://hbr. org/2016/01/how-one-fast-food-chain-keeps-its-turnover-rates-absurdly-low

17. Kinni, T. (2016, June 13). *How smart leaders build trust: The chairman of JetBlue explains how a high-trust culture makes a better company (and life).* Retrieved from https://www.gsb.stanford.edu/insights/ how-smart-leaders-build-trust

18. Vanderwood, M. W. (2018). *Leader self-perceptions of ethics in and out of the workplace and personal trustworthiness.*

Retrieved from https://scholarworks. waldenu.edu/cgi/viewcontent.cgi?arti cle=6711&context=dissertations

19. Bayraktaroglu, S., Ulukoy, M., & Izci, C. (2016). The relationship between systematic soldiering and organizational commitment in hospitality businesses. *Journal of Management & Economics Research*, *14*(2), 250–263. https://doi. org/10.11611/JMER178468

20. Branson, R. (2011, October 6). *Virgin's Richard Branson: Apple boss Steve Jobs was the entrepreneur I most admired.* Retrieved from https://www.telegraph. co.uk/technology/steve-jobs/8811232/ Virgins-Richard-Branson-Apple-boss-Steve-Jobs-was-the-entrepreneur-I-most-admired.html

21. Investopedia. (2017, September 12). *What is Tim Cook's Managerial Style?* Retrieved from https://www.investopedia. com/ask/answers/032515/what-tim-cooks-managerial-style.asp

22. Workplace Trends. (2015, July 20). *The millennial leadership survey.* Retrieved from https://workplacetrends. com/the-millennial-leadership-survey/

23. Sahai, K. (2017, August 18). *Four traits that make millennials more effective leaders.* Retrieved from https://www.forbes. com/sites/forbescoachescouncil/2017/ 08/18/four-traits-that-make-millennials-more-effective-leaders/#3e9b200c7303

24. Zak, P. J. (2017). *The neuroscience of trust.* Retrieved from https://hbr. org/2017/01/the-neuroscience-of-trust

Chapter 5

1. Zimmermann, C. (2018, August 30). *The FRED blog: The rise of the service economy.* Retrieved from https://fredblog. stlouisfed.org/2018/08/the-rise-of-the-service-economy/

2. Phillips, K. (2014, August 20). *How container shipping changed the world through globalization.* Retrieved from https://www.abc.net.au/radionational/ programs/rearvision/the-big-metal-box-that-changed-the-world/5684586

3. Intel. (2019). *Over 50 years of Moore's Law.* Retrieved from https:// www.intel.com/content/www/us/en/sili con-innovations/moores-law-technology. html

4. Wolfe, A. (2018, April 2). *Recent research from Deloitte shows just how much we use our smartphones.* Retrieved from https://www.journalofaccountancy. com/newsletters/2018/apr/how-often-use-phone-every-day.html

5. Hyken, S. (2019). *Social media response time, are you fast enough?* Retrieved from https://hyken.com/customer-care/ social-media-response-time-are-you-fast-enough/

6. Hirschi, A., Shockley, K. M., & Zacher, H. (2019). Achieving work-family balance: An action regulation model. *Academy of Management Review*, *44*(1), 150–171. https://doi.org/10.5465/amr.2016.0409

7. Hess, A. (2017, May 4). *The 20 best companies for work-life balance.* Retrieved from https://www.cnbc.com/2017/05/03/ the-20-best-companies-for-work-life-bal ance.html

8. Kurter, H. L. (2018, November 19). *The 4 outdated workplace rules employers still grip into.* Retrieved from https://www.forbes.com/sites/heidilyn nekurter/2018/11/19/the-4-outdated-workplace-rules-employers-still-grip-on to/#3d7988af122e

9. Lurie, M. (2018, September 16). *The disconnect between baby boomers and millennials when it comes to work ethic.* Retrieved from https://www.theladders. com/career-advice/the-disconnect-be tween-baby-boomers-and-millennials-when-it-comes-to-work-ethic

10. White, D, & White, P. (2014, December 23). *What to expect from Gen-X and millennial employees.* Retrieved from https://www.entrepreneur.com/arti cle/240556

11. Javitch, D. G. (2006, June 5). *The benefits of flextime.* Retrieved from https:// www.entrepreneur.com/article/159440

12. Hess, A. (2017, May 4). *The 20 best companies for work-life balance.* Retrieved from https://www.cnbc.com/2017/05/03/ the-20-best-companies-for-work-life-bal ance.html

13. Human Element. (2019). *Love your job-work at Human Element: Work/life balance.* Retrieved from https://www. human-element.com/careers

14. Vann, M., & Ling Kent, J. (2016, November 30). *Can work life balance be a reality? This company makes it possible.* Retrieved from https://www.nbcnews.com/nightly-news/work-life-balance-reality-company-makes-it-possible-n690346

15. Nikravan, L. (2016, November 22). *Cyber Monday shopping at work? You're not alone.* Retrieved from https://www.careerbuilder.com/advice/cyber-monday-shopping-at-work

16. Bresiger, G. (2017, July 29). *This is how much time employees spend slacking off.* Retrieved from https://nypost.com/2017/07/29/this-is-how-much-time-employees-spend-slacking-off/

17. Hyman, J. (2016, June 29). *Your employees are using social media at work; deal with it.* Retrieved from http://www.workforce.com/2016/06/29/your-employees-are-using-social-media-at-work-deal-with-it/

18. Society for Human Resource Management. (2016, January 19). *Managing and leveraging workplace use of social media.* Retrieved from https://www.shrm.org/resourcesandtools/tools-and-samples/toolkits/pages/managingsocialmedia.aspx

19. U.S. Department of Labor. (2009, July). *Wage and hour division: Fact sheet #53—The health care industry and hours worked.* Retrieved from https://www.dol.gov/whd/regs/compliance/whdfs53.htm

20. Gomez-Mejia, L. R., Balkin, D. B., & Cardy, R. L. (2012). *Managing human resources.* USA: Pearson.

21. Semler, R. (1993). *Maverick: The story behind the world's most unusual workplace.* New York, NY: Business Plus.

22. Wen Yi Ng, Abigail, & Andanari, K. (2018, June 28). *Millennials want diversity that's more than just skin-deep.* Retrieved from https://www.bloomberg.com/news/articles/2018-06-29/what-millennials-want-diversity-that-s-more-than-just-skin-deep

23. Schulte, B. (2015, May 5). *Millennials want a work-life balance. Their bosses just don't get why.* Retrieved from https://www.washingtonpost.com/local/millennials-want-a-work-life-balance-their-bosses-just-dont-get-why/2015/05/05/1859369e-f376-11e4-84a6-6d7c67c50db0_story.html?utm_term=.b45d6b49698e

24. Cilluffo, A., & Cohn, D'Vera. (2017, April 27). *10 demographic trends shaping the U.S. and the world in 2017.* Retrieved from https://www.pewresearch.org/fact-tank/2017/04/27/10-demographic-trends-shaping-the-u-s-and-the-world-in-2017/

25. Vespa, J., Armstrong, D. M., & Medina, L. (2018, March). *Demographic turning points for the United States: Population projections for 2020 to 2060.* Retrieved from https://www.census.gov/content/dam/Census/library/publications/2018/demo/P25_1144.pdf

26. Soergel, A. (2016, September 1). *Most of America's businesses run by white men: New government data show business owners are still a fairly homogenous group.* Retrieved from https://www.usnews.com/news/articles/2016-09-01/most-of-america-businesses-run-by-white-men-says-census-bureau

27. Jones, S. (2017, June 9). *White men account for 72% of corporate leadership at 16 of the Fortune 500 companies.* Retrieved from http://fortune.com/2017/06/09/white-men-senior-executives-fortune-500-companies-diversity-data/

28. Gerdeman, D. (2017, May 17). *Minorities who 'whiten' job resumes get more interviews: African American and Asian job applicants who mask their race on resumes seem to have better success getting job interviews, according to research by Katherine DeCelles and colleagues.* Retrieved from https://hbswk.hbs.edu/item/minorities-who-whiten-job-resumes-get-more-interviews

29. Graf, N., Brown, A., & Patten, E. (2019, March 22). *The narrowing, but persistent, gender pay gap.* Retrieved from https://www.pewresearch.org/fact-tank/2019/03/22/gender-pay-gap-facts/

30. Newport, F. (2018, May 22). *In U.S., estimate of LGBT population rises to 4.5%.* Retrieved from https://news.gallup.com/poll/234863/estimate-lgbt-population-rises.aspx

31. Compton, J. (2019, February 7). *LGBTQ families poised for 'dramatic growth,' national survey finds.* Retrieved from https://www.nbcnews.com/feature/nbc-out/lgbtq-families-poised-dramatic-growth-national-survey-finds-n968776

32. Chung, A., & Lawrence, H. (2018, June 4). *Most Americans oppose businesses refusing to serve gay people: Reuters/Ipsos poll.* Retrieved from https://www.reuters.com/article/us-usa-court-baker-poll/most-americans-oppose-businesses-refusing-to-serve-gay-people-reuters-ipsos-poll-idUSKCN1J02WN

33. Publix. (2019). *Committed to diversity: Variety makes everything better.* Retrieved from http://corporate.publix.com/about-publix/culture/committed-to-diversity

34. Satchell, M. (2017, December 5). *We're a best place for diversity!* Retrieved from https://blog.publix.com/careers/publix-is-a-great-place-to-work/were-a-best-workplace-for-diversity/

35. Morningstar. (2019). *Publix Supermarkets Inc: Key ratios.* Retrieved from https://financials.morningstar.com/ratios/r.html?t=PUSH

36. Fortune. (2018). *Publix Super Markets Inc. The best workplaces for diversity 2018.* Retrieved from http://fortune.com/best-workplaces-for-diversity/

37. Davis, A. B. (2019, May 6). *Personal interview* (MA-LPC).

38. Diversity. (2019). *Publix Supermarkets: Workforce diversity and inclusion.* Retrieved from https://www.diversity.com/Publix-Super-Markets

39. Gurchiek, K. (2018, March 19). *6 steps for building an inclusive workplace.* Retrieved from https://www.shrm.org/hr-today/news/hr-magazine/0418/pages/6-steps-for-building-an-inclusive-workplace.aspx

40. The University of Western Australia. (2019). *Code of conduct: Equity and justice—equity of access to employment and programs.* Retrieved from http://www.hr.uwa.edu.au/policies/policies/conduct/code/equity

Chapter 6

1. Ingraham, C. (2018, January 19). *Union membership remained steady in 2017. The trend may not hold.* Retrieved from https://www.washingtonpost.com/news/wonk/wp/2018/01/19/union-membership-remained-steady-in-2017-the-trend-may-not-hold/?utm_term=.a7873cf5d047

2. United States Department of Labor. (2009). *Timeline of OSHA's 40 year history.* Retrieved from https://www.osha.gov/osha40/timeline.html

3. United States Department of Labor. (2017, July 21). *Corporate-wide settlement agreements: TOMRA Recycling.* Retrieved from https://www.osha.gov/enforcement/cwsa/tomra-ny-recycling-llc-07212017

4. United States Department of Labor. (2016, August 1). *Worker falls 22 feet to death, 4 months after OSHA cites employer for failing to protect workers on the same job site.* Retrieved from https://www.osha.gov/news/newsreleases/region5/08012016. Louisville employer faces $320K in fines for serial disregard of fall protection.

5. O'Brien, S. A. (2018, August 22). *Uber to pay 56 workers $1.9 million for harassment and discrimination claims.* Retrieved from https://money.cnn.com/2018/08/21/technology/uber-settlement/index.html

6. U.S. Equal Employment Opportunity Commission. (2019, May 17). *EEOC press releases.* Retrieved from https://www.eeoc.gov/eeoc/newsroom/release/

7. Gomez-Mejia, L. R., Balkin, D. B., & Cardy, R. L. (2012). *Managing Human Resources* (7th ed.). USA: Pearson.

8. Rigoni, B., & Adkins, A. (2016, May 11). *What millennials want from a job.* Retrieved from https://hbr.org/2016/05/what-millennials-want-from-a-new-job

9. U.S. Equal Employment Opportunity Commission. (2018). *Discrimination by type.* Retrieved from https://www.eeoc.gov/laws/types/index.cfm

10. United States Department of Labor. (2018). *Occupational Safety and Health Administration: About OSHA.* Retrieved from https://www.osha.gov/laws-regs/oshact/section_1

11. Brainerd, J. (2017, August). *Paid family leave in the states.* Retrieved from http://www.ncsl.org/research/labor-and-employment/paid-family-leave-in-the-states.aspx

12. American Society for Quality. (2019). *What are the 5 s's (5s) of lean.* Retrieved from https://asq.org/quality-resources/lean/five-s-tutorial

13. Process Improvement Japan and

Australia. (2010). *How to motivate employees*. Retrieved from http://www.process-improvement-japan.com/how-to-motivate-employees.html

14. Rigoni, B., & Adkins, A. (2016, May 11). *What millennials want from a job*. Retrieved from https://hbr.org/2016/05/what-millennials-want-from-a-new-job

15. Hoagland, E. (2019). *Time: Photos-life in the Googleplex*. Retrieved from http://content.time.com/time/photogallery/0,29307,1947844,00.html

16. Johnson, T. (2018, June 29). *The real problem with tech professionals: High turnover*. Retrieved from https://www.forbes.com/sites/forbesbusinessdevelopmentcouncil/2018/06/29/the-real-problem-with-tech-professionals-high-turnover/#1b4867374201

17. Fagan, K. (2018, April 16). *Silicon Valley techies get free food and dazzling offices, but they're not very loyal—here's how long the average employee stays at the biggest tech companies*. Retrieved from https://www.businessinsider.com/average-employee-tenure-retention-at-top-tech-companies-2018-4

18. Radu, S. (2018, February 16). *How soon will you be working from home? Telecommuting might not just be a company perk in the next decade*. Retrieved from https://www.usnews.com/news/best-countries/articles/2018-02-16/telecommuting-is-growing-but-still-not-unanimously-embraced

19. Shoikhetbrod, A. A. (2018, April 6). *Telecommuting and employment law*. Retrieved from https://www.tullylegal.com/resources/articles/telecommuting-employment-law/

20. Mautz, S. (2018, April 2). *A 2-year Stanford study shows the astonishing productivity boost of working from home*. Retrieved from https://www.inc.com/scott-mautz/a-2-year-stanford-study-shows-astonishing-productivity-boost-of-working-from-home.html

21. Brunelli, L. M. (2019, April 1). *Work-at-home profile: Aetna*. Retrieved from https://www.thebalancecareers.com/aetna-work-at-home-company-profile-3542451

22. Barberio, J. (2017, November 6). *Aetna is hiring more than 200 work-from-home employees with full benefits*. Retrieved from https://www.workingmother.com/aetna-is-hiring-more-than-300-work-from-home-employees

23. Lavey-Heaton, M. (2014, March 10). *Working from home: How Yahoo, Best Buy and HP are making moves*. Retrieved from https://www.theguardian.com/sustainable-business/working-from-home-yahoo-best-buy-hp-moves

Chapter 7

1. Culbert, S. A. (2017). *Good people, bad managers: How work culture corrupts good intentions*. New York NY: Oxford University Press.

2. McGill University. (2010, July 6). *Mintzberg on managing*. Retrieved from https://www.youtube.com/watch?v=_NRWtd_SiU8

3. Kenny, B. (2007, April 25). *The coming crisis in employee turnover*. Retrieved from https://www.forbes.com/2007/04/24/employees-turnover-careers-lead-careers-cz_bk_0425turnover.html#5a00dbb7773a

4. Buffer. (2019). *About us*. Retrieved from https://buffer.com/about

5. Neugaard, B. (2019). *Halo effect: Psychology*. Retrieved from https://www.britannica.com/science/halo-effect

6. De Sio, S., Cedrone, F., Trovato Battagliola, E., Buomprisco, G., Perri, R., & Greco, E. (2018). The perception of psychosocial risks and work-related stress in relation to job insecurity and gender differences: A cross-sectional study. *BioMed Research International*, 1–6.

7. Kambayashi, R., & Kato, T. (2017). Long-term employment and job security over the past 25 years. *ILR Review*, 70(2), 359–394.

8. Metin Camgoz, S., Tayfur Ekmekci, O., Bayhan Karapinar, P., & Kumbul Guler, B. (2016). Job insecurity and turnover intentions: Gender differences and the mediating role of work engagement. *Sex Roles*, 75(11–12), 583–598.

9. Sullivan, B. (2016, July 7). *For older workers, getting a new job is a crapshoot*. Retrieved from https://www.cnbc.

com/2016/07/07/for-older-workers-getting-a-new-job-is-a-crapshoot.html

10. Burtless, G. (2017, October 22). *Age related health costs and job prospects of older workers.* Retrieved from https://siepr.stanford.edu/system/files/BURTLESS_Age-Related-Health-Costs_1st-Draft_Oct-2017.pdf

11. The Huffington Post. (2017, December 7). *7 cultures that celebrate aging and respect their elders.* Retrieved from https://www.huffpost.com/entry/what-other-cultures-can-teach_n_4834228

12. Center for Higher Ambition Leadership. (2016). *Who are your water carriers? Lessons from Herman Miller.* Retrieved from https://www.higherambition.org/14294/

13. Brasor, P. (2014, November 1). *Debating the merits of lifetime employment.* Retrieved from https://www.japantimes.co.jp/news/2014/11/01/national/media-national/debating-merits-lifetime-employment/#.XOwtRo97ns4

14. Heathfield, S. M. (2018, December 26). *What seniority means at work: Seniority means more in the public sector than in the private sector.* Retrieved from https://www.thebalancecareers.com/what-seniority-means-at-work-1919372

15. Sender, A., Arnold, A., & Staffelbach, B. (2017). Job security as a threatened resource: reactions to job insecurity in culturally distinct regions. *International Journal of Human Resource Management,* 28(17), 2403–2429. https://doi.org/10.1080/09585192.2015.1137615

16. Osman, I., Berbary, L., Sidani, Y., Al-Ayoubi, B., & Emrouznejad, A. (2011). Data Envelopment Analysis Model for the Appraisal and Relative Performance Evaluation of Nurses at an Intensive Care Unit. *Journal of Medical Systems*, 35(5), 1039–1062. https://doi.org/10.1007/s10916-010-9570-4

17. General Electric. (2019). *John F. Welch, Jr.: Chariman & CEO 1981–2001.* Retrieved from https://www.ge.com/about-us/leadership/profiles/john-f-welch-jr

18. Gomez-Mejia, L. R., Balkin, D. B., & Cardy, R. L. (2012). *Managing human resources.* USA: Pearson.

19. Olson, E. G. (2013, November 18). *Microsoft, GE, and the futility of ranking employees.* Retrieved from http://fortune.com/2013/11/18/microsoft-ge-and-the-futility-of-ranking-employees/

20. Jones, B., Smith, K., & Rock, D. (2018, June 20). *3 biases that hijack performance reviews, and how to address them.* Retrieved from https://hbr.org/2018/06/3-biases-that-hijack-performance-reviews-and-how-to-address-them

21. Chen, J. (2019, February 11). *Board of directors.* Retrieved from https://www.investopedia.com/terms/b/boardofdirectors.asp

22. Robbins, S. P., DeCenzo, D. A., & Coulter, M. A. (2014). *Fundamentals of management: Essential concepts and applications* (9th ed.). USA: Pearson.

23. Fox, J. (2018, August 24). *Why German corporate boards include workers: A brief history of "co-determination," which Elizabeth Warren now wants to bring to U.S. corporations.* Retrieved from https://www.bloomberg.com/opinion/articles/2018-08-24/why-german-corporate-boards-include-workers-for-co-determination

24. King Arthur Flour. (2019). *Why employee ownership matters.* Retrieved from https://www.kingarthurflour.com/our-story/article/employee-owned.html

Chapter 8

1. Jung, C. G. (1921). *Psychological types.* Retrieved from http://deenrc.files.wordpress.com/2008/03/carl-jung-psychological-types.pdf

2. Mosley, E. (2016, July 18). *The human need for recognition in the workplace.* Retrieved from https://www.wbjournal.com/article/the-human-need-for-recognition-in-the-workplace

3. Ward, B. (2019). The Impact of Personality on Job Satisfaction: A Study of Bank Employees in the Southeastern U.S. *The IUP Journal of Organizational Behavior, 18*(2), 60–79.

4. Merino, M. D., & Privado, J. (2015). Does employee recognition affect positive psychological functioning and well-being? *The Spanish Journal of Psychology,*

18. Retrieved from https://milligan.idm. oclc.org/login?url=https://search.ebsco host.com/login.aspx?direct=true&db=psy h&AN=2015–42476–001&site=eds-live& scope=site

5. Martin, R., Guillaume, Y., Thomas, G., Lee, A., & Epitropaki, O. (2016). Leader-Member Exchange (LMX) and performance: A meta-analytic review. *Personnel Psychology (69)*, 67–121.

6. Bolino, M. C. (2007). What about us? Relative deprivation among out-group members in Leader-Member Exchange relationships. *Academy of Management Annual Meeting Proceedings, 2007*(1), 1–5.

7. Karanika-Murray, M., Bartholomew, K. J., Williams, G. A., & Cox, T. (2015). Leader-Member Exchange across two hierarchical levels of leadership: Concurrent influences on work characteristics and employee psychological health. *Work Stress, 29*(1), 57–74.

8. Chung-kai Li, & Chia-hung Hung. (2009). The influence of transformational leadership on workplace relationships and job performance. *Social Behavior & Personality: An International Journal, 37*(8), 1129–1142.

9. Robbins, S. P., DeCenzo, D. A., & Coulter, M. A. (2014). *Fundamentals of management: Essential concepts and applications* (9th ed.). USA: Pearson.

10. Shu, C.-Y., & Lazatkhan, J. (2017). Effect of Leader-Member Exchange on employee envy and work behavior moderated by self-esteem and neuroticism. *Revista de Psicología Del Trabajo y de Las Organizaciones, 33*(1), 69–81.

11. Robbins, S. P, & Judge, T. A. (2012). *Organizational behavior* (15th ed.). Upper Saddle River, NJ: Prentice Hall.

12. Mahoney, J. T. (2004). *Behavioral Theory of the Firm*. Retrieved from https://us.sagepub.com/sites/default/files/upm-binaries/5029_Mahoney_Chapter_1.pdf

13. Hills, L. (2014). Managing cliques and exclusionary behavior within your medical practice team. *The Journal of Medical Practice Management: MPM, 29*(6), 373–377.

14. Brun, J.-P., & Dugas, N. (2008). An analysis of employee recognition: Perspectives on human resources practices. *The International Journal of Human Resource*

Management, 19(4), 716–730. https://doi. org/10.1080/09585190801953723

15. The PNC Financial Services Group. (2019). *Employees in the community.* Retrieved from https://www.pnc.com/en/about-pnc/corporate-responsibility/corporate-social-responsibility/communities-green/volunteerism.html

16. Rawland, A. (2011, February 1). *The County of San Bernardino Department of Behavioral Health: Employee recognition policy*. Retrieved from http://wp.sbcounty.gov/dbh/wp-content/uploads/2016/08/BOP3037.pdf

17. Seidel, L. (2010, October 2). *Good job! How to give recognition that promotes outstanding performance*. Retrieved from https://blog.smu.edu/hr/2010/10/02/good-job-how-to-give-recognition-that-promotes-outstanding-peformance/

18. eXp Realty. (2019, January 18). *eXp Realty exceeds 16,000 real estate agents across North America: Agent and broker growth increased 145% year-over-year*. Retrieved from https://www.globenewswire.com/news-release/2019/01/18/1701957/0/en/eXp-Realty-Exceeds-16–000-Real-Estate-Agents-Across-North-America.html

19. Gagnon, S. (2019, July 11). *Personal interview* (Realtor).

20. eXp World Holdings. (2019). ICON *Agent Award*. Retrieved from https://join.exprealty.com/icon-agent-award/

Chapter 9

1. Robbins, S. P., & Judge, T. A. (2009). *Organizational behavior*. Upper Saddle River, NJ: Pearson.

2. Bouton, K. (2015, July 17). *Recruiting for cultural fit*. Retrieved from https://hbr.org/2015/07/recruiting-for-cultural-fit

3. Morgan, B. (2018, January 16). *Chief culture officer and chief customer officer: A winning combination*. Retrieved from https://www.forbes.com/sites/blakemorgan/2018/01/16/chief-culture-officer-and-chief-customer-officer-a-winning-combination/#1e00a8833ab1

4. Rogel, C. (2014, March 17). *12 attributes to evaluate your organizational culture*. Retrieved from https://decision-wise.

com/12-attributes-to-evaluate-your-orga
nization-culture/

5. Dwivedi, S., Kaushik, S., & Luxmi. (2014). Impact of organizational culture on commitment of employees: An empirical study of BPO sector in India. *Vikalpa: The Journal for Decision Makers, 39*(3), 77–92. Retrieved from https://milligan. idm.oclc.org/login?url=https://search. ebscohost.com/login.aspx?direct=true& db=buh&AN=98850543&site=eds-live& scope=site

6. Tybout, A. M., & Calder, B. J. (2010). *Kellogg on marketing* (2nd ed.). Hoboken, NJ: John Wiley & Sons, Inc.

7. Toyota. (2018). *What are Toyota's mission and vision statements?* Retrieved from http://toyota.custhelp.com/app/ans wers/detail/a_id/7654/~/what-are-toyo tas-mission-and-vision-statements%3F

8. Bomey, N. (2018, February 22). *Toyota dominates Consumer Reports 2018 Top Picks for vehicles.* Retrieved from https:// www.usatoday.com/story/money/cars/ 2018/02/22/consumer-reports-2018-top-picks-vehicles/362272002/

9. Tybout, A. M., & Calder, B. J. (2010). *Kellogg on marketing* (2nd ed.). Hoboken, NJ: John Wiley & Sons, Inc.

10. Daft, R. L. (2008). *The leadership experience* (4th ed). Thompson/Southwestern: USA.

11. Lawn Care Academy. (2019). *Straight from the orient: The amazing zoysia grass.* Retrieved from https://www. lawn-care-academy.com/zoysia-grass. html

12. Christoffersen, T. (2017, June 1). *Our common core: Deliver WOW through service.* Retrieved from https://www.zap pos.com/about/stories/core-values-one

13. Dutch Bros Coffee. (2018). *Dutch Bros Coffee: Locations, menu, our story, news & events, coffee, love abounds.* Retrieved from https://www.dutchbros. com/our-story

14. Adams, S. (2016, June 29). *The coffee cult: How Dutch Bros. is turning its "bro-istas" into wealthy franchises.* Retrieved from https://www.forbes.com/ sites/susanadams/2016/06/15/the-coffee-cult-how-dutch-bros-is-turning-its-bro-istas-into-wealthy-franchisees/#5176 bd983694

15. Lambert, S., & Gonzalez, A. (November 15, 2013). Dutch Bros. Coffee. In Chris Carlson (executive producer). *Undercover Boss.* Los Angeles, CA: Columbia Broadcasting System.

16. Culverwell, W. (2014, August 14). *A chat with Dutch Bros.' Travis Boersma.* Retrieved from https://www.bizjournals. com/portland/blog/sbo/2014/08/a-chat-with-dutch-bros-s-travis-boersma.html

17. Schuyler, M., & Berkowitz, C. (2009). Developing talent through community involvement: A winning formula for Capital One. *People & Strategy, 32*(1), 46–53.

18. Henningfield, J., Pohl, M., & Tolhurst, N. (2006). *The ICCA handbook on corporate social responsibility.* Retrieved from http://www.untag-smd.ac.id/files/ Perpustakaan_Digital_1/CORPORATE %20SOCIAL%20RESPONSIBILITY%20 The%20ICCA%20handbook%20on%20 corporate%20social%20responsibility. pdf#page=84

19. Fox, J. (2012, April 18). *The social responsibility of a business is to increase ... what exactly?* Retrieved from https://hbr. org/2012/04/you-might-disagree-with-milton

20. Hategan, C.D., Sirghi, N., Curea-Pitorac, R., & Hategan, V.P. (2018). Doing well or doing good: The relationship between corporate social responsibility and profit in Romanian companies. *Sustainability* (4), 1041.

21. Rudominer, R. (2015). *Corporate social responsibility matters: Ignore millennials at your own peril.* Retrieved from http://csic.georgetown.edu/magazine/cor porate-social-responsibility-matters-ig nore-millennials-peril/

22. Hill, C. W. L., & Hult, G. T. M. (2015). *Global business today* (9th ed.). McGraw-Hill: New York, NY.

23. Velasquez, M. (2005, November 2). *Unocal in Burma.* Retrieved from https:// www.scu.edu/ethics/focus-areas/busi ness-ethics/resources/unocal-in-burma/

24. Cleveland Clinic. (2019). *Household chemicals: What's in my house?* Retrieved from http://www.cleveland clinic.org/healthinfo/Mobile/detail. aspx?MasterId=11397&Title=House hold%20Chemicals:%20What%27s%20 in%20My%20House?&Category=Type&

HEADERSTRING=Jm5ic3A7PiZuYn
NwOzxhIGhyZWY9Ii9oZWFFsdGh
pbmZvL01vYmlsZS9hdG96LmFFzcH
giPkEtdG8tWiBMaXN0N0PC9hPiZuYn
NwOz4mbmJzcDs8YSBocmVmPSIva
GVhbHHRoaW5tby9Nb2JpbGUvYXRRvei
5hc3B4P2NoYXI9UyI+UzwvYT4mb
mJzcDs+Jm5ic3A7PGEgaHJlZj0iL
2hlYWx0aGluZm8vTW9iaWxlL2F0b3ouYXNweFL2F
0b3ouYXNweD9jaGFyPVQiPlR1YWZsZHHk
mdG9waWJNJZD0xMTYxJmNoYXI9Uy
I+U2FmZXR5PC9hPg==

25. Spiller, H.A., & Griffith, J. R. K. (2009). The value and evolving role of the U.S. Poison Control Center system. *Public Health Reports, 124*(3), 359–363.

26. DeGeorge, R. T. (2006). *Business ethics (6th ed.).* Upper Saddle River, NJ: Pearson.

27. Tewari, R., & Pathak, T. (2014). Sustainable CSR for micro, small and medium enterprises. *Journal of Management & Public Policy, 6*(1), 34–44.

28. Opploans. (2019). *Financial opportunity, social responsibility, and commitment to our customers.* Retrieved from https://www.opploans.com/about-us/

29. Allafia. (2019). *Our history.* Retrieved from https://www.alaffia.com/pages/alaffia-history

30. Allafia. (2019). *The social enterprise model.* Retrieved from https://www.alaffia.com/pages/social-enterprise-model

31. Allafia. (2019). *Allafia's commitments.* Retrieved from https://www.alaffia.com/pages/alaffia-commitments

Chapter 10

1. Wren, D. A., & Bedeian, A. G. (2009). *The evolution of management thought* (6th ed). John Wiley & Sons, Inc.: USA.

2. Kass, S. J., Vodanovich, S. J., & Khosravi, J. Y. (2011). Applying the job characteristics model to the college education experience. *Journal of the Scholarship of Teaching and Learning, 11*(4), 56–68.

3. The Colonial Williamsburg Foundation. (2019). *Silversmith: Colonial silversmith required talent of an artist.* Retrieved from https://www.history.org/almanack/life/trades/tradesil.cfm

4. Brooks, S. (2014, October 17). *Sil-versmith in colonial times.* Retrieved from https://prezi.com/vlpfdyhawshm/silversmith-in-colonial-times/

5. Electricianschooledu.org. (2019). *Electrician schools: How to become an electrician.* Retrieved from https://www.electricianschooledu.org/

6. Wright, C. D. (1908). *The apprenticeship system in its relation to industrial education.* Retrieved from https://files.eric.ed.gov/fulltext/ED542849.pdf

7. Klein, C. (2019, January 4). *The original Luddites raged against the machine of the Industrial Revolution.* Retrieved from https://www.history.com/news/industrial-revolution-luddites-workers

8. Semler, R. (1993). *Maverick: The story behind the world's most unusual workplace.* New York, NY: Business Plus.

9. Manahan, C., & Lavoie, J. (2008). Who stays in rural practice?: An international [sic] review of the literature on factors influencing rural nurse retention. *Online Journal of Rural Nursing & Health Care, 8*(2), 42–53.

10. Lorenz, T. (2017, March 29). *How Asana built the best company culture in tech.* Retrieved from https://www.fastcompany.com/3069240/how-asana-built-the-best-company-culture-in-tech

11. Roepe, L. R. (2016, April 27). *Inside three companies that are innovating flexible schedules.* Retrieved from https://www.fastcompany.com/3059295/inside-three-companies-that-are-innovating-flexible-schedules

12. Porter, M., Williams, J.C., Grant, A., & Buckingham, M. (2019). *Five years of must reads from HBR: 2019 edition (HBR's 10 must reads).* Boston, MA: Harvard Review Press.

13. Green, P., Gino, F., & Staats, B. R. (2017). *Seeking to belong: How the words of internal and external beneficiaries influence performance.* Retrieved from pdfs.semanticscholar.org/1633/6a5b47d-62085808434945970cc75a81cdc37.pdf

14. Pozen, R. C. (2013, March 28). *The delicate art of giving feedback.* Retrieved from https://hbr.org/2013/03/the-delicate-art-of-giving-fee

15. Cappelli, P., & Tavis, A. (2016, October). *The performance management revolution.* Retrieved from https://hbr.

org/2016/10/the-performance-manage
ment-revolution

16. Adkins, A., & Rigoni, B. (2016, June 2). *Managers: Millennials want feedback, but won't ask for it.* Retrieved from https://www.gallup.com/workplace/236450/man agers-millennials-feedback-won-ask.aspx

17. Baldassarre, L., & Finken, B. (2015, August 12). *GE's real-time performance development.* Retrieved from https://hbr.org/2015/08/ges-real-time-perfor mance-development

18. Workopolis. (2016, December 22). *How GE replaced a 40-year-old perfor-mance review system.* Retrieved from https://hiring.workopolis.com/article/ ge-replaced-40-year-old-performance-re view-system/

19. Berger, S. M., & Ludwig, T. D. (2007). Reducing warehouse employee errors using voice-assisted technology that pro-vided immediate feedback. *Journal of Organizational Behavior Management, 27*(1), 1–31.

Chapter 11

1. Sullivan, E. (2016, July 13). *Self-ac-tualization: Psychology.* Retrieved from https://www.britannica.com/science/ self-actualization

2. Indeed. (2019). *HR manager job.* Retrieved from https://www.indeed.com/ q-HR-Manager-jobs.html

3. Stewart, A. J. & Kuenzi, K. (2018). The nonprofit career ladder: Exploring career paths as leadership development for future nonprofit executives. *Public Person-nel Management, 47*(4), 359–381.

4. Senge, P. M. (2006). *The fifth disci-pline: The art & practice of the learning organization.* New York, NY: Crown Busi-ness.

5. Gilley, J. W., Eggland, S. A., & Gilly, A. M. (2002). *Principles of human resource development* (2nd ed.). Perseus Publishing, USA.

6. Richman, N. (2015). Human resource management and human resource devel-opment: Evolution and contributions. *Creighton Journal of Interdisciplinary Leadership 1*(2), 120–129.

7. Bhalla, T. (2016, August 24). *Over-view of HRM & HRD.* Retrieved from https://www.slideshare.net/123trilochan/ overview-of-hrm-hrd

8. Evans, J. R., & Lindsay, W. M. (2016). *Managing for quality and performance excellence* (10th ed.). USA: Cengage Learn-ing.

9. Clevenger, D. (2009, June 5). *Human resources outsourcing: How HR depart-ments can do more by doing less in-house.* Retrieved from https://www.thebalance careers.com/human-resources-outsourc ing-1918386

10. Cheng, A. (2019, April 9). *With millennials in mind, outdoor retailer REI doubles down on rentals and used gear sales.* Retrieved from https://www.forbes. com/sites/andriacheng/2019/04/09/ with-millennials-in-mind-outdoor-gear-retailer-rei-to-double-down-on-rental-and-used-gear-sales/#63f73915141e

11. REI Co-op. (2019). *Who we are.* Re-trieved from https://www.rei.com/about-rei

12. Lyman, A. (2009). *REI—working together for a better world: Best company for 25 years.* Retrieved from https://www. rei.com/pdf/jobs/2009-Best-Company-for-25-Years-REI-for-REI.pdf

13. Chieh-Heng Ko, & Shu-Rung Lin. (2016). Exploring the effects of personal-ity traits on hotel employee job burnout. *International Journal of Organizational Innovation, 9*(2), 52–59.

14. Robbins, S. P., & Judge, T. A. (2009). *Organizational behavior* (13th ed.). Upper Saddle River, NJ: Pearson/Prentice Hall.

15. Saberr. (2019). *Saberr: Transform-ing teamwork.* Retrieved from https:// www.saberr.com/

16. O*Net Interest Profiler. (2019). *Welcome to the O*Net interest profiler.* Retrieved from https://www.mynextmove. org/explore/ip

17. O*Net Online. (2019). *Interests: Preferences for work environments and outcomes.* Retrieved from https://www. onetonline.org/find/descriptor/browse/ Interests/

18. Wen, T. (2017, August 21). *The new way your personality could be holding you back.* Retrieved from https://www.bbc. com/worklife/article/20170818-the-new-way-your-personality-could-be-holding-you-back

19. Briggs, S. P., Copeland, S., & Haynes, D. (2007). Accountants for the 21st century, where are you? A five-year study of accounting students' personality preferences. *Critical Perspectives on Accounting, 18*, 511–537.

20. The Myers and Briggs Foundation. (2019). *The 16 MBTI types.* Retrieved from https://www.myersbriggs.org/my-mbti-personality-type/mbti-basics/the-16-mbti-types.htm?bhcp=1

Chapter 12

1. Hawksworth, C. (2019). *How to avoid leading questions.* Retrieved from https://avius.com/blog/avoid-leading-questions/

2. Herzberg, F. (1966). *Work and the nature of man.* The World Publishing Company: Cleveland, OH.

Chapter 13

1. Redman, T. C. (2019, May 16). *Do your data scientists know the "why" behind their work?* Retrieved from https://hbr.org/2019/05/do-your-data-scientists-know-the-why-behind-their-work

2. UCLA Institute for Digital Research and Education. (2019). *What does Cronbach's alpha mean?* Retrieved from https://stats.idre.ucla.edu/spss/faq/what-does-cronbachs-alpha-mean/

Chapter 15

1. Kuijk, A. (2018). *Two Factor Theory by Frederick Herzberg.* Retrieved from https://www.toolshero.com/psychology/theories-of-motivation/two-factor-theory-herzberg/

2. Loannidis, J. P. (2007). *Limitations are not properly acknowledged in the scientific literature.* Retrieved from https://www.ncbi.nlm.nih.gov/pubmed/?term=Ioannidis%20JP%5BAuthor%5D&cauthor=true&cauthor_uid=17346604

3. Judge, T. A., Heller, D., & Mount, M. K. (2002). Five-Factor Model of personality and job satisfaction: A meta-analysis. *Journal of Applied Psychology, 87*(3), 530–541.

4. Rutledge, P. B. (2011, November 8). *Social networks: What Maslow misses.* Retrieved from https://www.psychologytoday.com/us/blog/positively-media/201111/social-networks-what-maslow-misses-0

5. Fain, P. (2015, September 4). *Call for help: Outsourced counseling designed as an employee benefit helps low-income students succeed in college, the Dell Scholars Program finds, and colleges may be following suit.* Retrieved from https://www.insidehighered.com/news/2015/09/04/outsourced-employee-style-counseling-can-work-first-generation-college-students

6. Housman, M., & Minor, D. (2015). *Toxic workers.* Retrieved from http://www.hbs.edu/faculty/Publication%20Files/16–057_d45c0b4f-fa19–49de-8f1b-4b12fe054fea.pdf

7. Browning, S., & Gagnon, S. (2017). *Personal interview* (Licensed Realtors).

Appendix

1. Goforth, C. (2015, November 16). *Using and interpreting Cronbach's alpha.* Retrieved from http://data.library.virginia.edu/using-and-interpreting-cronbachs-alpha/

2. Ward, B. (2019). The Impact of Personality on Job Satisfaction: A Study of Bank Employees in the Southeastern U.S. *The IUP Journal of Organizational Behavior, 18*(2), 60–79.

Bibliography

Adams, S. (2016, June 29). The coffee cult: How Dutch Bros. is turning its "bro-istas" into wealthy franchises. Retrieved from https://www.forbes.com/sites/susanad ams/2016/06/15/the-coffee-cult-how-dutch-bros-is-turning-its-bro-istas-into-wealthy-franchisees/#5176bd983694

Adkins, A., & Rigoni, B. (2016, June 2). Managers: Millennials want feedback, but won't ask for it. Retrieved from https://www.gallup.com/workplace/236450/managers-mil lennials-feedback-won-ask.aspx

Aguiar do Monte, P. (2012). Job dissatisfaction and labour turnover: Evidence from Brazil. International Journal of Human Resource Management, 23(8), 1717–1735.

Allafia (2019). Allafia's commitments. Retrieved from https://www.alaffia.com/pages/alaf fia-commitments

Allafia (2019). Our history. Retrieved from https://www.alaffia.com/pages/alaffia-history

Allafia (2019). The social enterprise model. Retrieved from https://www.alaffia.com/pages/ social-enterprise-model

American Society for Quality (2019). What are the 5 s's (5s) of lean. Retrieved from https:// asq.org/quality-resources/lean/five-s-tutorial

Baldassarre, L., & Finken, B. (2015, August 12). GE's real-time performance development. Retrieved from https://hbr.org/2015/08/ges-real-time-performance-development

Barberio, J. (2017, November 6). Aetna is hiring more than 200 work-from-home employ-ees with full benefits. Retrieved from https://www.workingmother.com/aetna-is-hiring-more-than-300-work-from-home-employees

Bassett-Jones, N., & Lloyd, G. C. (2005). Does Herzberg's motivation theory have staying power? Journal of Management Development, 24(10), 929–943.

Bayraktaroglu, S., Ulukoy, M., & Izci, C. (2016). The relationship between systematic sol-diering and organizational commitment in hospitality businesses. Journal of Manage-ment & Economics Research, 14(2), 250–263. https://doi.org/10.11611/JMER178468

Berger, S. M., & Ludwig, T. D. (2007). Reducing warehouse employee errors using voice-as-sisted technology that provided immediate feedback. Journal of Organizational Behav-ior Management, 27(1), 1–31

Bhalla, T. (2016, August 24). Overview of HRM & HRD. Retrieved from https://www. slideshare.net/123trilochan/overview-of-hrm-hrd

Bolino, M. C. (2007). What about us? Relative deprivation among out-group members in Leader-Member Exchange relationships. Academy of Management Annual Meeting Proceedings, 2007(1), 1–5.

Bomey, N. (2018, February 22). Toyota dominates Consumer Reports 2018 Top Picks for vehicles. Retrieved from https://www.usatoday.com/story/money/cars/2018/02/22/ consumer-reports-2018-top-picks-vehicles/362272002/

Bouton, K. (2015, July 17). Recruiting for cultural fit. Retrieved from https://hbr. org/2015/07/recruiting-for-cultural-fit

Brainerd, J. (2017, August). Paid family leave in the states. Retrieved from http://www.ncsl. org/research/labor-and-employment/paid-family-leave-in-the-states.aspx

Bibliography

Branson, R. (2011, October 6). Virgin's Richard Branson: Apple boss Steve Jobs was the entrepreneur I most admired. Retrieved from https://www.telegraph.co.uk/technology/steve-jobs/8811232/Virgins-Richard-Branson-Apple-boss-Steve-Jobs-was-the-entrepreneur-I-most-admired.html

Brasor, P. (2014, November 1). Debating the merits of lifetime employment. Retrieved from https://www.japantimes.co.jp/news/2014/11/01/national/media-national/debating-merits-lifetime-employment/#.XOwtRo97ns4

Bresiger, G. (2017, July 29). This is how much time employees spend slacking off. Retrieved from https://nypost.com/2017/07/29/this-is-how-much-time-employees-spend-slacking-off/

Briggs, S. P., Copeland, S., & Haynes, D. (2007). Accountants for the 21st century, where are you? A five-year study of accounting students' personality preferences. Critical Perspectives on Accounting, 18, 511–537.

Bromwich, J. E. (2018, January 31). We asked generation z to pick a name. It wasn't generation z. Retrieved from https://www.nytimes.com/2018/01/31/style/generation-z-name.html

Brooks, S. (2014, October 17). Silversmith in colonial times. Retrieved from https://prezi.com/vlpfdyhawshm/silversmith-in-colonial-times/

Browning, S., & Gagnon, S. (2017). Personal interview (Licensed Realtors).

Brun, J.-P., & Dugas, N. (2008). An analysis of employee recognition: Perspectives on human resources practices. The International Journal of Human Resource Management, 19(4), 716–730. https://doi.org/10.1080/09585190801953723

Brunelli, L. M. (2019, April 1). Work-at-home profile: Aetna. Retrieved from https://www.thebalancecareers.com/aetna-work-at-home-company-profile-3542451

Buffer (2019). About us. Retrieved from https://buffer.com/about

Bureau of Labor Statistics (2006, August 3). 100 years of U.S. consumer spending: Data for the nation, New York City, and Boston. Retrieved from https://www.bls.gov/opub/uscs/

Bureau of Labor Statistics (2014). Southeast information office: Occupational employment and wages in Memphis-May 2014. Retrieved from https://www.bls.gov/regions/southeast/news-release/2015/occupationalemploymentandwages_memphis_20150722.htm

Bureau of Labor Statistics (2016, August 30). Consumer expenditures—2015. Retrieved from https://www.bls.gov/news.release/cesan.nr0.htm

Bureau of Labor Statistics (2017, December 15). Employer costs for employee compensation. Retrieved from https://www.bls.gov/news.release/pdf/ecec.pdf

Bureau of Labor Statistics (2017, December 18). Employer costs for employee compensation for the regions-September 2017. Retrieved from https://www.bls.gov/regions/southwest/news-release/employercostsforemployeecompensation_regions.htm

Bureau of Labor Statistics (2018). Consumer Price Index. Retrieved from https://www.bls.gov/cpi/questions-and-answers.htm#Question_2

Burlingham, B. (2016, October 20). Decades later, the owners of Ann Arbor's iconic Zingerman's are still at odds over expansion. Retrieved from https://www.forbes.com/sites/boburlingham/2016/10/20/what-price-growth/#1d5c475f32e8

Burtless, G. (2017, October 22). Age related health costs and job prospects of older workers. Retrieved from https://siepr.stanford.edu/system/files/BURTLESS_Age-Related-Health-Costs_1st-Draft_Oct-2017.pdf

Cabell, B. (1997, August 20). It's official: Teamsters end UPS strike. Retrieved from http://www.cnn.com/US/9708/20/ups.update.early/

Cappelli, P., & Tavis, A. (2016, October). The performance management revolution. Retrieved from https://hbr.org/2016/10/the-performance-management-revolution

Center for Higher Ambition Leadership (2016). Who are your water carriers? Lessons from Herman Miller. Retrieved from https://www.higherambition.org/14294/

Chen, J. (2019, February 11). Board of directors. Retrieved from https://www.investopedia.com/terms/b/boardofdirectors.asp

Cheng, A. (2019, April 9). With millennials in mind, outdoor retailer REI doubles down on rentals and used gear sales. Retrieved from https://www.forbes.com/sites/andri acheng/2019/04/09/with-millennials-in-mind-outdoor-gear-retailer-rei-to-double-down-on-rental-and-used-gear-sales/#63f73915141e

Chib, M., & Anand, P. V. (2018). Understanding the impact of culture on job satisfaction, work motivation, work engagement, affect balance, emotional intelligence and happiness. International Journal of Social Sciences Review, 6(10), 1991–2001.

Chieh-Heng Ko, & Shu-Rung Lin (2016). Exploring the effects of personality traits on hotel employee job burnout. International Journal of Organizational Innovation, 9(2), 52–59.

Christoffersen, T. (2017, June 1). Our common core: Deliver WOW through service. Retrieved from https://www.zappos.com/about/stories/core-values-one

Chung, A., & Lawrence, H. (2018, June 4). Most Americans oppose businesses refusing to serve gay people: Reuters/Ipsos poll. Retrieved from https://www.reuters.com/article/us-usa-court-baker-poll/most-americans-oppose-businesses-refusing-to-serve-gay-people-reuters-ipsos-poll-idUSKCN1J02WN

Chung-kai Li, & Chia-hung Hung (2009). The influence of transformational leadership on workplace relationships and job performance. Social Behavior & Personality: An International Journal, 37(8), 1129–1142.

Cilluffo, A., & Cohn, D'Vera (2017, April 27). 10 demographic trends shaping the U.S. and the world in 2017. Retrieved from https://www.pewresearch.org/fact-tank/2017/04/27/10-demographic-trends-shaping-the-u-s-and-the-world-in-2017/

Cleveland Clinic (2019). Household chemicals: What's in my house? Retrieved from http://www.clevelandclinic.org/healthinfo/Mobile/detail.aspx?MasterId=11397&Title=Household%20Chemicals:%20What%27s%20in%20My%20House?&Category=Type&HEADERSTRING=Jm5ic3A7PiZuYnNwOzxhIGhyZWY9Ii9oZWFsdGGhpbmZvZvL01vYmlsZS9hdG96LmFzcHggiPkEtdG8tWiBMaXN0N0PC9hPiZuYnNwOz4mbbmJzcDs8YSBocmVmPSIvaGVhbHRoaW5mby81mby9Nb2JpbGUvYXRvei5hc3BsdGgiPlN0cmVmPSIvaGVhbHRoaW5mby81mby9Nb2JpbGUvYXRveiUyRmb3ouYXNweXXNweD9MTYxJmNoYXI9YXI9Ii9oZWFsdGgiPkEtdG8tWiBMaXN0N0PGEgaHJlZj0iL2hlYWx0aGluZm8vTW9iaWxlL2F0b3ouYXNweD9MTYxJmNoYXI9Ii9oZWFsdGgiPkEtdG8tWiBMaXN0N0PGEgaHJlZj0iL2hlYWx0aGluZm8vTW9iaWxlL2F0b3ouYXNweD9MTYxJmNoYXI9YXI9VS2FmZXR5PC9hPg==

Clevenger, D. (2009, June 5). Human resources outsourcing: How HR departments can do more by doing less in-house. Retrieved from https://www.thebalancecareers.com/human-resources-outsourcing-1918386

CNN Money (2018). Ultimate guide to retirement: Just how common are defined benefit plans? Retrieved from http://money.cnn.com/retirement/guide/pensions_basics.moneymag/index7.htm

The Colonial Williamsburg Foundation (2019). Silversmith: Colonial silversmith required talent of an artist. Retrieved from https://www.history.org/almanack/life/trades/tradesil.cfm

Compton, J. (2019, February 7). LGBTQ families poised for 'dramatic growth,' national survey finds. Retrieved from https://www.nbcnews.com/feature/nbc-out/lgbtq-families-poised-dramatic-growth-national-survey-finds-n968776

Culbert, S. A. (2017). Good people, bad managers: How work culture corrupts good intentions. New York NY: Oxford University Press

Culverwell, W. (2014, August 14). A chat with Dutch Bros.s' Travis Boersma. Retrieved from https://www.bizjournals.com/portland/blog/sbo/2014/08/a-chat-with-dutch-bros-s-travis-boersma.html

Curators of the University of University of Missouri (2017). Prices and wages by decade: 1910–1919. Retrieved from https://libraryguides.missouri.edu/pricesandwages/1910–1919#occupation

Daft, R. L. (2008). The leadership experience (4th ed). Thompson/Southwestern: USA.

David, F. R., & David, F. R. (2017). Strategic management: A competitive advantage approach—concepts and cases (16th ed.). USA: Pearson.

Davidson, P. (2016, November 10). Fast food workers strike, seeking $15 wage, political

Bibliography

muscle. Retrieved from https://www.usatoday.com/story/money/2015/11/10/fast-food-strikes-begin/75482782/

Davis, A. B. (2019, May 6). Personal interview (MA-LPC).

Deahl, J. (2016, October 6). Countries around the world beat U.S. on paid maternal leave. Retrieved from https://www.npr.org/2016/10/06/495839588/countries-around-the-world-beat-the-us-on-paid-parental-leaveparental-leave

DeGeorge, R. T. (2006). Business ethics (6th ed.). Upper Saddle River, NJ: Pearson.

De Sio, S., Cedrone, F., Trovato Battagliola, E., Buomprisco, G., Perri, R., & Greco, E. (2018). The perception of psychosocial risks and work-related stress in relation to job insecurity and gender differences: A cross-sectional study. BioMed Research International, 1–6.

Diversity (2019). Publix Supermarkets: Workforce diversity and inclusion. Retrieved from https://www.diversity.com/Publix-Super-Markets

Dutch Bros Coffee (2018). Dutch Bros Coffee: Locations, menu, our story, news & events, coffee, love abounds. Retrieved from https://www.dutchbros.com/our-story

Dwivedi, S., Kaushik, S., & Luxmi (2014). Impact of organizational culture on commitment of employees: An empirical study of BPO sector in India. Vikalpa: The Journal for Decision Makers, 39(3), 77–92. Retrieved from https://milligan.idm.oclc.org/login?url=https://search.ebscohost.com/login.aspx?direct=true&db=buh&AN=98850543&site=eds-live&scope=site

E. H., S., A., W., & B., P. (2016). Big city millenial workers in Indonesia and factors affecting their commitment to the organisation. Pertanika Journal of Social Sciences & Humanities, 2447–57.

The Economic Times (2018). Definition of 'Equity Theory.' Retrieved from https://economictimes.indiatimes.com/definition/equity-theory

Electricianschooledu.org (2019). Electrician schools: How to become an electrician. Retrieved from https://www.electricianschooledu.org/

Ertas, N. (2015). Turnover intentions and work motivations of millennial employees in federal service. Public Personnel Management, 44(3), 401–423.

Eschner, K. (2016, December 1). One hundred and three years ago today, Henry Ford introduced the assembly line: His workers hated it. Retrieved from http://www.smithsonianmag.com/smart-news/one-hundred-and-three-years-ago-today-henry-ford-introduced-assembly-line-his-workers-hated-it-180961267/

Evans, J. R., & Lindsay, W. M. (2016). Managing for quality and performance excellence (10th ed.). USA: Cengage Learning.

Evans, L., & Olumide-Aluko, F. (2010). Teacher job satisfaction in developing countries: A critique of Herzberg's Two- Factor theory applied to the Nigerian Context. International Studies in Educational Administration (Commonwealth Council For Educational Administration & Management (CCEAM)), 38(2), 73–85.

eXp Realty (2019, January 18). eXp Realty exceeds 16,000 real estate agents across North America: Agent and broker growth increased 145% year-over-year. Retrieved from https://www.globenewswire.com/news-release/2019/01/18/1701957/0/en/eXp-Realty-Exceeds-16-000-Real-Estate-Agents-Across-North-America.html

eXp World Holdings (2019). ICON Agent Award. Retrieved from https://join.exprealty.com/icon-agent-award/

Fagan, K. (2018, April 16). Silicon Valley techies get free food and dazzling offices, but they're not very loyal—here's how long the average employee stays at the biggest tech companies. Retrieved from https://www.businessinsider.com/average-employee-tenure-retention-at-top-tech-companies-2018-4

Fain, P. (2015, September 4). Call for help: Outsourced counseling designed as an employee benefit helps low-income students succeed in college, the Dell Scholars Program finds, and colleges may be following suit. Retrieved from https://www.insidehighered.com/news/2015/09/04/outsourced-employee-style-counseling-can-work-first-generation-college-students

Bibliography

Federal Reserve Bank of St. Lous (2017). Real gross domestic product per capita. Retrieved from https://fred.stlouisfed.org/series/A939RX0Q048SBEA

Fortune (2018). Publix Super Markets Inc. The best workplaces for diversity 2018. Retrieved from http://fortune.com/best-workplaces-for-diversity/

Fox, J. (2012, April 18). The social responsibility of a business is to increase ...what exactly? Retrieved from https://hbr.org/2012/04/you-might-disagree-with-milton

Fox, J. (2018, August 24). Why German corporate boards include workers: A brief history of "co-determination," which Elizabeth Warren now wants to bring to U.S. corporations. Retrieved from https://www.bloomberg.com/opinion/articles/2018–08–24/why-german-corporate-boards-include-workers-for-co-determination

Frank, K. (2016, February 10). The 6 responsibilities of a Zingerman's servant leader. Retrieved from http://www.zingtrain.com/webinars/6-responsibilities-zingermans-servant-leader

French Jr., J. R. P., & Raven, B. (1959). The bases of social power. Retrieved from http://web.mit.edu/curhan/www/docs/Articles/15341_Readings/Power/French_&_Raven_Studies_Social_Power_ch9_pp150–167.pdf

Friedman, T. L. (2005). The world is flat: A brief history of the twenty-first century. USA: Farrar, Straus and Giroux.

Gagnon, S. (2019, July 11). Personal interview (Realtor).

General Electric (2019). John F. Welch, Jr.: Chairman & CEO 1981–2001. Retrieved from https://www.ge.com/about-us/leadership/profiles/john-f-welch-jr

Gerdeman, D. (2017, May 17). Minorities who 'whiten' job resumes get more interviews: African American and Asian job applicants who mask their race on resumes seem to have better success getting job interviews, according to research by Katherine DeCelles and colleagues. Retrieved from https://hbswk.hbs.edu/item/minorities-who-whiten-job-resumes-get-more-interviews

Gilley, J. W., Eggland, S. A., & Gilly, A. M. (2002). Principles of human resource development (2nd ed.). Perseus Publishing, USA.

Glassdoor.com (2018). Zingerman's salaries. Retrieved from https://www.glassdoor.com/Salary/Zingermans-Salaries-E270584.htm

Global Rich List (2018). Income: Global rich list. Retrieved from http://www.globalrichlist.com/#na

Goforth, C. (2015, November 16). Using and interpreting Cronbach's alpha. Retrieved from http://data.library.virginia.edu/using-and-interpreting-cronbachs-alpha/

Gomez-Mejia, L. R., Balkin, D. B., & Cardy, R. L. (2012). Managing human resources. USA: Pearson.

Graf, N., Brown, A., & Patten, E. (2019, March 22). The narrowing, but persistent, gender pay gap. Retrieved from https://www.pewresearch.org/fact-tank/2019/03/22/gender-pay-gap-facts/

Green, P., Gino, F., & Staats, B. R. (2017). Seeking to belong: How the words of internal and external beneficiaries influence performance. Retrieved from https://pdfs.semanticscholar.org/1633/6a5b47d62085808434945970cc75a81cdc37.pdf

Greenhouse, S. (2014, February 10). Labor battle at Kellogg plant in Memphis drags on. Retrieved from https://www.nytimes.com/2014/02/11/business/kellogg-workers-in-4th-month-of-lockout-in-memphis.html

Gurchiek, K. (2018, March 19). 6 steps for building an inclusive workplace. Retrieved from https://www.shrm.org/hr-today/news/hr-magazine/0418/pages/6-steps-for-building-an-inclusive-workplace.aspx

Halkos, E. (2015). Employee discount and purchase programs—a smart employee benefits strategy. Retrieved from http://www.corporatewellnessmagazine.com/voluntary-benefits/discount-purchase-programs/

Hategan, C.D., Sirghi, N., Curea-Pitorac, R., & Hategan, V.P. (2018). Doing well or doing good: The relationship between corporate social responsibility and profit in Romanian companies. Sustainability (4), 1041

Bibliography

Hawksworth, C. (2019). How to avoid leading questions. Retrieved from https://avius.com/blog/avoid-leading-questions/

Heathfield, S. M. (2018, December 26). What seniority means at work: Seniority means more in the public sector than in the private sector. Retrieved from https://www.thebalancecareers.com/what-seniority-means-at-work-1919372

Henningfield, J., Pohl, M., & Tolhurst, N. (2006). The ICCA handbook on corporate social responsibility. Retrieved from http://www.untag-smd.ac.id/files/Perpustakaan_Digital_1/CORPORATE%20SOCIAL%20RESPONSIBILITY%20The%20ICCA%20handbook%20on%20corporate%20social%20responsibility.pdf#page=84

Herzberg, F. (1966). Work and the nature of man. New York, NY: The World Publishing Company.

Herzberg, F. (1966). Work and the nature of man. The World Publishing Company: Cleveland, OH.

Herzberg, F., Mausner, B., & Snyderman, B. B. (1959). The motivation to work. New York, NY: John Wiley & Sons, Inc.

Hess, A. (2017, May 4). The 20 best companies for work-life balance. Retrieved from https://www.cnbc.com/2017/05/03/the-20-best-companies-for-work-life-balance.html

Hill, C. W. L., & Hult, G. T. M. (2015). Global business today (9th ed.). McGraw-Hill: New York, NY.

Hills, L. (2014). Managing cliques and exclusionary behavior within your medical practice team. The Journal of Medical Practice Management: MPM, 29(6), 373–377.

Hirschi, A., Shockley, K. M., & Zacher, H. (2019). Achieving work-family balance: An action regulation model. Academy of Management Review, 44(1), 150–171. https://doi.org/10.5465/amr.2016.0409

Hoagland, E. (2019). Time: Photos-life in the Googleplex. Retrieved from http://content.time.com/time/photogallery/0,29307,1947844,00.html

Housman, M., & Minor, D. (2015). Toxic workers. Retrieved from http://www.hbs.edu/faculty/Publication%20Files/16-057_d45c0b4f-fa19-49de-8f1b-4b12fe054fea.pdf

Hsieh, J. S. (2016). Spurious or true? An exploration of antecedents and simultaneity of job performance and job satisfaction across the sectors. Public Personnel Management, 45(1), 90–118. doi:10.1177/0091026015624714

The Huffington Post (2017, December 7). 7 cultures that celebrate aging and respect their elders. Retrieved from https://www.huffpost.com/entry/what-other-cultures-can-teach_n_4834228

Human Element (2019). Love your job-work at Human Element: Work/life balance. Retrieved from https://www.human-element.com/careers

Hunt, J. (2017). Nurturing children's natural love of learning. Retrieve from http://www.naturalchild.org/jan_hunt/unschooling.html

Hyken, S. (2019). Social media response time, are you fast enough? Retrieved from https://hyken.com/customer-care/social-media-response-time-are-you-fast-enough/

Hyman, J. (2016, June 29). Your employees are using social media at work; deal with it. Retrieved from http://www.workforce.com/2016/06/29/your-employees-are-using-social-media-at-work-deal-with-it/

Indeed (2019). HR manager job. Retrieved from https://www.indeed.com/q-HR-Manager-jobs.html

Ingraham, C. (2018, January 19). Union membership remained steady in 2017. The trend may not hold. Retrieved from https://www.washingtonpost.com/news/wonk/wp/2018/01/19/union-membership-remained-steady-in-2017-the-trend-may-not-hold/?utm_term=.a7873cf5d047

Intel (2019). Over 50 years of Moore's Law. Retrieved from https://www.intel.com/content/www/us/en/silicon-innovations/moores-law-technology.html

Investopedia (2017, September 12). What is Tim Cook's Managerial Style? Retrieved from https://www.investopedia.com/ask/answers/032515/what-tim-cooks-managerial-style.asp

Javitch, D. G. (2006, June 5). The benefits of flextime. Retrieved from https://www.entre preneur.com/article/159440

Jenkins, R. (2017, August 21). This is how similar generation z will be to millennials: A different generation entering the workforce, but they will share many similarities to millennials. Here are nine similarities between generation z and millennials. Retrieved from https://www.inc.com/ryan-jenkins/this-is-how-similar-generation-z-will-be-to-millen.html

Johnson, T. (2018, June 29). The real problem with tech professionals: High turnover. Retrieved from https://www.forbes.com/sites/forbesbusinessdevelopmentcouncil/2018/06/29/the-real-problem-with-tech-professionals-high-turnover/#1b4867374201

Jones, B., Smith, K., & Rock, D. (2018, June 20). 3 biases that hijack performance reviews, and how to address them. Retrieved from https://hbr.org/2018/06/3-biases-that-hijack-performance-reviews-and-how-to-address-them

Jones, S. (2017, June 9). White men account for 72% of corporate leadership at 16 of the Fortune 500 companies. Retrieved from http://fortune.com/2017/06/09/white-men-senior-executives-fortune-500-companies-diversity-data/

Judge, T. A., Heller, D., & Mount, M. K. (2002). Five-Factor Model of personality and job satisfaction: A meta-analysis. Journal of Applied Psychology, 87(3), 530–541.

Jung, C. G. (1921). Psychological types. Retrieved from http://deenrc.files.wordpress.com/2008/03/carl-jung-psychological-types.pdf

Kambayashi, R., & Kato, T. (2017). Long-term employment and job security over the past 25 years. ILR Review, 70(2), 359–394.

Kane, J. (2012, October 22). Health costs: How the U.S. compares with other countries. Retrieved from https://www.pbs.org/newshour/health/health-costs-how-the-us-compares-with-other-countries

Karanika-Murray, M., Bartholomew, K. J., Williams, G. A., & Cox, T. (2015). Leader-Member Exchange across two hierarchical levels of leadership: Concurrent influences on work characteristics and employee psychological health. Work Stress, 29(1), 57–74.

Kass, S. J., Vodanovich, S. J., & Khosravi, J. Y. (2011). Applying the job characteristics model to the college education experience. Journal of the Scholarship of Teaching and Learning, 11(4), 56–68.

Kelly, J. (2019, October 25). More than half of US workers are unhappy in their jobs: Here's why and what needs to be done now. Retrieved from https://www.forbes.com/sites/jackkelly/2019/10/25/more-than-half-of-us-workers-are-unhappy-in-their-jobs-heres-why-and-what-needs-to-be-done-now/#66b286520247

Kenny, B. (2007, April 25). The coming crisis in employee turnover. Retrieved from https://www.forbes.com/2007/04/24/employees-turnover-careers-lead-careers-cz_bk_0425turnover.html#5a00dbb7773a

Khalili, O. (2010). How to grow your business by giving your employees a calling-with Chip Conley. Retrieved from http://causecapitalism.com/how-to-grow-your-business-by-giving-your-employees-a-calling-with-chip-conley/

Kidwell, R. E., & Scherer, P. M. (2001). Layoffs and their ethical implications under scientific management, quality management and open-book management. Journal of Business Ethics, 29(1/2), 113–124.

Kiechel III, W. (2012). The management century. Harvard Business Review, 90(11), 62–75.

Kim, S. (2008). The auto industry's forgotten legacy. Diversity. Retrieved from http://content.time.com/time/nation/article/0,8599,1865121,00.html

King Arthur Flour (2019). Why employee ownership matters. Retrieved from https://www.kingarthurflour.com/our-story/article/employee-owned.html

Kinni, T. (2016, June 13). How smart leaders build trust: The chairman of JetBlue explains how a high-trust culture makes a better company (and life). Retrieved from https://www.gsb.stanford.edu/insights/how-smart-leaders-build-trust

Klein, C. (2019, January 4). The original Luddites raged against the machine of the Industrial Revolution. Retrieved from https://www.history.com/news/industrial-revolution-luddites-workers

Bibliography

Kremer W., & Hammond, C. (2013, September 1). Abraham Maslow and the pyramid that beguiled business. Retrieved from http://www.bbc.com/news/magazine-23902918

Kruse, K. (2012, October 16). 100 best quotes on leadership. Retrieved from https://www.forbes.com/sites/kevinkruse/2012/10/16/quotes-on-leadership/#7c1a4a382feb

Kuijk, A. (2018). Two Factor Theory by Frederick Herzberg. Retrieved from https://www.toolshero.com/psychology/theories-of-motivation/two-factor-theory-herzberg/

Kurter, H. L. (2018, November 19). The 4 outdated workplace rules employers still grip into. Retrieved from https://www.forbes.com/sites/heidilynnekurter/2018/11/19/the-4-outdated-workplace-rules-employers-still-grip-onto/#3d7988af122e

Lalwani, S., & Lalwani, S. J. (2017). Relevance of Herzberg's hygiene theory in today's context: An analysis of motivators and hygiene factors in present scenario in Indian context. Singaporean Journal of Business Economics and Management Studies, 5(7), 19–25.

Lambert, S., & Gonzalez, A. (November 15, 2013). Dutch Bros. Coffee. In Chris Carlson (executive producer). Undercover Boss. Los Angeles, CA: Columbia Broadcasting System.

Landrum, S. (2017, November 10). Millennials aren't afraid to change jobs, and here's why. Retrieved from https://www.forbes.com/sites/sarahlandrum/2017/11/10/millennials-arent-afraid-to-change-jobs-and-heres-why/#1a59086219a5

Lavey-Heaton, M. (2014, March 10). Working from home: How Yahoo, Best Buy and HP are making moves. Retrieved from https://www.theguardian.com/sustainable-business/working-from-home-yahoo-best-buy-hp-moves

Lawn Care Academy (2019). Straight from the orient: The amazing zoysia grass. Retrieved from https://www.lawn-care-academy.com/zoysia-grass.html

Loannidis, J. P. (2007). Limitations are not properly acknowledged in the scientific literature. Retrieved from https://www.ncbi.nlm.nih.gov/pubmed/?term=Ioannidis%20JP%5BAuthor%5D&cauthor=true&cauthor_uid=17346604

Long, G. I. (2013). Differences between union and nonunion compensation, 2001–2011. Retrieved from https://www.bls.gov/opub/mlr/2013/04/art2full.pdf

Long, H. (2018, October 5). Amazon's $15 minimum wage doesn't end debate over whether it's creating good jobs. Retrieved from https://www.washingtonpost.com/business/economy/amazons-15-minimum-wage-doesnt-end-debate-over-whether-its-creating-good-jobs/2018/10/05/b1da23a0-c802–11e8–9b1c-a90f1daae309_story.html?noredirect=on&utm_term=.74e5c99c4400

Lorenz, T. (2017, March 29). How Asana built the best company culture in tech. Retrieved from https://www.fastcompany.com/3069240/how-asana-built-the-best-company-culture-in-tech

Lurie, M. (2018, September 16). The disconnect between baby boomers and millennials when it comes to work ethic. Retrieved from https://www.theladders.com/career-advice/the-disconnect-between-baby-boomers-and-millennials-when-it-comes-to-work-ethic

Lyman, A. (2009). REI - working together for a better world: Best company for 25 years. Retrieved from https://www.rei.com/pdf/jobs/2009-Best-Company-for-25-Years-REI-for-REI.pdf

Mahoney, J. T. (2004). Behavioral Theory of the Firm. Retrieved from https://us.sagepub.com/sites/default/files/upm-binaries/5029_Mahoney_Chapter_1.pdf

Manahan, C., & Lavoie, J. (2008). Who stays in rural practice?: An international [sic] review of the literature on factors influencing rural nurse retention. Online Journal of Rural Nursing & Health Care, 8(2), 42–53.

Martin, C. C. (2008). Getting high on Gen Y: How to engage the entitlement generation. Career Planning & Adult Development Journal, 24(3), 19–22.

Martin, R., Guillaume, Y., Thomas, G., Lee, A., & Epitropaki, O. (2016). Leader-Member Exchange (LMX) and performance: A meta-analytic review. Personnel Psychology (69), 67–121.

Mautz, S. (2018, April 2). A 2-year Stanford study shows the astonishing productivity boost of working from home. Retrieved from https://www.inc.com/scott-mautz/a-2-year-stanford-study-shows-astonishing-productivity-boost-of-working-from-home.html

Maxwell, J. C. (2011). The 360 degree leader: Developing your influence from anywhere in the organization. Nashville, TN: Thomas Nelson.

McGill University (2010, July 6). Mintzberg on managing. Retrieved from https://www.youtube.com/watch?v=_NRWtd_SiU8

McKay, G. (2015). Personal interview (Ph.D.)

Merino, M. D., & Privado, J. (2015). Does employee recognition affect positive psychological functioning and well-being? The Spanish Journal of Psychology, 18. Retrieved from https://milligan.idm.oclc.org/login?url=https://search.cbscohost.com/login.aspx?direct=true&db=psyh&AN=2015-42476-001&site=eds-live&scope=site

Metin Camgoz, S., Tayfur Ekmekci, O., Bayhan Karapinar, P., & Kumbul Guler, B. (2016). Job insecurity and turnover intentions: Gender differences and the mediating role of work engagement. Sex Roles, 75(11–12), 583–598.

Mindrila, D., & Balentyne, P. (2019). Scatterplots and correlation. Retrieved from https://www.westga.edu/academics/research/vrc/assets/docs/scatterplots_and_correlation_notes.pdf

Mohamad, M. M., Sulaiman, N. L., Sern, L. C., and Salleh, K. M. (2015). Measuring the validity and reliability of research instruments. Procedia-Social and Behavioral Sciences, 204, 164–171.

Morgan, B. (2018, January 16). Chief culture officer and chief customer officer: A winning combination. Retrieved from https://www.forbes.com/sites/blakemorgan/2018/01/16/chief-culture-officer-and-chief-customer-officer-a-winning-combination/#1e00a8833ab1

Morgan, J. (2014, December 15). The top 10 factors for on-the-job employee happiness. Retrieved from https://www.forbes.com/sites/jacobmorgan/2014/12/15/the-top-10-factors-for-on-the-job-employee-happiness/#7a9a52e25afa

Morningstar (2019). Publix Supermarkets Inc: Key ratios. Retrieved from https://financials.morningstar.com/ratios/r.html?t=PUSH

Mosley, E. (2016, July 18). The human need for recognition in the workplace. Retrieved from https://www.wbjournal.com/article/the-human-need-for-recognition-in-the-workplace

Murray, A. (2017, January 10). Are millennial leaders different? Retrieved from http://fortune.com/2017/01/10/are-millennial-leaders-different/

The Myers and Briggs Foundation (2019). The 16 MBTI types. Retrieved from https://www.myersbriggs.org/my-mbti-personality-type/mbti-basics/the-16-mbti-types.htm?bhcp=1

National Right to Work Committee (2018). Right to work. Retrieved from https://nrtwc.org/facts/right-work-mean/

NBC News (2010, November 10). France raises retirement age despite protests. Retrieved from http://www.nbcnews.com/id/40103988/ns/world_news-europe/t/france-raises-retirement-age-despite-protests/#.Wo74F-dG0dU

Neugaard, B. (2019). Halo effect: Psychology. Retrieved from https://www.britannica.com/science/halo-effect

Newman, M. A. & Guy, M. E. (1998). Taylor's triangle, Follett's web. Administrative Theory & Praxis, 20(3), 287–297.

Newport, F. (2018, May 22). In U.S., estimate of LGBT population rises to 4.5%. Retrieved from https://news.gallup.com/poll/234863/estimate-lgbt-population-rises.aspx

Newton, R. R., & Rudestam, K. E. (1999). Your statistical consultant: Answers to your data analysis questions. Sage Publications, Inc: Thousand Oaks, CA.

Nikravan, L. (2016, November 22). Cyber Monday shopping at work? You're not alone. Retrieved from https://www.careerbuilder.com/advice/cyber-monday-shopping-at-work

1940s.org (2013, May 8). From the 1940s decade—famous firsts and inventions. Retrieved from http://1940s.org/from-the-1940s-decade-famous-firsts/

Bibliography

Oakleaf, L. (2016). Elton Mayo and the Hawthorne experiments: Jacob Robertson and Garrett Carothers. Retrieved from https://oer.missouriwestern.edu/rsm424/chapter/elton-mayo-and-the-hawthorne-experiments/

O'Brien, S. A. (2018, August 22). Uber to pay 56 workers $1.9 million for harassment and discrimination claims. Retrieved from https://money.cnn.com/2018/08/21/technology/uber-settlement/index.html

Olsen, E.J. (2014, July 21). Zingerman's co-founder to be honored at White House event. Retrieved from http://www.zingermanscommunity.com/2014/07/zingermans-co-founder-to-be-honored-at-white-house-event/

Olson, E. G. (2013, November 18). Microsoft, GE, and the futility of ranking employees. Retrieved from http://fortune.com/2013/11/18/microsoft-ge-and-the-futility-of-ranking-employees/

O*Net Interest Profiler (2019). Welcome to the O*Net interest profiler. Retrieved from https://www.mynextmove.org/explore/ip

O*Net Online (2019). Interests: Preferences for work environments and outcomes. Retrieved from https://www.onetonline.org/find/descriptor/browse/Interests/

Opploans (2019). Financial opportunity, social responsibility, and commitment to our customers. Retrieved from https://www.opploans.com/about-us/

Ortiz, M. (2012). Traditionalists to millennials. Rdh, 32(10), 26–29.

Osman, I., Berbary, L., Sidani, Y., Al-Ayoubi, B., & Emrouznejad, A. (2011). Data Envelopment Analysis Model for the Appraisal and Relative Performance Evaluation of Nurses at an Intensive Care Unit. Journal of Medical Systems, 35(5), 1039–1062. https://doi.org/10.1007/s10916–010–9570–4

Pangaribuan, C. H., Wijaya, F. H., Djamil, A. B., Hidayat, D, & Putra, O. P. B. (2020). An analysis on the importance of motivation to transfer learning in VUCA environments. Management Science Letters, 2, 271

Patton, M. (2016, February 29). U.S. role in global economy declines nearly 50%. Retrieved from https://www.forbes.com/sites/mikepatton/2016/02/29/u-s-role-in-global-economy-declines-nearly-50/#5996bc015e9e

Pew Research Center (2015, June 18). The rise in dual income households. Retrieved from http://www.pewresearch.org/ft_dual-income-households-1960–2012–2/

Phillips, K. (2014, August 20). How container shipping changed the world through globalization. Retrieved from https://www.abc.net.au/radionational/programs/rearvision/the-big-metal-box-that-changed-the-world/5684586

The PNC Financial Services Group (2019). Employees in the community. Retrieved from https://www.pnc.com/en/about-pnc/corporate-responsibility/corporate-social-responsibility/communities-green/volunteerism.html

Porter, M., Williams, J.C., Grant, A., & Buckingham, M. (2019). Five years of must reads from HBR: 2019 edition (HBR's 10 must reads). Boston, MA: Harvard Review Press.

Pozen, R. C. (2013, March 28). The delicate art of giving feedback. Retrieved from https://hbr.org/2013/03/the-delicate-art-of-giving-fee

Pringle, C. D., DuBose, P. B., & Yankey, M.D. (2010). Personality characteristics and choice of academic major: Are traditional stereotypes obsolete? College Student Journal, 44(1), 131–142.

Process Improvement Japan and Australia (2010). How to motivate employees. Retrieved from http://www.process-improvement-japan.com/how-to-motivate-employees.html

Publix (2019). Committed to diversity: Variety makes everything better. Retrieved from http://corporate.publix.com/about-publix/culture/committed-to-diversity

Radu, S. (2018, February 16). How soon will you be working from home? Telecommuting might not just be a company perk in the next decade. Retrieved from https://www.usnews.com/news/best-countries/articles/2018–02–16/telecommuting-is-growing-but-still-not-unanimously-embraced

Raff, D. M. G., & Summers, L. H. (1987). Did Henry Ford pay efficiency wages? Journal of Labor Economics, 5(4), 57–86.

Bibliography

Rajput, N., Bali, R. & Kesharwani, S. (2013). Does motivational strategies and issues differ across generations: An analytical study. Global Journal of Enterprise Information System, 5(1), 2–10.

Ravenelle, A. J. (2019). "We're not Uber": Control, autonomy and entrepreneurship in the gig economy. Conference Papers—American Sociological Association, 1–31.

Rawland, A. (2011, February 1). The County of San Bernardino Department of Behavioral Health: Employee recognition policy. Retrieved from http://wp.sbcounty.gov/dbh/wp-content/uploads/2016/08/BOP3037.pdf

Redman, T. C. (2019, May 16). Do your data scientists know the 'why' behind their work? Retrieved from https://hbr.org/2019/05/do-your-data-scientists-know-the-why-behind-their-work

REI Co-op (2019). Who we are. Retrieved from https://www.rei.com/about-rei

Reshef, Y. Fredrick Winslow Taylor (1865–1915): Principles of scientific management. Retrieved from https://web.stanford.edu/class/sts175/NewFiles/Taylorism

Ricci, T. (2012). Frank Bunker Gilbreth: Biography. Retrieved from https://www.asme.org/engineering-topics/articles/construction-and-building/frank-bunker-gilbreth

Richman, N. (2015). Human resource management and human resource development: Evolution and contributions. Creighton Journal of Interdisciplinary Leadership 1(2), 120–129.

Rigoni, B., & Adkins, A. (2016, May 11). What millennials want from a job. Retrieved from https://hbr.org/2016/05/what-millennials-want-from-a-new-job

Robbins, S. P. (1998). Organizational behavior: Concepts, controversies, applications. (8th ed.). Upper Saddle River, NJ: Prentice Hall.

Robbins, S. P., & Judge, T. A. (2009). Organizational behavior (13th ed.). Upper Saddle River, NJ: Pearson/Prentice Hall.

Robbins, S. P, & Judge, T. A. (2012). Organizational behavior (15th ed.). Upper Saddle River, NJ: Prentice Hall.

Robbins, S. P., DeCenzo, D. A., & Coulter, M. A. (2014). Fundamentals of management: Essential concepts and applications (9th ed.). USA: Pearson.

Roepe, L. R. (2016, April 27). Inside three companies that are innovating flexible schedules. Retrieved from https://www.fastcompany.com/3059295/inside-three-companies-that-are-innovating-flexible-schedules

Rogel, C. (2014, March 17). 12 attributes to evaluate your organizational culture. Retrieved from https://decision-wise.com/12-attributes-to-evaluate-your-organization-culture/

Rudominer, R. (2015). Corporate social responsibility matters: Ignore millennials at your own peril. Retrieved from http://csic.georgetown.edu/magazine/corporate-social-responsibility-matters-ignore-millennials-peril/

Rutledge, P. B. (2011, November 8). Social networks: What Maslow misses. Retrieved from https://www.psychologytoday.com/us/blog/positively-media/201111/social-networks-what-maslow-misses-0

Saberr (2019). Saberr: Transforming teamwork. Retrieved from https://www.saberr.com/

Sahai, K. (2017, August 18). Four traits that make millennials more effective leaders. Retrieved from https://www.forbes.com/sites/forbescoachescouncil/2017/08/18/four-traits-that-make-millennials-more-effective-leaders/#3e9b200c7303

Satchell, M. (2017, December 5). We're a best place for diversity! Retrieved from https://blog.publix.com/careers/publix-is-a-great-place-to-work/were-a-best-workplace-for-diversity/

Schulte, B. (2015, May 5). Millennials want a work-life balance. Their bosses just don't get why. Retrieved from https://www.washingtonpost.com/local/millennials-want-a-work-life-balance-their-bosses-just-dont-get-why/2015/05/05/1859369e-f376-11e4-84a6-6d7c67c50db0_story.html?utm_term=.b45d6b49698e

Schuyler, M., & Berkowitz, C. (2009). Developing talent through community involvement: A winning formula for Capital One. People & Strategy, 32(1), 46–53

Seidel, L. (2010, October 2). Good job! How to give recognition that promotes outstanding

Bibliography

performance. Retrieved from https://blog.smu.edu/hr/2010/10/02/good-job-how-to-give-recognition-that-promotes-outstanding-peformance/

Semler, R. (1993). Maverick: The story behind the world's most unusual workplace. New York, NY: Business Plus.

Sender, A., Arnold, A., & Staffelbach, B. (2017). Job security as a threatened resource: reactions to job insecurity in culturally distinct regions. International Journal of Human Resource Management, 28(17), 2403–2429. https://doi.org/10.1080/09585192.2015.11 37615

Senge, P. M. (2006). The fifth discipline: The art & practice of the learning organization. New York, NY: Crown Business.

Sheetz, M. (2017, August 4). Technology killing off corporate America: Average life span of companies under 20 years. Retrieved from https://www.cnbc.com/2017/08/24/tech nology-killing-off-corporations-average-lifespan-of-company-under-20-years.html

Shoikhetbrod, A. A. (2018, April 6). Telecommuting and employment law. Retrieved from https://www.tullylegal.com/resources/articles/telecommuting-employment-law/

Shu, C.-Y., & Lazatkhan, J. (2017). Effect of Leader-Member Exchange on employee envy and work behavior moderated by self-esteem and neuroticism. Revista de Psicología Del Trabajo y de Las Organizaciones, 33(1), 69–81.

Simms, M. (2009). Insights from a Management Prophet: Mary Parker Follett on Social Entrepreneurship. Business & Society Review (00453609), 114(3), 349–363.

Singh, R. (2016). The impact of intrinsic and extrinsic motivators on employee engagement in information organizations. Journal of Education for Library & Information Science, 57(2), 197–206.

Smerek, R. E., & Peterson, M. (2006). Examining Herzberg's theory: Improving job satisfaction among non-academic employees at a university. Research in Higher Education, 48(2), 229–250.

Society for Human Resource Management (2016, January 19). Managing and leveraging workplace use of social media. Retrieved from https://www.shrm.org/resourcesand tools/tools-and-samples/toolkits/pages/managingsocialmedia.aspx

Soergel, A. (2016, September 1). Most of America's businesses run by white men: New government data show business owners are still a fairly homogenous group. Retrieved from https://www.usnews.com/news/articles/2016–09–01/most-of-americas-business es-run-by-white-men-says-census-bureau

Spiller, H.A., & Griffith, J. R. K. (2009). The value and evolving role of the U.S. Poison Control Center system. Public Health Reports, 124(3), 359–363.

Stewart, A. J. & Kuenzi, K. (2018). The nonprofit career ladder: Exploring career paths as leadership development for future nonprofit executives. Public Personnel Management, 47(4), 359–381.

Sullivan, B. (2016, July 7). For older workers, getting a new job is a crapshoot. Retrieved from https://www.cnbc.com/2016/07/07/for-older-workers-getting-a-new-job-is-a-crapshoot.html

Sullivan, E. (2016, July 13). Self-actualization: Psychology. Retrieved from https://www.britannica.com/science/self-actualization

Tatsuse, T., & Sekine, M. (2010). Explaining global job satisfaction by facets of job satisfaction: The Japanese civil servants study. Environmental Health and Preventative Medicine, 16(2), 133–137.

Taylor, B. (2016, January 26). How one fast-food chain keeps its turnover rates absurdly low. Retrieved from https://hbr.org/2016/01/how-one-fast-food-chain-keeps-its-turn over-rates-absurdly-low

Tewari, R., & Pathak, T. (2014). Sustainable CSR for micro, small and medium enterprises. Journal of Management & Public Policy, 6(1), 34–44.

Toyota (2018). What are Toyota's mission and vision statements? Retrieved from http://toyota.custhelp.com/app/answers/detail/a_id/7654/~/what-are-toyotas-mission-and-vision-statements%3F

Bibliography

Twarog, J. (2018). Mandatory, permissive, & illegal subjects of bargaining. Retrieved from https://www.local1222.org/index.cfm?zone=/unionactive/view_article.cfm&HomeID=42683

Tybout, A. M., & Calder, B. J. (2010). Kellogg on marketing (2nd ed.). Hoboken, NJ: John Wiley & Sons, Inc.

UAW (2015, October 13). UAW history. Retrieved from https://uaw.org/solidarity-magazine/uaw-history/

UCLA Institute for Digital Research and Education (2019). What does Cronbach's alpha mean? Retrieved from https://stats.idre.ucla.edu/spss/faq/what-does-cronbachs-alpha-mean/

United States Department of Labor (2009). Timeline of OSHA's 40 year history. Retrieved from https://www.osha.gov/osha40/timeline.html

United States Department of Labor (2016, August 1). Worker falls 22 feet to death, 4 months after OSHA cites employer for failing to protect workers on the same job site. Retrieved from https://www.osha.gov/news/newsreleases/region5/08012016

United States Department of Labor (2017, July 21). Corporate-wide settlement agreements: TOMRA Recycling. Retrieved from https://www.osha.gov/enforcement/cwsa/tomra-ny-recycling-llc-07212017

United States Department of Labor (2018, January 1). Changes in basic minimum wages in non-farm employment under state law: Selected years 1968 to 2017. Retrieved from https://www.dol.gov/whd/state/stateMinWageHis.htm

United States Department of Labor (2018). Occupational Safety and Health Administration: About OSHA. Retrieved from https://www.osha.gov/laws-regs/oshact/section_1

U.S. Department of Labor (2009, July). Wage and hour division: Fact sheet #53—The health care industry and hours worked. Retrieved from https://www.dol.gov/whd/regs/compliance/whdfs53.htm

U.S. Equal Employment Opportunity Commission (2018). Discrimination by type. Retrieved from https://www.eeoc.gov/laws/types/index.cfm

U.S. Equal Employment Opportunity Commission (2019, May 17). EEOC press releases. Retrieved from https://www.eeoc.gov/eeoc/newsroom/release/

The University of Western Australia (2019). Code of conduct: Equity and justice—equity of access to employment and programs. Retrieved from http://www.hr.uwa.edu.au/policies/policies/conduct/code/equity

Vanderwood, M. W. (2018). Leader self-perceptions of ethics in and out of the workplace and personal trustworthiness. Retrieved from https://scholarworks.waldenu.edu/cgi/viewcontent.cgi?article=6711&context=dissertations

Vann, M., & Ling Kent, J. (2016, November 30). Can work life balance be a reality? This company makes it possible. Retrieved from https://www.nbcnews.com/nightly-news/work-life-balance-reality-company-makes-it-possible-n690346

Varghese, S. (2010, November 3). Henry Ford, William Sarnoff and leadership today. Retrieved from https://www.forbes.com/2010/11/03/ford-sarnoff-mayo-harvard-leadership-managing-varghese.html

Velasquez, M. (2005, November 2). Unocal in Burma. Retrieved from https://www.scu.edu/ethics/focus-areas/business-ethics/resources/unocal-in-burma/

Vespa, J., Armstrong, D. M., & Medina, L. (2018, March). Demographic turning points for the United States: Population projections for 2020 to 2060. Retrieved from https://www.census.gov/content/dam/Census/library/publications/2018/demo/P25_1144.pdf

Ward, B. (2019). The Impact of Personality on Job Satisfaction: A Study of Bank Employees in the Southeastern U.S. The IUP Journal of Organizational Behavior, 18(2), 60–79.

Weinzweig, A. (2000). Servant leadership. Retrieved from http://www.zingtrain.com/content/servant-leadership

Wen, T. (2017, August 21). The new way your personality could be holding you back. Retrieved from https://www.bbc.com/worklife/article/20170818-the-new-way-your-personality-could-be-holding-you-back

Bibliography

Wen Yi Ng, Abigail, & Andanari, K. (2018, June 28). Millennials want diversity that's more than just skin-deep. Retrieved from https://www.bloomberg.com/news/articles/2018–06–29/what-millennials-want-diversity-that-s-more-than-just-skin-deep

White, D, & White, P. (2014, December 23). What to expect from Gen-X and millennial employees. Retrieved from https://www.entrepreneur.com/article/240556

Wiedmer, T. (2015). Generations do differ: Best practices in leading traditionalists, boomers, and generations X, Y, and Z. Delta Kappa Gamma Bulletin, 82(1), 51–58.

Wilkie, D. (2015, October 21). If 1 in 3 workers wants to quit, HR had better figure out why. Retrieved from https://www.shrm.org/resourcesandtools/hr-topics/employee-relations/pages/many-employees-plan-to-quit.aspx

Windhorst, B., & McMenamin, D. (2016, January 23). Long time coming: End comes for David Blatt's bumpy Cavs tenure. Retrieved from http://www.espn.com/nba/story/_/id/14629892/nba-final-unraveling-david-blatt

Wolfe, A. (2018, April 2). Recent research from Deloitte shows just how much we use our smartphones. Retrieved from https://www.journalofaccountancy.com/newsletters/2018/apr/how-often-use-phone-every-day.html

Workopolis (2016, December 22). How GE replaced a 40-year-old performance review system. Retrieved from https://hiring.workopolis.com/article/ge-replaced-40-year-old-performance-review-system/

Workplace Trends (2015, July 20). The millennial leadership survey. Retrieved from https://workplacetrends.com/the-millennial-leadership-survey/

Works, R. (2016). Trends in employer costs for defined benefit plans. Beyond the Numbers: Pay and Benefits 5(2), 1–9.

The World Bank (2016). GDP per capita, PPP (current international $). Retrieved from https://data.worldbank.org/indicator/NY.GDP.PCAP.PP.CD

Wren, D. A., & Bedeian, A. G. (2009). The evolution of management thought (6th ed). John Wiley & Sons, Inc.: USA.

Wright, C. D. (1908). The apprenticeship system in its relation to industrial education. Retrieved from https://files.eric.ed.gov/fulltext/ED542849.pdf

Wronski, L., & Cohen, J. (2019, July 26). A third of US workers seriously considered quitting their job in the last 3 months. Here's why. Retrieved from https://www.cnbc.com/2019/07/16/third-of-us-workers-considered-quitting-their-job-in-last-3-months.html

Zaiontz, C. (2019). Cronbach's alpha. Retrieved from http://www.real-statistics.com/reliability/internal-consistency-reliability/cronbachs-alpha/

Zak, P. J. (2017). The neuroscience of trust. Retrieved from https://hbr.org/2017/01/the-neuroscience-of-trust

Zimmermann, C. (2018, August 30). The FRED blog: The rise of the service economy. Retrieved from https://fredblog.stlouisfed.org/2018/08/the-rise-of-the-service-economy/

Zingerman's Community of Businesses (2018). Mission and guiding principles. Retrieved from http://www.zingermanscommunity.com/about-us/mission-guiding-principles/

Zingtrain (2018). Why open book management is an excellent way to run a business! Retrieved from http://www.zingtrain.com/content/why-open-book-management-excellent-way-run-business

Index

Index

Index